PRAISE FOR *A FOREST OF SYMBOLS*

"The undertaking represented by this book is of capital importance... We must learn to discover or rediscover the liturgy of the Holy Mass such as our Church has transmitted it, starting with an authentic allegorical or mystical explanation, which in a certain way forms the essence of each of our rites, in the same way that a tree's sap, invisible beneath its bark, provides it with moisture and gives it life and growth."

—**ROBERT CARDINAL SARAH**, from the Foreword

"For almost a millennium, theologians saw in the Holy Mass an allegory of the life of Christ, a symbolic unfolding of the ages of the world, a pageant of mysteries. Under the withering chill of rationalism, this treasure-chest of meditation was first mocked, then forgotten. Fr. Barthe explains why we should recover the mystical interpretation of the Mass and then shows how it is done, reconnecting us with our forefathers in the Roman rite. A potent tonic to restore our lost memories!"

—**PETER A. KWASNIEWSKI**, author of *Reclaiming Our Roman Catholic Birthright*

"Drawing on Amalarius of Metz, Innocent III, St. Thomas Aquinas, William Durandus, and Jean-Jacques Olier, among others, Abbé Claude Barthe has synthesized the best insights from the tradition of the *expositio Missae*—a genre of Mass commentary, focused on the mystical meaning of the rites, that flourished from the ninth century through the seventeenth. If the mystical meaning is to the Mass what the spiritual sense is to Sacred Scripture, then *A Forest of Symbols* reads like a liturgical *lectio divina*."

—**URBAN HANNON**, editor, *The Josias*

"Allegory is a classic method by which Christians have sought to achieve a deeper understanding and appreciation of the liturgy's meaning, especially for the Eucharistic sacrifice. The liturgy is a collection of texts, chants, actions, and symbols that might rightly be considered a kind of 'sacred drama' that points to ever deeper meanings. Fr. Barthe's book aims to provide the reader with a revived allegorical approach to liturgy that is informed by the great allegorists of yesteryear alongside insights offered by more recent scholarship and commentary."

—**SHAWN TRIBE**, editor of *Liturgical Arts Journal*

"Historical-critical investigation of the liturgy is an important task, yet without deep contemplation on its fundamental nature and spirit, the faithful will not be able to live the liturgy in the way the Second Vatican Council desired—as the 'source and summit' of their Christian life. In this highly accessible commentary, Abbé Claude Barthe leads us in this essential spiritual reflection on the mystical qualities of the Holy Sacrifice of the Mass. From the preparation of the altar to the end of the Last Gospel, each aspect of the Mass is examined with reference to the Bible, the Fathers, and the Catholic tradition, with the allegorical meaning of even the smallest ritual details explained. In an age disfigured by scientism, literalism, and rationalism, in which the corrosive idea that liturgy is 'manufactured' seems so pervasive, Abbé Barthe's work is a sure guide through the glorious 'forest of symbols' given us in the traditional liturgy, and provides an excellent way for us to rediscover the spiritual power and beauty of the Mass in our lives."

—MATTHEW HAZELL, scholar of comparative liturgics

A FOREST OF SYMBOLS

A Forest of Symbols

THE TRADITIONAL MASS AND ITS MEANING

ABBÉ CLAUDE BARTHE

Translated by David J. Critchley

Foreword by Robert Cardinal Sarah

Angelico Press

Original title: *La messe: une forêt de symboles: Commentaire allégorique ou mystique de la messe romaine traditionelle avec indications historiques et rituelles*

First published in the USA
by Angelico Press 2023

For information, address:
Angelico Press, Ltd.
169 Monitor St.
Brooklyn, NY 11222
www.angelicopress.com

ppr 978-1-62138-916-3
cloth 978-1-62138-917-0

Book and cover design by Michael Schrauzer

Te igitur, clementissime Pater... (Wherefore, O most merciful Father, we humbly pray and beseech thee... that thou wouldst vouchsafe to receive and bless... this holy and unblemished sacrifice...) To enable us to understand the mystery of the most Holy Sacrifice of the Mass, and to draw aside in an instant the curtain that conceals it from us, we must understand that this sacrifice is the heavenly sacrifice. It was for that purpose that Our Lord, made a priest after the order of Melchisedech for all eternity, was entrusted by the Father with the task of offering him the sacrifice for ever. [1]

1 Jean-Jacques Olier, *L'esprit des cérémonies de la grand'messe de paroisse selon l'usage romain* (Paris: Langlois, 1656), Préface.

CONTENTS

NOTE BY THE TRANSLATOR

THIS TRANSLATION FOLLOWS THE POCKET EDItion (Le Chesnay: Via Romana, 2020), which includes the preface by Cardinal Sarah. The numbering of the chapters and pages of this edition differs from that found in the original edition (Versailles: Via Romana, 2011).

Scriptural quotations are taken from the 1752 edition of Challoner's revision of the Douay-Rheims translation, which like the text of the Mass follows the Vulgate. Translations of the prayers of the Mass are taken from the translation of Abbot Fernand Cabrol OSB, ed. 13 (Tours: A. Mame and Sons, 1949), with minor changes. Quotations from other authors in translation are the work of the present translator unless otherwise stated. References to French-language books and sources have been replaced with references to equivalent English-language publications when possible.

The translator wishes to thank the author, Abbé Claude Barthe, for his assistance and encouragement; Dr Raymond Davis for sharing his liturgical knowledge; M. Benoît Mancheron, of Via Romana, for his assistance in matters of copyright; and Dr Peter Kwasniewski for his encouragement and for his editing of the final text for publication.

PREFACE

IT GIVES ME GREAT PLEASURE TO PRESENT THE new edition of a work of Abbé Claude Barthe on the allegorical meaning of the rites of the Mass. The book, which focuses on the Extraordinary Form of the Roman rite, is well documented and accessible, but is above all eminently spiritual and doctrinal.

The truth is, as Abbé Barthe rightly reminds us, that following the decline of mystical commentary on the Mass that started at the end of the seventeenth century, and because of the poverty of contemporary catechesis, which goes back at least fifty years, the majority of the faithful know nothing of the allegorical meaning of the Mass—something that prevents a right understanding, in conformity with Catholic doctrine, of the Mystery of the Faith celebrated in the liturgy. This leads to a withering, not to say a collapse, of their spiritual life, marked notably by an abandonment of the adoration of the Holy Sacrament. We observe as well, with great distress, a growing lack of interest in the Holy Mass, which in these recent years has too often been reduced to a celebration dominated by activity and wholly cheerful in spirit, something that has inevitably far too often led to a massive loss of enthusiasm for attendance at the Sunday Mass.

Now, Romano Guardini (1885–1968), in the Introduction to his book, *Sacred Signs*, states clearly that, from childhood, Christians must acquire a full and fruitful knowledge of the visible signs that the baptized have received and assimilated and that they use to express "the 'invisible grace.'"[1] The undertaking represented by this book is therefore of particular, indeed capital, importance, and so is vital for the future of our Christian communities, and parochial communities in particular,

1 Romano Guardini, *Sacred Signs*, trans. Grace Branham (Saint Louis: Pio Decimo Press, 1956), 10.

because it constitutes without doubt an instructional resource for which there is the greatest need. This book has the potential to help pastors of souls just as much as the faithful who are disoriented to differing degrees by a liturgical creativity contemptuous of the organic way in which rites develop. We must learn to discover or rediscover the liturgy of the Holy Mass such as our Church has transmitted it, starting with an authentic allegorical or mystical explanation, which in a certain way forms the essence of each of our rites, in the same way that a tree's sap, invisible beneath its bark, provides it with moisture and gives it life and growth. If we pay attention only to the bark, or outer covering, of our rites, there is a danger that over time those rites will lose their deep and original meaning. Because, if our rites are thought of as a purely human construct, and therefore changeable at our will, they can become the object of distortions, of substitutions, not to mention abusive suppressions, thus suffering all the fantasies of a poor-quality creativity.

Now, we should recall here the golden rule that can be seen throughout the Second Vatican Council's Constitution on the Liturgy, *Sacrosanctum Concilium*: this expresses an untouchable principle, which should be highlighted at the start of all liturgical instruction: the liturgy is not a human creation, and that includes the most elaborate or innovative liturgies, but it is first and foremost the work of God; that is why it is welcomed into the Church, the spouse of Our Lord Jesus Christ. And it is the Church alone that is charged with transmitting it, in the etymological sense of the word: in reality, the noun "tradition" is formed of the Latin words *trans* and *dare*, and means "handing on," that is, more precisely, passing on faithfully to others what one has oneself received by tradition.[2] That is why the

---

2 On the importance of the concept of transmission, founded on the Latin word *tradere*—itself the origin of the noun "tradition"—we should remember what Father Bertrand de Margerie, SJ, said: "The Lord has given us, handed on to us, transmitted to us (*tradidit*) by a transmission that is at once both verbal and real the sacramental sentences by means of which he makes present, by the power of the Spirit the Paraclete, his own holy Body and Blood. The chalice is that which the Lord handed (*tradidit*) to the Apostles and it is thanks to this transmission (*ex traditione*) that the Church preserves the mystery of the Body and Blood of the Lord." *Vous ferez ceci en mémoire de moi* (Montréal: Bellarmin, & Paris: Beauchesne, 1989), 114.

Constitution *Sacrosanctum Concilium* affirms: "No one else at all, not even a priest, may, of his own authority, add to, take from, or modify, anything in the Liturgy."[3]

For all that, Vatican II approved at the same time a necessary *aggiornamento* of the rites, which has been given effect in the liturgical books published after the Council, in particular the missal of Paul VI, which is now in its third edition:[4]

> while the substance of the rites is to be preserved, they themselves should be simplified. Doublets and any additions of little value that have accrued in the course of the centuries are to be omitted. Certain things that have fallen out through the wearing processes of time are to be reinstated after the ancient model of the holy Fathers, according as that may seem advisable or necessary.[5]

This is an immense and delicate task, which will require for its success patience, perseverance, faithfulness, and a firm determination, following the basic and incontrovertible criterion that Pope Benedict has never ceased to make clear and to develop with a view to a true reception of the conciliar renovation of the liturgy: namely, that we must read and understand the changes that Vatican II wished to see within the unity that characterizes the development of the rite itself, without introducing any artificial ruptures.[6]

We know that, starting from the first and second centuries, the words of Our Lord Jesus Christ at the Last Supper on Maundy Thursday, when he instituted the sacraments of the Most Holy Eucharist and of Holy Orders, have been encased, with the authority of the apostles and their successors, aided by

3 *Sacrosanctum Concilium* (1964), §22.

4 *Missale Romanum*, editio typica tertia (Rome: CLV-Ed. Liturgiche, 2002).

5 *Sacrosanctum Concilium* §50.

6 Here is a quotation from Cardinal Joseph Ratzinger which expresses his thought on this subject well: "The orthodox forms of a rite are living realities, born of a dialogue between the Church and its Saviour; they are expressions of the life of the Church, in which are condensed the faith, the prayer, and even the life of generations, and in which are embodied in a concrete form at one and the same time the action of God and the response of man" (Address given in Rome on 24 October 1998, to mark the tenth anniversary of the motu proprio *Ecclesia Dei*).

the Holy Spirit, in a liturgy composed of rites that were fairly similar in both East and West, as evidenced by the *Didache*, the *Epistle* of St Clement, the *Epistle* ascribed to Barnabas, and the writings of St Ignatius, St Justin, and St Irenaeus. Then the rites rapidly developed and were set in order in the four main regions of the Mediterranean world, corresponding to the four different cultural areas touched by the gospel, as much in the East as in the West. This led to the existence, in the fourth century, of the rites of Antioch and Alexandria in the East, and of the Roman and Gallican rites, which were similar to each other, in the West. The principal rites of the Mass in the Roman liturgy were fixed between the sixth century, most especially by Pope St Gregory the Great (590–604), and the eighth and ninth centuries, the Carolingian age, particularly with the unification of the rules and liturgies of the Benedictine abbeys by St Benedict of Aniane (750–821).

The great liturgist Mgr Aimé-Georges Martimort (1911–2000) said in 1951: "An exact and scrupulous fulfilment of the ceremonial instructions is already enough to provide the faithful with a thorough grounding in the divine meaning of the liturgical actions."[7] Now, every ceremonial action has its own meaning. Here are three examples. First, the liturgical kiss: when the priest kisses the altar, which is the symbol of Christ the Redeemer, as are the Gospel-book and the cross, he expresses an attitude of veneration, of respect, and of gratitude towards God, all in the form of a mark of a deep acceptance of God's presence. Second, the bows: they express the relationships that unite us with God, with his saints and with those who celebrate the Work of God with us. There are two sorts of bow: an inclination of the head and an inclination of the whole body. Thus, one inclines the head when the three divine Persons are named together, and at the names of Jesus, of the blessed Virgin Mary, and of the saint in whose honor the Mass is being said; and one inclines the whole body, in what is called a deep bow, in front of the altar, at the prayers *Munda cor meum* (Cleanse my heart . . .), *In spiritu humilitatis* (In a humble spirit . . .), and at the words of the Roman Canon, *Supplices*

7 Aimé-Georges Martimort, "Le Sens du sacré," in *La Maison Dieu*, No. 25 (1951): 61.

te rogamus (We most humbly beseech thee . . .). Finally, a specific action: the Commixture of the Bread and Wine, that is to say, the placing of a fragment of the consecrated host in the chalice before the Communion, recalls the Resurrection that has reunited for ever, and for the life of eternity, the body and soul of Our Lord Jesus Christ.

So let us have no doubt that respect for the actions, which are all part of the ceremonial, allows us to maintain a heightened sense for the sacred, as much among the priests as among the faithful, that is to say, not a necessarily subjective and fleeting feeling, but a determining element of what the *Catechism of the Catholic Church* calls "the virtue of religion,"[8] provided always that we rediscover the vital sap of the actions and attitudes, starting from a practical mystagogy, which in the field of liturgy is called the "ceremonial" – starting from an explanation of the allegorical or spiritual sense of the rites, as our author has done in this excellent work written for Catholics and, more widely, for today's people of good will, who are eager to meet the living God, Father and Son and Holy Spirit, in the mysteries of the Catholic faith that we celebrate in our churches, our chapels, and our oratories.

May this book of Abbé Claude Barthe contribute to a realization of the wishes of the Second Vatican Council, which gave this justification for the decisions that it had taken relating to a liturgical *aggiornamento*: that the faithful should be encouraged "to take a full, intelligent, active part" in the liturgy;[9] something which requires that the totality of liturgical signs be made available to them, these "forests of symbols" dear to the poet Charles Baudelaire, which include the ceremonial, and

8 *Catechism of the Catholic Church* §2144. The Catechism supports its statement with this magnificent quotation from St John Henry Newman: "Are these feelings of fear and awe Christian feelings or not? . . . I say this, then, which I think no one can reasonably dispute. They are the class of feelings we *should* have – yes, have in an intense degree – if we literally had the sight of Almighty God; therefore they are the class of feelings which we shall have, *if* we realize His presence. In proportion as we believe that He is present, we shall have them; and not to have them, is not to realize, not to believe that He is present." Sermon 2, "Reverence, a Belief in God's Presence," *Parochial and Plain Sermons* (London, Oxford, and Cambridge: Rivingtons, 1868), vol. 5, 21–22.

9 *Sacrosanctum Concilium* §14.

also the beauty of the liturgical ornaments, the sacred vessels and the choral chant, and in first place the Gregorian chant; so that the entirety of the elements put to the service of a liturgy celebrated with dignity and magnificence to the glory of God, in accordance with the wishes of the Church, may constitute the true pedagogy of the sacred that goes with an *ars celebrandi* focused on the proclamation of the gospel of salvation.

Robert Cardinal Sarah
March 19, 2019

INTRODUCTION
The Mystical Meaning of the Liturgy

THE ALLEGORICAL OR MYSTICAL MEANING, OR again the spiritual meaning, of the liturgy as a whole and of the Mass especially, has for a long time been poorly understood. Today's task is to rediscover this meaning, just as we have rediscovered the whole importance of the spiritual sense of Scripture. The purpose of this work therefore is to put right an omission that long predates the period of chaos that has overtaken Christian worship since the 1960s.

The Christian liturgy, and the Roman liturgy in particular, developed and thrived, in the Middle Ages especially, within a tradition of commentary and meditation that was fundamental for its understanding. To enter the liturgy of the Mass without this key is like trying to understand a cathedral assisted only by an architectural summary and a background knowledge of Christianity. In fact, nowadays you are lucky if you have this background knowledge of Christianity. But even so, such a collection would not lead you into these "forests of symbols" to which Baudelaire refers in his poem *Correspondances*, in which he sees nature as a "temple" of "living pillars," itself a metaphorical counterpart for a religious structure.

This is not the time to dwell on the difficulty of entering liturgy today, in a secular world, a land without water, a universe that is rational and focused on technical solutions. The osmosis that used to exist between daily life and the cultic life, lived out in communal, family, royal, or military ceremonies, has totally disappeared. Worship has been at best reduced to a cultural activity, or even to a folk activity, to make it socially acceptable to a modernity that is much more radically all-embracing than the most highly developed forms of the Christian ideal found in Late Antiquity or in the Middle Ages. The great liturgical crisis, which exploded at the end of the 1960s, has also contributed greatly to the invasion of the sanctuary by the profane (a modern profanity, uncomprehending of and hostile to the sacred, having nothing in common with the profanity of the ancient world), in the name of a process of "inculturation," which started in certain sections of what is called the Liturgical Movement, and which reached its full extent in the reform of Pope Paul VI (1963–1978). Just as Christian worship was adapted, for example, after the Spanish and Portuguese conquests, to the cultures of South America, so it was thought that it needed to be adapted today to the modern world. But the promoters of this "inculturation" into modernity did not realize that they were naively trying to domesticate and incorporate into the Christian liturgy a worldliness that was not a matter of culture, but was essentially anti-liturgical, since it was radically anti-Christian.

To recover the joyful experience of Christian worship, we have therefore to undertake a demanding training, starting with the recollection that is always indispensable in matters related to prayer – in this case, the public prayer of the Church – but with the additional difficulty that arises from the immersion in the modern world of a Church that is suffering from a crisis of identity. If today this effort itself makes it more difficult to enter the world of worship, it is also one of the most efficacious defenses against the toxicity of modernity. The practice of divine worship is itself a radical form of antimodern prayer – something about which the revolutions, whether violent or peaceful, that succeeded Luther's premodern revolution were not mistaken.

But we will leave aside this difficulty, so characteristic of our age. The instruments of the liturgy – bells, oil, sacred vestments, prayers, and chants – play on a particular register, where memory and poetry, particularly scriptural and catechetical poetry, are based on the world of sense, but only in order constantly to go beyond it. Liturgy therefore requires active enquiry, and at the same time a very receptive state, what in the language of mysticism one might call a "passive" state. Just like Scripture, the Christian liturgy speaks almost immediately to the soul of all believers, but it penetrates deeply only into those who listen to it attentively. We must therefore go through the church door, sign ourselves with holy water, and allow ourselves to be submerged in the luminous shadow of the sacred place, as Moses and Elijah were before us. A sacred preparation takes place, like that of the priest who prepares to celebrate the holy mysteries and who performs a series of actions, accompanied by prayer, as he clothes his body, and even more his soul, in the sacred vestments.

That is what the minister is really doing (as are the faithful): he is clothing himself in the New Man of whom St Paul speaks, he is putting on Christ, in the place of the Old Man of sin. Or again, he is arming himself with spiritual armor, ready for the combat in which the Christian and spiritual life consists (Eph 5:10–18). Thus the priest puts the amice first on his head, and then on his shoulders as a "helmet of salvation." He then slips on the alb of purity, representing a heart cleansed by the Blood of the Lamb, of which we catch a glimpse in the Apocalypse. He then puts the cincture around his waist, representing chastity, and on his left arm he puts the maniple, which represents the weight of a sheaf (in Latin, *manipulus*) of good works. Next he hangs over his back the stole of the immortality promised by Christ, which represents Christ's priestly authority, shared to different degrees by the ministers who wear it: the bishop (who wears it uncrossed), the priest (over whose breast the bishop crossed the stole on the day of his ordination, to represent the binding quality of obedience) and the deacon (who wears it as a shoulder sash or cross-belt, like an equerry, since that is the relationship that he holds to the bishop). Finally, over this assemblage of vestments, the priest or bishop puts the chasuble of the life celestial that he should already be leading on earth, in the same way as the holy liturgy is heaven descended onto earth.

If we are to achieve this understanding of the divine cult, we must recognize the fundamental parallelism between the Bible and the liturgy. Holy Scripture was written, certainly, to be studied and to be understood in its theological import, but it was also written to be meditated upon in *lectio divina*. That means that the knowledge of the sacred texts, in the manner of the Fathers of the Church and the medievals, such as St Bernard

(1090–1153) or St Thomas Aquinas (c. 1225–1274), starts, continues, and finishes in meditation: the Bible in reality is both human speech and divine speech, and God unveils its meaning progressively by granting knowledge of that meaning from on high. According to the principle of St Gregory, Scripture is received by the preaching of the masters and deepened under the action of grace. Scripture "grows in a certain way alongside those who read it."[1] St Bonaventure (1221–1274) applied the term "revelation" to this progressive discovery by the Christian soul, under the guidance of the Church, of the spiritual sense of Holy Scripture. This is ultimately nothing other than its Christic sense. Just as Holy Scripture, including the Old Testament, is the speech of Christ who reveals himself definitively, so the liturgy is the prayer of Christ who extends himself and spreads himself out in the souls of the faithful.

The Mass, since that will be the subject of our discussion, is therefore an assemblage of actions, words, vestments, objects, texts, forming ceremonies that open for us a supernatural reality, with different levels or, if you prefer, steps, of depth. We have already noted that the implicit biblical references are continual, and refer both to the biblical text and to the way in which it is understood. We must insist here on the link between Scripture and the liturgy and between the spiritual reading of the one and the spiritual reading of the other. When we speak of an allegorical or spiritual meaning, or again of a mystical interpretation of the liturgy, we mean the same thing as when we speak of a similar meaning of Holy Scripture. It is quite remarkable that when William Durand (c. 1230–1296), bishop of Mende, or Durandus as he is usually known, the most famous author of spiritual commentary on the liturgy, introduces his work, the *Rationale Divinorum Officiorum* or *Explanation of Divine Service*, he gives as something that is self-evident, needs no explanation, and is the key to the understanding of divine worship, the four classic senses of Scripture, which are listed, for example, by St Thomas Aquinas.[2]

---

1 St Gregory, *Homiliae in Ezechielem* I, VII, 8–10 (*Patrologia Latina* [hereafter *PL*], vol. 76, cols. 843–46).

2 Durandus, *Rationale, prooemium*, 9–12; St Thomas Aquinas, *Summa theologiae* Ia, q1, a10.

First is the *historical* or *literal* sense (the story narrated in the passage, for example, the story of David sinning and repenting, with its theological implications). Then there are the three *spiritual* senses, that is: the *allegorical* sense, by which the Old Testament looks ahead to the New (as the manna in the desert signifies the Eucharist); the *tropological* or *moral* sense (thus, the combat of Jacob with the angel shows that obtaining the Kingdom of heaven through virtue requires the violent conquest of oneself);[3] and the *anagogical* sense, which is ordered towards heavenly things (God's rest on the seventh day of creation foretells the peace of eternal blessedness).

The literal or historical sense is basic. It represents the foundations on which rests the entire building of the understanding of the holy texts: all interpretation is based on the sacred history such as it is presented by the biblical text. The Fathers of the Church also compare it to the bark of a tree: it is immediately accessible, it is the "letter" in contrast to the "spirit," that is, the spiritual sense or the deeper sense (for "the written code," if one goes no further, "kills, but the spirit gives life"—2 Cor 3:6). Among the spiritual meanings, the most important is the allegorical, as St Paul terms it at one point (Gal 4:24), though he also calls it the figurative or typical sense (1 Cor 10:11), which links the Old Testament to the New, to Christ and to the Church. Because the allegorical sense is the most important of the spiritual senses, to the point where it covers both the moral sense and the anagogical sense, we will often use the phrase "allegorical meaning" to mean the totality of the spiritual interpretation. Here therefore the word "allegorical" is understood in the technical sense used in the interpretation of Scripture: it is the Christic sense of Scripture (and of the liturgy). This meaning is Christ himself, the immolated Lamb, who opens up the meaning of the entirety of Scripture, and without whom Scripture remains a book that is closed, sealed, and incomprehensible. The entire Old Testament, underneath the letter, looks ahead to Christ. But even in the New Testament, which by definition contains Christ directly, we must not content ourselves with the letter,

3 See Mt 11:12.

Christic though it may be. Each text, for example from the Gospels, reveals beyond the literal sense, beyond the surface Christic sense, a deeper Christic sense: for example, the Good Samaritan is the image of Jesus, who brings healing to the wounded while the priests of the Old Covenant are incapable of doing so; the best wine "served last" at the marriage of Cana is the Gospel compared to the Old Testament, etc. Just as the spiritual sense of the Old Testament looked forward to the New Testament, so this deeper and spiritual sense of the New Testament depends on a contrast with, or explanation of, the Old Testament. In summary, we can say with Pope Pius XII (1939–1958) in his encyclical *Divino Afflante* that the Letter is the sacred teaching, which by its nature speaks of Jesus Christ, even before his coming, and that the Spirit is Jesus Christ himself.[4]

When we come to the liturgy, the literal sense is equally fundamental, and more so today than ever. Knowledge of the spirit presupposes (and reinforces) that of the letter, which is the bearer of the theology of the Mass. Reference to the theology of the Mass currently creates an immense problem: how many Catholics know the theology of the Mass, or know what we might otherwise call the letter of the Christian liturgy? How many Catholics know, as those who had been catechized as children used once to know in their own fashion, that "in this divine sacrifice, which is carried out in the Mass, the same Christ is contained and immolated in a bloodless manner who offered himself once for all in a bloody sacrifice on the altar of the Cross (Heb 9:14, 27)," as the Council of Trent (1545–1563) recalled?[5] *A fortiori*, an even smaller proportion could recall in detail what Pope Pius XII said in his encyclical on the sacred liturgy, *Mediator Dei*: the sacrifice of the altar, entirely directed towards the sacrifice of Golgotha, is completed by the arrival of Christ in glory, under the form of the two kinds or species; it is an act of oblation and of immolation that is realized in the double consecration:

---

4 *Divino Afflante* (1943), §26.

5 Heinrich Denzinger and Adolf Schönmetzer, *Enchiridion symbolorum: definitionum et declarationum de rebus fidei et morum* (Barcinone: Herder, 1965), 33rd ed. (hereafter DS), no. 1743.

> On the cross He completely offered Himself and all His sufferings to God, and the immolation of the victim was brought about by the bloody death, which He underwent of His free will. But on the altar, by reason of the glorified state of His human nature, "death shall have no more dominion over Him" (Rom 6:9), and so the shedding of His blood is impossible; still, according to the plan of divine wisdom, the sacrifice of our Redeemer is shown forth in an admirable manner by external signs that are the symbols of His death. For by the "transubstantiation" of bread into the body of Christ and of wine into His blood, His body and blood are both really present: now the Eucharistic species under which He is present symbolize the actual separation of His body and blood. Thus the commemorative representation of His death, which actually took place on Calvary, is repeated in every sacrifice of the altar, seeing that Jesus Christ is symbolically shown by separate symbols to be in a state of victimhood.[6]

This last passage, which in its way states authoritatively what St Thomas Aquinas said in his *Summa theologiae*[7] and in his *Summa contra gentiles*,[8] brings to a close the long debate of post-Tridentine theology reflecting on the Council's magisterial pronouncements that affirmed both the uniqueness of Christ's sacrifice and the reality of the sacrifice carried out in the course of each Mass. Pius XII made clear in *Mediator Dei* that the sacrifice of the Mass, a sacrificial act that could be repeated without limit, although entirely contained within the unique sacrifice of the Cross, is produced by the presence on the altar of the glorified Christ under the form of the two distinct kinds. This act of oblation and immolation takes concrete form in the two kinds, and is realized by their double consecration. Of course, even if the two kinds are separate, nevertheless through concomitance, the Body exists together with the Blood, the soul, and the divinity of the Lord, just as

6 Pope Pius XII, *Mediator Dei* (1947), §70; DS 3848.
7 St Thomas Aquinas, *Summa theologiae* IIIa, q74, a1 and q78, a3, ad 2 and ad 7.
8 St Thomas Aquinas, *Summa contra gentiles* IV, ch. 61.

his Blood exists inseparably from his Body, his soul, and his divinity.[9]

We will observe in the course of what follows that what appears to me to be the most important dogmatic point made in the Roman Canon (a real standard of faith regarding the Eucharistic sacrifice) was made by St Gregory with regard to this very issue: he said that it was particularly appropriate that the Lord's Prayer, the *Pater noster*, like the Canon that it concludes, is said or sung over the two Eucharistic species while they are still in the separate state in which they were offered, before they are brought together when a particle of the host is put in the chalice.[10] The Mass strictly speaking, the sacramental oblation, therefore runs from the offering of the oblation to the *Pater noster* inclusive, as St Caesarius of Arles (c. 470–542) made clear.[11] What precedes this sacrificial offering – the Entrance and the readings – and what follows it – the Communion – are the preparation for the sacrifice and the application of its fruits.

We see here how the letter and the spirit explain each other. We must not forget that an understanding of the spirit presupposes an understanding of the letter: an understanding of the tree (the symbolism of the Mass) presupposes an understanding of its roots (the doctrine of the sacrifice of the altar). It is true – thanks particularly to the fact that the liturgy is made up entirely of instructive symbols – that the spirit helps us very considerably to rediscover the meaning of the letter. Speaking of branches and leaves – allegorical symbolism, in the technical sense explained above – is another way of recovering the deep roots, the doctrine of the Eucharistic sacrifice, which have enabled the foliage above to branch out. That is why mystagogy, that is, the teaching on the sacraments given to new initiates by the Fathers of the Church, was as much doctrinal as spiritual. The consequence is that, if for more than fifty years there has been an extraordinary catechetical landslide in our basic religious culture in general and in the doctrine of the Eucharistic sacrifice in particular, as a representation of the salvific Passion and, in a connected way, of the real presence and of the priestly

9 St Thomas Aquinas, *Summa contra gentiles* IV, ch. 64.
10 St Gregory, *Epistles*, Bk. IX, Ep. 26 (*PL* 77:964–65).
11 St Caesarius of Arles, Sermon 73, 2.

ministry *in persona Christi*, we have all the more need to recover the mystical understanding of the Mass.

This clarification, which is as much a matter of fact as of poetry, is of immense pedagogical importance for the faith and so for the devotion of the faithful. For Durandus, as for all the spiritual commentators on the ceremonies of the Church (on its architecture, on its ornaments, and on its sacred vessels), the allegorical sense of the liturgy, like that of Scripture, remains inexhaustible and, we might say, limitless; though with this qualification, given by Durandus himself, that Christian worship, which contains countless references to the Old Testament, belongs nevertheless to the New Testament, of which it is an extension. When we take part in the divine liturgy, just as when we read a text of the Gospels, we must in some sense ascend from our initial knowledge of Christ, which reveals its active presence in the divine offices, and rise to a more intimate experience of his living presence, just like the disciples who stepped out from the crowd and came up to Jesus to listen to his Sermon on the Mount (Mt 5:1).

St Paul criticized the Jews who rejected Christ for holding fast to the letter of, and thus falsifying, the Old Testament, as if the veil that covered the face of Moses when it was shining with divine light had stayed in place over their hearts, blinding them and preventing them from seeing in the Law the foreshadowing of Jesus Christ, Messiah and Lord (2 Cor 3:15). In the same way, it is important in the ceremonies of the Mass not to confine ourselves to the letter, which would leave the doctrinal significance of the Mass warped and jejune, but to penetrate to the spirit, or to the deeper meaning that is perpetually capable of becoming deeper still. Thus in the lit candle we will see the *Lumen Christi*, the divine light with which Christ's humanity shines. In fact, even before that, we shall see in the wax a representation of Christ with his most pure Body, and in the wick, his holy soul that makes visible to us his divinity, which is the flame. The liturgy itself will help us to see more complex allegories, comparing the paschal wax, in the *Exultet* sung on Easter Eve, with the column of fire that, as a prefiguring of Christ, went before the Hebrews in the desert at night. And then we will understand that the divine flame, grace, spreads to the candles of the faithful, that is, to their souls whose wax is recast in the mold of Christ.

Moreover, this spiritual commentary on the liturgy is already at work in the New Testament, particularly in the Apocalypse, but also in the Epistle to the Hebrews and in the Gospel according to St John. The Apocalypse itself proceeds in this way to complex mystical interpretations of cultic objects that will go on to serve as models for patristic and medieval authors: the seven lamps are the seven spirits of God (4:5); the gold cups full of perfume represent the prayers of the saints (5:8 and 8:3–4); and the fine linen with which the Spouse is clothed signifies the virtues of the saints (19:8).

Here it is particularly important to underline the twofold character of the liturgical scenes in the Apocalypse: they are at the same time both sacrificial and royal. They describe this triumph of the sacrificed Christ that all the Christian liturgies will go on to elaborate. One could furthermore, on this subject, point to interlinked references between the Apocalypse and the Gospels, particularly the Gospel of St John: the epiphanies, or solemn appearances of the king, when he is enthroned in majesty, seen in the baptismal Epiphany of the Lamb of God (Jn 1:28–34) and in the slaughtered Lamb on its throne (Rev 5:6); the royal entries, or the great procession along the highway prepared for Priest and King to enable him to enter his country, his city, or his Temple, seen in Christ's solemn Entry into Jerusalem (Jn 12:12–19) and in the Lamb on Mount Sion followed by the procession of men without spot (Rev 14:1–5); and the public and royal banquet, seen especially in the marriage of the king's firstborn at Cana (Jn 2:1–11) and in the marriage of the Lamb (Rev 19:7). Moreover we find this liturgical coloring of the book of the Apocalypse, whose sources are in the Gospels (that is to say, are based on Christ's words and actions as they are reported by the inspired authors) in the most liturgical of the four Passion narratives, that of St John: the *Ecce Homo* of Christ clad in the crown of thorns and the purple mantle (Jn 19:5); the procession to Golgotha and the royal superscription (Jn 19:17–21); and the Church, the Spouse of the Lamb, issuing from the side of the new Adam with the blood and water of the sacraments (Jn 19:34). So, as we note the fundamentally priestly and royal character of the book of the Apocalypse (consider the institution of a royal people of priests, 1:6, 5:10, 20:6), we can legitimately say that the great visionary canvas of Scripture's final book contains the spiritual archetypes of all the forms that Christian worship will go on to take.

One could cite many other references, particularly related to the three main aspects mentioned above of the reverence that was given to rulers, and developed in many profound ways, first in the world of the biblical and Hellenistic periods, then in the Christian society of Late Antiquity, and finally in the medieval world; namely first, the solemn entry of the king; second, the appearance of the king to receive his subjects' solemn homage; and third and last, the participation of the king's favored friends in festive celebrations. Christian worship has thus borrowed, as much as it has inspired, the ceremonial that accompanied public life in the periods of its greatest development. So, we will find that, along with other elements of this type, such as lengthy prayers modelled on petitions to the sovereign, gestures demonstrating allegiance, and the reproduction in the communion rites of rituals associated with the receiving of gifts, all Christian liturgies will contain the following three elements.

First, the solemn entrances, of which three are particularly important: the entry at the Introit (the entry of Christ in the form of his ministers); the entry of the Gospel (the Gospel procession, the entry of Christ in the form of his word, corresponding to the Little Entrance of the Gospel in the liturgy of St John Chrysostom); and the entry of the oblations (corresponding to the Great Entrance in the liturgy of St John Chrysostom, the entry of Christ in the form of the Eucharistic elements).

Second, acts of adoration of the Lord that take place at various times but particularly at the elevations, introduced in the medieval period, of the consecrated elements.

Third, the communion rites at the sacred banquet reuniting the friends of the Lord.

In summary, the Apocalypse is a key source for one of the essential lines of spiritual interpretation of the Mass: the triumph of the immolated Christ, given in communion to his disciples. This victorious aspect of the sacrifice of Christ, which is repeated on the altar and whose merits are applied to the church, is certainly at the root of all mystical interpretation of the Christian Mass and of the Roman Mass in particular.

This spiritual interpretation of the elements of Christian worship, drawn partly from the continuation in the Apocalypse of the allegorical method of interpreting Scripture, was developed in the teaching of the Fathers concerning the sacraments. "When the wine in the chalice is mixed with water, it is the people being united with Christ," said St Cyprian (d. 258),[12] giving an interpretation that refers back to the Apocalypse: "The waters that thou sawest . . . are peoples, and nations, and tongues" (Rev 17:15). It is worth dwelling on this comment, because it is a typical example where the allegory explains the selection of the text that accompanies the rite: in the Roman Mass, the prayer *Deus qui humanae substantiae . . .* , an ancient prayer for the feast of Christmas, refers to the union of the faithful with Christ and accompanies the addition of some water to the wine that is going to be consecrated. Ever since the Late Antique period, the great period when the Roman liturgy and the other great Eastern liturgies were formed, the mystical sense has linked together the parts of the sacred action. Thus Theodore of Mopsuestia (c. 350–428), in the course of preaching on the symbolic meaning of each ceremony, explains why in the Syrian rite the deacons continually agitate fans around the altar from the moment when the consecrated bread and wine are deposited on it in turn: this was what people did in daily life when the corpse of a notable was being carried in an open coffin.[13] By acting thus, the Syrian deacons similarly demonstrate the respect that is due to the holy Body that lies lifeless on the altar as a victim immolated but incorruptible. A mystical author of the end of the fifth century or the beginning of the sixth, who exercised an immense influence on the Middle Ages under the name of Dionysius the Areopagite, wrote regarding the censing of the church by the bishop:

12 St Cyprian, Epistle 63 (*PL* 4:384).
13 Alphonse Mingana, ed. and trans., *Commentary of Theodore of Mopsuestia on the Lord's Prayer, and on the Sacraments of Baptism and the Eucharist*, Woodbrooke Studies, vol. vi (Cambridge: W. Heffer & Sons, 1933), ch. V, 86.

> And in the same way you will see the Hierarch bringing forward the sweet perfume from the more holy place into the sacred areas outside and teaching us by his return to the same place that a share in things divine occurs in all holy persons to the extent that they are worthy, and that it cannot be diminished or set in motion in any way and that it stands unchangeably within its own characteristic in accordance with its divine foundation.[14]

We should also mention St Isidore of Seville (c. 560–636), who was famous for his mystical etymologies, so as not to leave out Visigothic and Merovingian allegory; and we must remind ourselves of the Eastern links of this allegorical approach: Germanus I (c. 634–c. 733), Patriarch of Constantinople, provides us among other themes with the fundamental theme of "heaven on earth," by referring to the Apocalypse, which presents the earthly liturgy as a concelebration with the choirs of angels that worship before the throne of the Lamb.

It was however in the Carolingian period that the spiritual interpretation of the Mass unfolded to its full extent, at the very moment when in Frankish territory the Roman rite underwent an almost definitive development under the simultaneous influence of several different factors: borrowings from the Gallican liturgy; a strong belief in the efficacity of the sacrifice, leading to a multiplication of private Masses and the development of Masses for the Dead; and the widespread introduction of self-deprecating passages said by the celebrant expressing his unworthiness, the famous *apologiae*, which recall a literary genre not uninfluenced by the *Confessions* of St Augustine (354–430) and which we find represented in the Offertory prayers, and in the confession described as "Prayers at the Foot of the Altar." This was moreover roughly the same period as that in which the Byzantine rite entered its last great phase of development, itself borrowing extensively (in this case, from the monastic liturgy of Palestine). A short allegorical commentary on the Mass—a type of composition later given the technical name of *expositio missae*—written at the start of the ninth century, by an author later wrongly named

14 Pseudo-Dionysius, *Ecclesiastical Hierarchy*, Bk. 4, ch. 3, 3.

as Germanus of Paris, is the oldest example of this liturgical literature that has survived to our own day, along with another almost contemporary document, called *Dominus Vobiscum*. Then, with the great Amalarius of Metz (c. 780 – c. 850), collaborator of Charlemagne and Louis the Pious, compiler of extracts from St Gregory and St Augustine, the *expositiones missae* become a specific genre of ecclesiastical literature. One of Amalarius's principal ideas, which he acquired as part of an already well-established tradition and which became a key element in the spiritual interpretation of the Eucharistic sacrifice, is that there is a link between the unfolding of the Mass and the history of salvation: the Mass represents the mission of Jesus Christ, from the proclamation of his arrival on earth, to which the Introit corresponds, sung by the choir, who in their turn represent the choir of prophets who foretold Christ's arrival, up to his Ascension, to which corresponds the *Ite missa est*, the dismissal of the faithful (we will return to this), with which those assisting at the Mass are dismissed just as Christ dismissed his apostles on the Mount of Olives.

From the ninth century to the end of the twelfth century, the age of the cathedrals, this genre of explanatory descriptions of the allegory of the Mass, the *expositiones missae*, underwent an extraordinary flowering. This was also the great period of the medieval spiritual commentaries on Holy Scripture. Continuing with the work of Lothar of Segni, who became Pope Innocent III (1198 – 1216), all these commentaries led up to one of the Middle Ages' most inspired encyclopedists, Durandus, who was a legal expert as well as an outstanding scholastic theologian. Just as St Thomas Aquinas was able to create a *Summa theologiae*, Durandus composed what one could really call a *Summa liturgiae*, which would go on to be reissued as a fundamental guide to the allegorical explanation of the liturgy until the great decline of mystical commentary on Scripture and the liturgy at the end of the seventeenth century.

Already starting in the sixteenth century, however, the allegorical interpretation was increasingly regarded as "Gothic," like the architectural style based on the pointed arch. Nevertheless, just as in the seventeenth century people such as Henri Du Mont (1610 – 1684) and Guillaume-Gabriel Nivers

(1632–1714) composed plainchant, so people at this period continued to practice the *expositio missae*. Thus Jean-Jacques Olier (1608–1657), parish priest of St Sulpice in Paris, and founder of France's *grands séminaires* designed to form candidates for the priesthood, wrote for his clergy the *Explication des cérémonies de la grand'messe de paroisse selon l'usage romain* (an adaptation of the work's true title, *L'esprit des cérémonies de la messe*—"*esprit*" being understood in the technical sense of "allegorical meaning"), which was published in 1657. Olier, while imprinting the spirituality of his own period on the work, picked up the images that had been used thousands of times, like biblical metaphors woven through the liturgy, answering each other, interlinking, and enriching the text:

> The grains of incense, thrown into the fire three times, indicate therefore the faithful of the Church, thrown into the burning furnace of the bosom of God, who pour themselves out into praise, and are consumed in him through Jesus Christ . . . The body of the censer, which contains the burning charcoal, represents Christ's humanity, the basis of which consists in glory and is consumed by the divine fire.[15]

But what has been called "the crisis of the European mind"[16] was growing unavoidably, with its complex thrust that comprised a positive element, the demands of rationality, but also a negative element, rationalism. This led to a crisis of the mystical sense in the interpretation of Scripture and the liturgy, as well as elsewhere a crisis in mysticism, in the sense of passive prayer, something that is a separate story, though caused by the same developments. This decline accompanied the rise of scientific criticism in the study of the Bible. Though this criticism was a positive development, its rational method was often confused with rationalism, and in fact the application of the historico-critical method to the Bible, as with the liturgy, progressively eliminated all interest in tracing the spiritual meaning. Even from the point of view of the historical knowledge of the text, this is an aberration in that we cannot separate the

15 Olier, *L'esprit des cérémonies*, Bk. III, chs. i & iv.
16 Paul Hazard, *The Crisis of the European Mind 1680–1715*, trans. by J. Lewis May (New York: New York Review, 2013).

development of the spiritual hermeneutic of both Bible and liturgy from the story of their transmission and composition. The result was that until recently, despite the resurgence of interest prompted by the work of Henri de Lubac (1896–1991),[17] medieval spiritual interpretation has been treated with the greatest condescension. And if the spiritual exegesis of the Bible is now regaining its former glory, that is still far from the case for the spiritual exegesis of the liturgy. Now, without understanding this wave of allegory in which an entire Christian and sacral society was immersed, we can no more understand, even scientifically, the Roman liturgy, and the Roman Mass especially, than we can understand the planning and construction of the early Christian basilicas and of their successors, the cathedrals.

My purpose here will therefore be the very limited one of encouraging a wish, not just to rediscover this vein of allegorical interpretation, which should for example be given its full and proper place in all the missals published for the use of the faithful, but also to practice it. By that I mean nothing more than to point out a route, the traces of which have often been erased. The practical focus of my work means that naturally I have to a certain extent summarized the long interpretative tradition, as if it underwent relatively little change from beginning to end. Nevertheless a linear development does exist, following an evolutionary path that leads to a growing comprehensiveness, not so different from that of the *lex credendi* in its theologico-magisterial pronouncements. With this in mind, it is good intellectual practice, as we survey the ways in which sacred doctrine was taught and prayed, to place ourselves within this all-embracing theological perspective. This long interpretative tradition (eight centuries, if one restricts oneself to the *expositiones missae* properly so-called, from the ninth to the seventeenth century) nevertheless deserves, and will perhaps one day receive, many historical investigations of its continuities and developments.

It is also not my purpose today to continue to develop this style of commentary along traditional lines, since that can be left to those with the aptitude for it, as Paul Claudel (1868–1955)

---

17 Henri de Lubac, *Medieval Exegesis: The Four Senses of Scripture*, trans. by Mark Sebanc et al., 3 vols. (Grand Rapids, MI: Eerdmans, 1998–2009).

demonstrated in the exegetical world.[18] I wish only to revive it, while giving each and every one access to this tradition. In doing so, I do not hide, nor am hiding from myself, that my exposition of the tradition will be innovative in one way. It would, for example, not be realistic to list all the meanings that Amalarius, Rupert of Deutz (c. 1070–1129), Ivo of Chartres (c. 1040–1116), Durandus, or Olier have given for the censer. On the other hand, it is certainly valuable to insist on what seems to lie at the heart of their interpretations: incense is the sacrificial prayer that the humanity of Christ offers before his Father. It is impossible to avoid a certain amount of selection, of translation into contemporary thought, of filtering through the knowledge of tradition. I beg the kind reader to excuse the failings of this necessarily personal action, bearing in mind that I am only trying to make accessible to him the traditional material that I am putting before him.

Two keys to the spiritual reading of the Mass, which have already been described as fundamental, are particularly important.

The first key, which we can call *victory*, is taken from the Apocalypse and has driven the formation of the Eucharistic liturgy throughout: the *sacrificium missae* is the triumph of the immolated Christ, given in communion to his disciples. The Mass reminds us of what has been called a "theology of victory."[19]

The second key, which we can call *history*, has underpinned the entire interpretative tradition of the Eucharistic sacrifice: in all the allegorical explanations of divine worship, the unfolding of the Mass corresponds to the history of salvation. My explanation will be no different from that of St Francis de Sales (1567–1622), who stated what seemed to him to be incontrovertible and to be part of a tradition going back at least to Carolingian times:

> From the time [the priest] goes up to the altar until the Gospel, consider the advent of our Lord and His life

18 Michel Malicet, Dominique Millet-Gérard, Xavier Tilliette, eds., *Paul Claudel, Le poète et la Bible*, 2 vols. (Paris: Gallimard, 1998–2004).
19 François Heim, *La Théologie de la victoire: de Constantin à Théodose*, Théologique Historique 89 (Paris: Beauchesne, 1992).

> in this world . . . . From the Gospel till the end of the Creed, consider the preaching of our Savior . . . . From the Creed to the *Pater noster*, apply your heart to the mysteries of the death and passion of our Redeemer, actually and essentially represented in this holy sacrifice . . . .[20]

---

20 St Francis de Sales, *Introduction to the Devout Life* (London and New York: Longmans, Green and Co., 1891), part 2, ch. xiv, 69.

THE ARRANGEMENT OF THIS WORK

OUR DESCRIPTION OF THE CEREMONIES OF THE Roman Mass will be divided into three parts:

PART 1: *The Preparation for the Sacrifice*, otherwise known as the Mass of the Catechumens, leading up to what in ancient times was their dismissal.

1. *The Holy Preparations*: after surveying the framework of the Mass and the celebrating ministers and their assistants, we will consider the liturgical vestments, the cleansing of the congregation and of the church, the confessions of the ministers, their move to the altar, and the censing of the altar where the sacrifice is due to take place.
2. *The Ceremony of the Entrance*: we will consider the prayers and ceremonies from the Introit to the homily, and in particular the solemn entry of the ministers of the Mass, highlighted by the Introit, and the solemn entrance of the Gospel, that is to say, the Gospel procession and the censing of the Gospel.

PART 2: *The Mass Properly So-called: the Eucharistic Sacrifice*, containing two sets of prayers.

1. *The Offertory*, from the *Credo* to the Secret, including the solemn entrance of the oblations, that is, their unveiling and their censing.
2. The Roman Eucharistic Prayer, the Canon, from the introductory Preface to the concluding *Pater noster*.

PART 3: *The Communion*, from the Fraction to the Last Gospel: a ritual unit focused on the application of the fruits of the sacrifice, in which each one of the elements, all very closely connected together, has undergone changes, and which comprises the Fraction, the consumption of the sacred elements, the prayers of thanksgiving, the blessing, and the dismissal.

In sum, the key to the mystical interpretation of each part is:

PART 1: The fulfilment of the Scriptures in the Gospel, with the movement from the epistle side to the gospel side, or again the movement from the proclamation by the subdeacon to the chant of the deacon.

PART 2: The death on the Cross, indicated by the separation of the holy elements.

PART 3: The Resurrection, the reunion of the soul and body of the Savior, indicated by the Commixture.

PART 1

The Preparation for the Sacrifice

EXTENDING UP TO THE GOSPEL AND THE HOMILY, AND DEMONSTRATING THE FULFILMENT OF THE SCRIPTURES IN THE GOSPEL

I *The Holy Preparations*

1 THE FRAMEWORK

> In this sacrifice, the Son of God offers to the glory of the eternal Father all that he has ever done or suffered: he offers what he has done himself and through others, what he has suffered himself and through others; with the result that everything that is seen to be expressed in the ceremonies serves to explain to the faithful, and to put before their eyes, what happens in the secret offering of Jesus Christ, who offers along with himself this admirable sacrifice of the Church, clothed in his merits and his praise; whether in one or the other Testament, whether among the angels or among men: in one word, reaching out to his full extent he offers himself to the eternal Father, to obtain mercy for his Church, and to consummate his body so that it may be glorified.[1]

We will here discuss the Roman Mass in its traditional form, and will focus on the solemn Mass, which is a sung Mass celebrated by a priest, assisted by a deacon and a subdeacon.[2] One

---

1 Olier, *L'esprit des cérémonies*, Bk. I, ch. i.

2 The celebrant is equally assisted by inferior clergy: (1) by two acolytes, the acolyteship being in itself one of the minor orders, but in the course of a solemn Mass the acolyte's function is generally exercised by simple clerics or by laymen temporarily treated as clerics, charged with carrying the candles during the entrance and the Gospel chant, with bringing the cruets of water and wine to the altar, with washing the hands of the celebrant, with ringing bells and hand bells, etc.; (2) by a thurifer carrying the censer with its burning charcoal and the incense-boat containing the grains of incense; (3) by two, four, or six clerics carrying lit torches from the *Sanctus* until after the Elevation or the Communion; (4) and possibly by at least one cleric overseeing the choreography of the ceremony, the Master of Ceremonies or *ceremoniarius*. For the actual movements in the ceremony, see Louis Hébert, *Leçons de liturgie à l'usage des séminaires*, ed. 29, rev. Auguste Fayard (Paris: Berche et Pagis, 1952), vol. III, ch. iii; Louis Stercky, *Manuel de liturgie et cérémonial selon le rit romain*, 17th ed., rev. Joseph Antoine Haegy and Léon le Vavasseur (Paris: J. Gabalda, 1940), vol. I, sect. 2, ch. 1.

could reasonably maintain that the Mass *par excellence* is that of the bishop, clothed in the fullness of his priesthood. But the bishop's special Mass, the pontifical Mass, is surrounded by the ceremonial of a real ecclesiastical court, governed by the *Caeremoniale Episcoporum* or *Ceremonial of Bishops*, and until about the sixteenth century was practically invisible to the people (as for a long time was the ceremonial of royal courts), being celebrated in the cathedral choir, which up until this point had generally been closed off from public view by a rood or chancel screen. A solemn Mass celebrated by a priest is in some ways a midpoint, situated between the pontifical Mass, the solemn Mass celebrated by a bishop, and the low Mass, a Mass celebrated by a minister (whether priest or bishop) without solemnity, and which is said rather than sung.[3]

The Sacred Ministers: Christ Yesterday, Today, and Always

The special characteristic of a solemn Mass is that it revolves around the actions of three sacred ministers: the priest, the deacon, and the subdeacon, who all belong to the major orders.[4] And the three of them, from one point of view, are simply one; and when a single bench without a back (called the *sedilia*) is available, they all sit on it together. This is because the three ministers of the solemn Mass all represent the same Jesus Christ in three different states: yesterday, today, and world without end.

---

3 It is possible to characterise the different types of Mass briefly, without distinguishing between prelates superior or inferior to a bishop, or between the bishop of the area and another bishop, who may or may not have the delegated rights of the bishop of the area. Thus there are (1) *the pontifical Mass of the bishop*, which is theoretically the baseline for all other Masses, and may be celebrated either at the bishop's throne, or at a chair or faldstool; (2) *a solemn Mass celebrated by a priest*, which can be either an ordinary solemn Mass or one at which the priest is assisted by the bishop, in which case the bishop can assist from his throne, wearing a cope (*pluviale* or *cappa*, a long silk mantle), and in which he either may be deeply involved (to the point where one could practically call it a pontifical Mass) or may assist from his stall, wearing a mozetta, in which case his involvement is more modest; (3) *a priest's sung Mass* or *Missa cantata*, with or without the use of incense, and somewhere in between a solemn Mass and a low Mass, which is quite widespread because of the small number of clergy generally available in parishes; (4) *a low Mass*, or *Missa lecta* (literally, a "read Mass"), which can be said either by a priest or by a bishop who is accompanied by two chaplains.

4 Even if, theologically speaking, the subdeacon is closer to the minor orders, that is, to the acolytes, exorcists, lectors, and porters.

The subdeacon represents the Old Testament, Jesus Christ yesterday, who was proclaimed partly in the sayings of the prophets, and partly in figures by the saintly individuals who preceded his coming. As is appropriate, the subdeacon always occupies the lowest rank, that of incompleteness. He walks in front of the priest and deacon in a procession (because in a liturgical procession the lowest rank walks at the front); he takes up position on the left when he is needed to support the priest's cope or when the ministers sit on their shared bench; and he generally stands in the sanctuary (the sacred space surrounding the altar) when the ministers are at the altar.

The deacon represents the New Testament, Jesus Christ today, proclaimed in his fullness by the apostles and their successors, the bishops, who are the propagators of the Gospel. He walks behind the subdeacon, as is appropriate to the fullness of Revelation, supports the priest's cope from the right, sits on the right of the priest on the bench, and generally stands on the second step at the altar, just below the celebrant.

The celebrant himself is most fully identified with Jesus Christ today and world without end, as he presently is and always will be, in glory in heaven. The celebrant is the instrument and the representative of Christ glorious and victorious, the Christ who makes himself really present on the altar in the elements of bread and wine in order to accomplish there his sacrifice for the remission of sins and to the glory of his Father. The priest who celebrates at the altar is the image of Jesus Christ priest and victim, but an unbloody victim in his heavenly state. He acts *in persona Christi*, in the person of Christ, wearing his chasuble, the yoke that is sweet and light, as if it were a heavenly vesture, although it is often marked on the back (particularly in chasubles of the French pattern) with the Cross of sacrifice. He is the first in dignity and he walks at the back of the procession, Alpha and Omega, like Christ "the first-born of creation," but also preparing to bring creation to an end. He stands at the altar on the highest step or level, which represents the holy Mount of Golgotha or again the Mountain of the Ascension (without forgetting Tabor and the Mount of the Beatitudes). This highest step puts him as it were above the three great angelic hierarchies, at the highest point of heaven (2 Cor 12:3).

The Sacrifice of the Lamb, Expressed in the Flame, the Incense, and the Stone

As always in the allegorical interpretation of Scripture and the Liturgy, Jesus Christ is figured by the principal objects used in divine worship. Thus the candles, whether the six candles of the altar[5] or the two candlesticks carried by the acolytes, are figures of Jesus Christ consumed in the glory of his Father in this august sacrifice, in which he is always a torch burning and shining before the majesty of God: "a burning and shining light" (Jn 5:35). In fact, in the Jerusalem that descends from heaven to earth, according to the vision of St John, "the Lamb is the lamp thereof" (Rev 21:23). The wax is a "precious substance" made by chaste mother bees, according to the *Exultet*, a chant in honor of the glory of the Paschal Candle, which links them to the Virgin Mary. The virgin wax that the virgin bees bring to birth is the Body of Jesus Christ, whose soul is consumed by the flame of his divinity. The wax is thus the most expressive sign of the presence of divinity in the Holy Sacrament, like the burning bush that burnt and was never consumed, prefiguring the humanity of Jesus Christ in the sacrament of the altar, which burns always without ever being consumed (Ex 3:2).[6]

Similarly, the censer containing the burning charcoal represents, as we have seen, the humanity of Jesus Christ consumed in the divine fire; while the grains of incense, thrown into the flames three times before receiving the priest's blessing, symbolize the faithful of the Church who are thrown into the burning furnace of Christ's Sacred Heart, and whose prayer

5 Seven candles are used at the pontifical Mass of the diocesan bishop, like the seven-branched candlestick, since the bishop possesses the fullness of priesthood. The seven candles also resemble the seven sacred orders (priest, deacon, subdeacon, acolyte, exorcist, reader or lector, porter) which, issuing in a manner of speaking from the hands of the bishop at ordination, carry out the ministry of Christ in its various manifestations: opening the gate of heaven (porters), driving away demons (exorcists), enlightening souls (acolytes), etc. For more on the seven orders, see Peter Kwasniewski with Athanasius Schneider, *Ministers of Christ: Recovering the Roles of Clergy and Laity in an Age of Confusion* (Manchester, NH: Crisis Publications, 2021).

6 The principal sign of the real presence in the tabernacle is the silk canopy, creating a real *tabernaculum*, a holy tent like that belonging to the Ark of the Covenant. Even so, it is obligatory to keep one or more lamps (always an odd number) burning in front of the tabernacle day and night.

fuses with Christ's own, forming the sacrificial prayer that Christ's humanity offers up in front of his Father.

Similarly, too, the altar is a figure of Christ: like the many altars mentioned in the Bible, it is prefigured by the rock in the desert from which living water flowed for the people of Israel – and we recall that "the rock was Christ" (1 Cor 10:4) – or again by the stone on which Jacob sacrificed after having laid his head on it and seen in his dream the mystical ladder leading to heaven (Gen 28:10 ff.). The stone altar, consecrated in its entirety by the holy chrism,[7] or at least containing a consecrated stone bearing five crosses, like the five wounds of Christ, and enshrining the relics of martyrs, saints who have most perfectly reproduced Christ's expiatory sacrifice, also matches the comparison of Christ to the corner stone, the living stone *par excellence*. The three cloths of white linen that cover the altar are the Savior's humanity in its purity: quite apart from the Trinitarian symbolism, which affirms that the divinity of Jesus Christ has been united with the consecrated humanity, they also demonstrate the three parts of Jesus's humanity, according to the division of the Epistle to the Thessalonians (5:23): body, soul, and spirit. Ever since the sixteenth century the altar has usually supported the tabernacle (*tabernaculum* or tent) containing the consecrated reserved hosts, all of which was prefigured by the gold vase containing the manna deposited in the Ark, in the Holy of Holies of the Tabernacle, while one approaches this holy humanity by steps similar to those that led to heaven on Jacob's ladder.

The Church, a Place of Ambiguity midway between Heaven and Earth

It is of the greatest importance that the word designating the sacred building, the church, the place where the holy mysteries are celebrated, is the same as that designating the spiritual building, the Church, the Spouse of Jesus Christ. The Old Testament images of the Temple, of the Tabernacle, the assembled people of Israel, the stone on which Jacob dreamed, the ladder of which

---

7 Chrism, scented oil recalling the sweet smell of Christ, is a royal oil, used for the consecration of bishops, kings, churches, and candidates for confirmation. It represents a spiritual anointing by the Holy Spirit, the divine Person who made Jesus the Christ, that is, the Lord's Anointed One *par excellence* (Is 61:1–2).

Jacob dreamed, the holy mountains of Sinai, Tabor, and Carmel, are only images. True worship, "in spirit and in truth," is by its nature separate from any particular place (Jn 4:23–24). Being worship of the "last days," it is by definition transitory. In the heavenly Jerusalem, which is going to descend onto earth, there will very significantly no longer be a Temple: the Savior himself will be its Temple (Rev 21:22), that is, firstly Christ's physical body, and secondly his Mystical Body. Christ is the definitive Temple. The stone building, as beautiful and sumptuous, or as plain and simple, as it is, represents the Christ who is the Head and the Church who is his Spouse. It represents the real Temple, but is not itself the Temple of the New Covenant.

The dedication or consecration of a church, one of the most beautiful and lengthy ceremonies of the *Roman Pontifical* (the book containing the ceremonies proper to bishops), expresses this idea in various ways and particularly by the twelve anointings of the holy chrism made by the bishop on the walls or pillars of the building, recalling the apostles of the Lord on whom his Church rests. The Mass for the anniversary of the dedication, which in liturgical terms is a Feast of the Lord, affirms the sacred character of the building ("How terrible is this place! This is no other but the house of God, and the gate of heaven" says the Introit, quoting Gen 28:17) just as much as it affirms its spiritual character. The building is what it is only through the habitation within it of Jesus Christ, who said to Zacchaeus, who was due to receive him, "This day is salvation come to this house" (Lk 19:9). Just as the stone church with its altar is assembled from many stones, so the Church, the Spouse of Christ, is assembled from Christians, or "living stones" (1 Cor 3:9, 16; 1 Pet 2:4–8).

We should recall that a pagan temple, which was understood to be the residence of the god, was in reality little more than the *cella* where the cult statue stood, and was not strictly speaking a place of assembly for the people, who stayed outside or in the surrounding courts. By contrast, the precinct of the Temple in Jerusalem that was reserved for the people was for this reason already a sacred place, but was distinct from the place where God lived, the Holy of Holies. Christian churches, images of the Church, the assembly of the baptized that has been called together, are on the contrary the special assembly places of the holy people in their Head, Christ, and in his members. From this came Christianity's preferred adoption of the form of the civil basilica (which was a covered forum and place of assembly for the citizens) as the standard model for the Christian sacred building.

In addition, the people assemble in the church not in a state of disorder but in a pattern ordered by degree. In the *nave*, which recalls the ship of the Church, are the "living stones," the baptized faithful, stones sealed with Christ, the foundation and corner stone (the first stone to be laid in position, blessed according to the rite in the *Roman Pontifical*, is the Christic foundation: he "laid the foundation upon a rock"—Lk 6:48). The walls, so the medievals used to say, are made of stones, of the baptized, joined by a mortar comprising lime (burning charity), sand (earthly matters and affection for them), and water (the grace of life in Christ). The building's length is patience, its width charity, and its height hope. The columns, particularly those that received the twelve anointings with oil, are the apostles. And if there are transepts, extending across the church and separating the nave from the choir, giving the church the form of a cross, we can compare the stone church to a man with a body, arms, and a head, or rather to the Man-God, the Body of Christ on the Cross.

The *choir* (whose name derives from *chorus*, the team of singers, giving rise to medieval etymologies embroidering the idea of *chorea*, dance, or *corona*, a crown), which in the old basilicas is also the *presbyterium*, belongs to the priests and singers, and is the place where the clergy,[8] who are the representatives of Christ the Head, take their place. In Christian states, it is also where certain magistrates, "the clergy of the exterior world," take their place, since they are the defenders of the Church, as was the Emperor Constantine, "the bishop of those outside."

At the end of the choir, or sometimes in front of it, but always more prominent, is the *sanctuary*, the *sanctuarium*, the sacred area around the altar.

---

8 Or of those regarded as comparable to the clergy. In France, from at least the sixteenth century, there is evidence that each small parish contained lay singers who wore a long surplice, a cope, and a square cap (the biretta), and sang before a large music-desk, which was part of the furniture of each church.

The entire building, just like the entire people assembled in prayer, encourages us to think of a procession that is oriented, that is, facing towards the East (or at least theoretically so), and more precisely towards the Crucifix placed to the East. For there, suspended over, or resting on, the altar of sacrifice, will always be found the representation of the Cross of Christ, towards which ministers and faithful turn. All the sacred rites, the Mass, the Divine Office, are therefore oriented, turned towards the Lord, while the participants, like the wise virgins waiting for the bridegroom, take part waiting and watching for the glorious return of their Lord, who will appear like lightning shining from the East (Mt 24:27).

2 THE LITURGICAL VESTING IN THE SACRISTY

In every church or cathedral there is an important room, a necessary addition to the place of worship. This room, to be honest, is a real liturgical location where practical preparations are made, which permits reflection and recollection, and in which complete silence must be maintained. The room concerned is the sacristy, the *sacrarium*,[9] a sacred location where the holy vessels are stored, or again a *secretarium*, a separated area where such items can be protected.

In this place that is both separate and sacred, the ministers put on their liturgical vestments and prepare themselves spiritually for the ceremony in which they are going to participate. This separate and sacred room is doubly representative.

First, it is the symbol of the Virgin Mary, the "secret chamber" of the king, linking to various images in the Song of Songs (chamber, storeroom, secret garden). Mary's womb was like a sacristy: there the Son of God put on his fleshly vestments before entering the world for the great liturgy that he was going to carry out there, which ended with the holy Sacrifice of Calvary.

Second, it also symbolizes the soul, within which each of us clothes himself with ornaments of grace, piety, virtue, and

---

9 Today, if we are to be wholly correct, the *sacrarium* of a cathedral is a sacristy laid out as a chapel, specially reserved as a place where the bishop dons his liturgical vestments, when he does not do so at his throne or at his faldstool.

penitence, with which he will carry out his spiritual exercises and his good works.

Olier adds his own special and delightful touch to the office of the sacristan, a touch that has enchanted generations of seminarians charged with fulfilling this office. He sees in the sacristan, who is normally a cleric, and sometimes even a priest, according to the *Caeremoniale Episcoporum*,[10] the image of God the Father who sends a priest to offer sacrifice on the altar, and must do so with that same love that was shown by the eternal Father entrusting his Son with the mission of saving the world: "We therefore need for this holy service of the sacristy a venerable man, of a most complete sanctity, who would be seen as the image of God the Father."[11]

The symbolism of the sacred vestments has already been mentioned in the Introduction. It is drawn particularly from the "Preparation for the Mass" found in the Roman missal, which is followed by a prayer attributed to St Ambrose (but in fact composed by John of Fécamp), divided into seven, with one part of the prayer for each day of the week. All these prayers are inspired by ancient prayers of the greatest interest. The prayers corresponding to the different vestments that the priest puts on, explaining their symbolic importance, are as follows. All of them, as we shall see, allude to scriptural images.

The *surplice* is a linen vestment with long sleeves, worn over the cassock during the ceremonies. It is a reduced form of the alb, which may have appeared towards the twelfth century. The Tridentine missal, according to a rubric[12] that later fell into disuse, provided for the priest to wear his other vestments, the alb and the chasuble, over the top of the surplice, but this usage has been retained only for the two vested canons of the pontifical Mass, who wear their cope, chasuble, dalmatic, or tunicle over the surplice and the amice. "*Indue me*... (Clothe me, O Lord, in the new man, who is created by God in justice and the sanctity of truth)."

10 *Caeremoniale Episcoporum*, Bk. I, ch. vi, 1.
11 Olier, *L'esprit des cérémonies*, Bk. I, ch. iii.
12 Rubrics are instructions printed in liturgical books in red letters, *rubrae*, which give the details of the ceremonies to be carried out, or indications of this sort grouped together at the start of a book or chapter.

The *amice* is a rectangle of linen cloth put on over the head, and then fastened over the neck, covering the collar, possibly deriving from the old *amictus Romanus* that used to cover the priest's head during the Holy Sacrifice. "*Impone, Domine*... (Place upon me, O Lord, the helmet of salvation, that I may overcome the assaults of the devil)."

The *alb* is a long white (*alba*) robe of linen cloth covering all the body down to the ankles, the ancient priestly "tunicle" from the fourth century onwards, and restricted to liturgical use since at least the eighth century. "*Dealba me*... (Purify me, O Lord, and cleanse my heart, so that, washed in the Blood of the Lamb, I may enjoy eternal bliss)."

The *cincture* or girdle is a linen cord used to fasten the alb above the waist, and is mentioned as an accessory of the alb from the ninth century, but is undoubtedly earlier. "*Praecinge me*... (Gird me, O Lord, with the cincture of purity, and quench in my heart the fire of concupiscence, that the virtue of continence and chastity may abide in me)."

The *maniple* is a silk ornament of the liturgical color of the day, in the form of a small stole carried by the priest, the deacon, and the subdeacon on the left forearm, like a sheaf, *manipulus*, or napkin, and is a sign of the duties of a consul that has entered the liturgy. "*Merear, Domine*... (May I deserve, O Lord, to bear the maniple of weeping and sorrow, that I may receive the reward for my labors with rejoicing)."

The *stole* is a long strip of silk of the liturgical color of the day that goes around the neck of the priest and the deacon. The priest crosses the stole over his chest; the deacon crosses it on his right hip using the cincture; and the bishop wears it in front without crossing it at all. It is assuredly the oldest of the specifically liturgical forms of clothing. "*Redde mihi*... (Restore unto me, O Lord, the stole of immortality, which was lost through the guilt of our first parents: and, although I am unworthy to approach thy sacred Mysteries, nevertheless grant unto me eternal joy)."[13]

---

13 The crossing of the stole over the breast, as noted in the Introduction, is a ceremony within the ordination rite that symbolizes the ordinand's submission to the bishop, whose fellow worker he is. The priest wears the stole crossed only when he is celebrating Mass.

The *chasuble* is an outer garment, and we cannot be sure that it became a specifically liturgical form of clothing until towards the eighth century. It is today the proper garment for the celebrant of the Holy Sacrifice. "*Domine, qui dixisti*... (O Lord, Who said, 'My yoke is easy and My burden light': grant that I may bear it well and follow after Thee with thanksgiving. Amen)." The shape of the chasuble has varied according to period and place: it can be more or less ample, but it at least covers the shoulders and falls in front of and behind the body. It is made of silk of the liturgical color of the day, i.e., of white, red, green, violet, or black, sometimes of cloth of gold (which in solemn celebrations stands for all the colors except violet and black) or of silver (which stands for white).[14]

The deacon and subdeacon wear respectively a *dalmatic*, which is a vestment originating in imperial and aristocratic courts, introduced to Rome from Dalmatia, and adopted by the pope, priests, and deacons, and a *tunicle*. Dalmatics and tunicles are generally of the same pattern and fabric as the priest's chasuble. Their essential distinguishing feature is that they have short sleeves.[15]

---

14 Rose can replace violet at *Gaudete* and *Laetare* Masses in the middle of Advent and Lent. Other colours exist or have existed: in Lyon (and anciently in Paris) ash-grey was used in Lent; yellow, blue (used almost identically to green), brown and red or *fulva* were used in Paris; while blue is used today in Spain and its former territories for the Virgin Mary. The colour associated with a given feast can vary: Corpus Christi used to be in red, but is today in white. Currently white is used for Feasts of the Lord, of the Virgin Mary, of Confessor Saints, and of Virgin Saints who were not martyred; red is used for the flames of the Holy Spirit and for the blood of martyrs; violet is used for periods of penitence such as Lent, Advent, and vigils; black is used for Masses for the Dead and for Good Friday; green, symbolizing Christian hope, is used for the Sundays after Epiphany and after Pentecost.

15 At solemn Masses during the week (with some exceptions), and on Sundays in Advent and Lent (except for *Gaudete* and *Laetare* Sundays), the deacon and the subdeacon replace the dalmatic and the tunicle with chasubles that are folded in front of the chest. Chasubles worn by the principal ministers of the altar and folded up at certain moments (not necessarily in penitential periods) and unfolded at other moments were one of the characteristics of the Roman rite. The sacred ministers, all representatives of Christ, each wore a chasuble, so it seems, ever since a time in the distant past. The folded chasuble, kept in penitential Masses, which have a particularly traditional character, is a sign of the ministers' identity with Christ. The folded chasubles of the deacon and subdeacon are a sign of

The *cope*, once called the pluvial, is the vestment used for processions, and for the ministers of the Divine Office (as also for dignitaries from the cathedral chapter at a diocesan bishop's pontifical Masses). The celebrant of the Mass puts on the cope on Sunday, before the Holy Sacrifice, when he is getting ready for the Aspersion, or in general before every ceremony that precedes the Mass, such as the blessing of ashes or of palms. It is a vestment of silk, falling as far as the ankle and open in front. Its origin is debated: because of the false hood that can be seen on the back of the cope, it might be a modification of the monastic and clerical *cappa*, today worn only by bishops, and it is possible that at Rome it did not become specifically liturgical before the twelfth century. One of the most noticeable particularities of French vestments was the wearing of the cope by singers, not just in the Divine Office or in processions, but also at the Sunday high Mass. The cope is the vestment of the elect, clothed in the new heaven (Heb 1:12), a symbolism identical to that of the heavenly veils that cover the oblations (in current Roman practice, the veil that covers the chalice and the paten on which the host rests prior to the Offertory) and the sacred vessels. There is no prayer to accompany the wearing of the cope, since heavenly prayer is pure contemplation, without the utterance of any formula.

The sacred ministers also wear a *biretta*, a cap of square shape, and the headgear of magistrates, doctors, and clerics. The clerical Roman biretta has a tuft of silk and three appendages, called peaks or horns, three in number because clerical authority comes from the Trinity.[16]

The departure from the sacristy resembles the entrance of Christ into the world. Contrary to a widespread opinion, the emergence of the priest and his ministers, unlike the arrival of a bishop in the sanctuary, is not a real procession; and because

penitence, suitably replacing the "joyful" dalmatic and the tunicle (for, at ordinations, the bishop puts the dalmatic on the deacon as a "vestment of joy," *vestimentum laetitiae*, and puts the tunicle on the subdeacon as an "garment of joy," *indumentum laetitiae*). The folded chasuble is also a sign of incompleteness, in the same way that the back of the chasuble of the newly ordained priest is folded until the end of the ordination ceremony, the moment when the bishop has just conferred on him through the liturgy the power to forgive sins.

16 It can also be used as part of the choir vestments. The current Roman form of the biretta was made obligatory in France towards 1840.

the sacristy is generally adjacent to the choir, it does not allow for a long route towards the sanctuary. To tell the truth, the departure from the sacristy anticipates the real entry of Christ and his ministers, corresponding to his entry into the world, which is symbolized by the Introit, much as the real rising of the king at Versailles might take place before the official ceremony of the *levée*. Be that as it may, Jesus Christ appears before the eyes of the faithful in three manifestations, as we have seen: the subdeacon, symbolizing the Old Testament that foretells the coming of Christ (particularly in the case of St John the Baptist, the last of the prophets), and the deacon, who symbolizes the New Testament, and who by walking with the subdeacon indicates that the Old and New Testaments form a single whole, whose fullest realization is in the Christ, both priest and victim, symbolized by the celebrant himself.

We should note that the movement of these ministers, despite what we have just said, sometimes turned into a real procession, before (or sometimes after) the Sunday high Mass, which either processed round the interior of the church, or moved outside the church to a calvary or a statue. This was the practice in many French parishes, which is why so many French towns and villages have a *Rue de la Procession*.

3 THE CLEANSING OF THE CLERGY AND THE FAITHFUL; THE CONFESSION OF THE MINISTERS

The Aspersion of Holy Water

The rite of the aspersion of holy water takes place on Sundays, because it recalls baptism and was originally attached to Easter Sunday, the Sunday recalled by every Sunday, the day of the Lord. The ceremony is not complete if it is not preceded in the sacristy by the exorcism and blessing of the salt and water before the high Mass, which we could describe as a preparatory rite that gives the aspersion all its meaning.[17] Just as Elisha cured the unwholesomeness of the water by scattering a little salt on it (4 Kgs 2:20), so this same salt, accompanying the priest's exorcisory prayers, removes what is unwholesome from the people,

17 The blessing of the fire on Holy Saturday, which with the reforms of Pius XII became a most theatrical event, was originally a preparatory blessing of this sort.

symbolized by the water, as in "The waters that you saw . . . are peoples, and nations, and tongues" (Rev 17:15). It sanctifies and cleanses those who are soiled, and renders the devices of the devil ineffective. The people or water is cleansed and purified, ready to be sanctified by the word of God, which can never lose its savor.

The aspersion itself, which follows when the ministers have entered the church, is really a combination of blessing and exorcism, almost a domestic rite. It resembles the aspersions seen in monasteries when a tour was made of the cloister, or the individual cells were visited. The final prayer of this ceremony, *Exaudi nos, Domine* . . . (Hear us, O holy Lord, almighty Father, eternal God: and vouchsafe to send thy holy angel from heaven, to guard, cherish, protect, visit, and defend all that dwell in this house), which is that of the blessing prescribed by the Ritual when the priest blesses a house as he enters it to carry out a ceremony, refers to the *habitaculum*, the house where one lives, for which one requests a visit from the Angel of God.

This is also a first reference to "the Angel of God," that is, to Christ himself, who is asked to come down to this place. During the aspersion, the ancient chant *Asperges* is sung (Thou shalt sprinkle me with hyssop, O Lord, and I shall be cleansed; thou shalt wash me, and I shall be made whiter than snow), or at Eastertide, *Vidi aquam* (I saw water flowing from the right side of the temple, Alleluia; and all to whom that water came were saved, and they shall say: Alleluia, Alleluia),[18] with the first verse of the penitential psalm *Miserere* (Have mercy on me, O God, according to thy great mercy—Ps 50:2), or at Eastertide, *Confitemini Domino* (Give praise to the Lord, for he is good: for his mercy endureth forever—Ps 117:1), to the end that all soiling of unclean spirits be driven from the building as much as from the hearts of the faithful.

That is the real effect of the blessed and exorcised water, virtually the same as that of baptismal water, and of the water with

18 The text is taken from Ezekiel 47, where the Lord shows Ezekiel the City built on a mountain and facing the south where the glorious Temple was to be found. This Temple is the body of Christ, of which he said, "Destroy this temple, and in three days I will raise it up" (Jn 2:19). The waters which flow from the Temple and from the open side of Christ on the Cross (Jn 19:14) are the fountain of baptism.

which we mark ourselves on entering the church.[19] There is a link between this water and the Blood of Christ, since immersion in the waters of baptism represents in reality immersion in the cistern of Christ's propitiatory Blood: "For if the blood of goats and of oxen, and the ashes of an heifer being sprinkled, sanctify such as are defiled, to the cleansing of the flesh: How much more shall the blood of Christ, who by the Holy Ghost offered himself unspotted unto God, cleanse our conscience from dead works, to serve the living God?" (Heb 9:13–14).

After the aspersion, the priest puts aside the heavenly cope and clothes himself in the chasuble that represents the clothing of Jesus Christ, both in his state of glory in heaven and in his sacramental and unbloody state of weakness on the altar.

The Confession of the Ministers

These prayers of confession are collectively called "prayers at the foot of the altar." Reverting to the category of *apologiae*,[20] they form the ministers' own preparation prior to approaching the altar. With head uncovered (apart from bishops and comparable prelates who wear a skull cap),[21] with hands "linked," that is to say, brought together,[22] the priest identifies himself with

19 There are three sorts of holy water: the first is the lustral, or purificatory, water which is used for the dedication of a church or an altar; the second is ordinary holy water, with which we are sprinkled or sprinkle ourselves; the third is the water consecrated by the holy oils for the administration of the sacrament of baptism. Once upon a time there used to be a fourth sort, for the ordeal by water and intended to elicit a "judgment of God."

20 Or *apologiae sacerdotis*, confessions by the priest, in the sense of requests for forgiveness, confessions of unworthiness. People also used the term *excusationes*, accusations in front of the altar, etc. An example is given by the *oratio ante altare*, the prayer before the altar of a ninth-century sacramentary: "O God, who makest the unworthy worthy, accept with favour these pleasing sacrifices, which I offer for my sins and my offences and for my innumerable errors, and for all those who are present here and also for all faithful Christians."

21 The skull cap, a small hemispherical headcovering, was worn by most clergy until the beginning of the twentieth century, and covered the tonsure, giving rise to the famous anticlerical slogan, "Down with the skull cap!" It was in practice abandoned under Pope Pius XI (1922–1939) apart from bishops, for whom it was now violet, cardinals, who wear red skull caps, and some other senior clergy.

22 Joining the hands together is itself a prayer, indicating an attitude of complete submission to God, resembling that of a feudal vassal to his superior.

the publican of the Gospel, who beats his breast while confessing his sin (Lk 18:13). Even so, while doing this, the priest identifies himself with Christ, who despite not having committed any sins himself, "bore our sins in his body" (1 Pet 2:24), and thus represents the publican *par excellence*.

At the start of these prayers of confession, the priest and his ministers greet the altar again[23] and then mark themselves with a first sign of the cross. This is of great importance, since right from the beginning it identifies the priest sacrificing *in persona Christi* with the holy victim, the same Christ. The sign of the cross, a summary of faith in Christ, is moreover the most specific cultic symbol, unlike other gestures known also from the usage of the courts of Late Antiquity, like processions and censings. One can surely make the same observation regarding the liturgical kiss of peace on the cheek or on the shoulder, a sign of the virtue of charity that sums up all Christian life.

The sign of the cross is followed by the psalm *Judica me* (Ps 42), with the antiphon *Introibo ad altare Dei* (I will go in to the altar of God), which is verse 4 of the same psalm, explaining the choice of this text for the initial moment of the celebration. The *Confiteor* that follows the psalm, the principal act in this preparation by the ministers, is one among numerous similar formulations found in the old missals. Its recital reminds us of the growth in the practice of repeated confession between the end of Late Antiquity and the start of the High Middle Ages. St Ambrose (c. 339–397), bishop of Milan, says that the psalm *Introibo . . . ad Deum qui laetificat juventutem meam* (I will go . . . unto God, who giveth joy to my youth), was used for the passage of the newly baptized from the baptistery to the altar.[24] Thus the ministers, as they approach the altar, express their wish to recover the baptismal purity of spiritual children.

The totality of these penitential gestures and prayers also recalls the abasement of Christ, who "bowed the heavens, and came down" (Ps 17:9) and emptied himself in taking the form of a servant (Phil 2:7). Was not the incarnate Son of God, the Righteous One, the first to accuse himself (Prov 18:17) and to

23 All genuflect in front of the cross. But if the Blessed Sacrament is not present in the tabernacle, the priest bows deeply.

24 St Ambrose, *De Mysteriis*, ch. 8, 43.

affirm his confidence in the coming consolation: "I said I will confess against myself my injustice to the Lord: and thou hast forgiven the wickedness of my sin" (Ps 31:5)?

4 THE APPROACH TO THE ALTAR AND THE CENSING OF THE ALTAR

The Ascent to the Altar

There follow some versicles and responses – ℣. Thou shalt turn again, O God, and quicken us. ℟. And thy people shall rejoice in thee. ℣. Show us, O Lord, thy mercy. ℟. And grant us thy salvation. ℣. O Lord, hear my prayer. ℟. And let my cry come unto thee. ℣. The Lord be with you. ℟. And with thy spirit. – which prepare in the classic way for a prayer. This preparation for a prayer by a series of verses and responses has a penitential coloring. The prayer in this case is *Aufer a nobis* (Take away from us our iniquities, we beseech thee, O Lord: that we may be worthy to enter with pure minds into the Holy of Holies), heralded by the *Dominus vobiscum*. This prayer, which the priest says with lowered voice, using the royal "we" that belongs to priestly prayers, is an old prayer from the *Leonine Sacramentary*.[25] Attached to it is a second prayer, *Oramus te* . . . (We beseech thee, O Lord, by the

---

25 The sacramentary, *Liber Sacramentorum*, or *Sacramentarium*, is the ancestor of the missal. The oldest, known as the *Leonine Sacramentary*, does not date to the time of Pope St Leo the Great (440–461), but was compiled in the second half of the sixth century. The sacramentary was a collection of all the priestly functions and all the formulae used by the priest for the entirety of the liturgical year. It was used alongside the antiphonaries (containing the antiphons, the processional psalms, and the psalmody that followed the readings), the lectionaries, and the *ordines Romani*, books explaining the conduct of the ceremony and the actions that had to be completed. From the ninth to the tenth century, the sacramentary gradually gave place to the "plenary missal," a book which gathered together not just the prayers that were priestly, strictly speaking, but also the elements of the epistolary, the evangeliary, the sacramentary, and the antiphonary. All these become priestly in a certain sense, particularly because of the frequency of private Masses, a Western phenomenon, which habituated the priest to say, or at least to follow by recitation, all the prayers and readings. The missal edited by Azevedo from material in the Lateran archives, and published as that of Innocent III (r. 1198–1216) – *Vetus Missale Romanum Monasticum Lateranense cum praefatione, notis, & nonnullis opusculis, quæ omnia nunc primum in lucem eduntur*, ed. Emmanuele de Azevedo SJ, Rome, 1752 – could practically be used "as is," with few exceptions, for the celebration of the traditional Mass today.

merits of thy saints whose relics are here, and of all the saints, that thou wouldst vouchsafe to forgive me all my sins), which alludes to the holy martyrs "whose relics are here." This is a more recent prayer, and the oldest manuscripts in which it occurs date to the twelfth century. It is a prayer of the *apologia* type, accompanying and explaining the action being undertaken, namely the kissing of the altar stone containing the cavity holding the relics.

The reverence and solemnity of this approach to the altar were especially underlined by particular practices preserved by the French liturgies until the nineteenth century: for example, in Paris, the deacon and subdeacon used to make a new genuflection when they arrived at the altar steps, while the priest bowed in preparation for kissing the altar; or again the priest used to kiss the altar cross that the subdeacon would present to him (just as the bishop kisses the Gospel, when he has come up to the altar, before the first censing).

This first kiss given to the altar, like all those that will follow, is a kiss of respect, friendship, intimacy, and the establishment of peace. It recalls the first verse of the Song of Songs: "Let him kiss me with the kiss of his mouth." The kiss is that of the holy marriage between humanity and divinity in the form of the Son of God incarnate, but also that of the glorious and victorious Christ returning to his Father at the Ascension. This symbolism is parallel to that of the marriage of Christ and the Church, of the divine fiancé and his fiancée: "He hath clothed me with the garments of salvation: and with the robe of justice he hath covered me, as a bridegroom decked with a crown, and as a bride adorned with her jewels" (Is 61:10).

The Censing of the Altar

Was the Christian use of incense, known since at least the time of Tertullian (c. 160 – c. 220), initially restricted to burials?[26] Incense was frequently used in the fourth century in processions. But should we treat the use of incense in the Mass as originally a Gallican custom?

26 The references to the use of incense in the Temple, such as the heavenly ceremony described in the Apocalypse (8:3–4), seem to disprove the hypothesis that the first Christians objected to the use of incense in worship as if it were a pagan practice.

One unavoidable scriptural reference is that of gold cups full of perfumes representing the prayers of the saints (Rev 5:8): incense ascends like the sweet smell of Jesus Christ and of the souls of the saints. Incense is a sacrificial prayer, as it was in the Old Testament and in pagan areas, with the grains of incense being consumed, a form of divine honor *par excellence*, and it was indirectly a rite of purification, with the sweet smell of the prayer driving away assaults of the devil. The humanity of Jesus Christ, consumed (or consummated, as the classical writers used to say) in the sacrifice, lifts his prayer up to the Father, the only prayer that the Father finds acceptable, to which are joined the prayers of the saints, thrown like grains of incense into the burning furnace of love of Christ's holy soul.

The incense that the Magi brought (Mt 2:12) certainly signified the honor that they were paying to God made a Child, but also, and perhaps even more so, the honor that was already being paid to the Father by this Child in the arms of his Mother, a Child whose sacrifice started at the moment when he was conceived: "When he cometh into the world, he saith: Sacrifice and oblation thou wouldest not . . . . Then said I: Behold I come: in the head of the book it is written of me: that I should do thy will, O God" (Heb 10:5–7). One's attention is called above all to the golden censer (or incense scoop) held by the Angel of the Apocalypse (Rev 8:3–4), who draws near to the altar and offers the incense with the prayers of the saints, as we have just seen. This Angel is, of course, Christ himself, and his golden censer (or scoop) is his precious humanity: "Let my prayer be directed as incense in thy sight; the lifting up of my hands, as evening sacrifice" (Ps 140:2).

The rite prescribes the censing of the altar cross, the successive censing of the relics placed to the right, and then to the left, of the cross, then the censing of the altar table, close to the steps, on the top, at the sides, and in front. In other words, the cloud of incense entirely surrounds the altar, and proclaims the sacrifice that is going to take place on it. The rubricists (liturgical experts who specialize in the rubrics), who understand that the history and the symbolism of the liturgy are inextricably linked, emphasize that the censing of the altar possesses one curious detail, identical to a detail relating to the altar candles:

just as one starts by lighting the candles on the right, which are apparently less "worthy" since they are to the left of the cross, so one starts the censing on the right of the altar, where these candles are. This perhaps derives from the fact that the censing was originally a processional rite. The candles placed on the altar were originally held by the acolytes: those on the right of the altar, the more worthy ones, by the acolytes on the right, and those on the left by the acolytes on the left. This minute detail has the virtue that it reminds us that every liturgy, even when the clergy and the faithful are stationary in front of the altar, remains a symbolic procession towards the heavenly fatherland. The entire building, and the people assembled in prayer, together recall a hierarchical procession organized and oriented towards Christ, a procession that advances, like the Virgins in the Gospel, towards the Bridegroom, who will not be slow in appearing (Mt 25:1–11) on the altar for the Mass, and who will soon appear in the heavens for the Judgement.

II *The Ceremony of the Entrance*

EXTENDING FROM THE INTROIT TO THE HOMILY

5 THE INTROIT

The Roman Mass, in its present state, contains a certain number of "chants" whose texts are generally taken from Holy Scripture, although sometimes they are the Church's own compositions. These chants *de facto* fall into two categories. The first category comprises chants that one could describe as meditative chants (the Gradual, the Alleluia, the Tract or Sequence), following either the epistle or other readings preceding the epistle (in those Roman Masses that have several readings before the Gospel, for example, the Masses for Ember Saturdays). The second category comprises three chants that one could describe as processional chants, to the extent that they may accompany movements of a processional type: the Introit, corresponding to the entrance procession of the clergy; the Offertory chant, corresponding to the hierarchical procession of the oblations characteristic of the ancient Roman Mass (at the moment when in other liturgies the Entrance of the Oblations takes place); and the Communion chant corresponding to the "procession" of Christ towards those who are going to receive communion. (It will be noted in addition that three great priestly prayers are to be found today concluding these three actions directly or indirectly: the Collect concluding the entrance of the clergy, the Secret concluding the Offertory, which may have been preceded by another prayer of oblation, and the Postcommunion.)

The composition of these three chants, like the aspersion chant, is in theory based on the liturgical chant of the Psalms of the Divine Office, that is to say, they are composed, or were composed, or are thought to have been composed, first, of an antiphon (a refrain that introduces and concludes the chant, consisting of a sentence taken from a psalm or another text);[1] second, a psalm, reduced to just a single verse; third, ever since Pope St Damasus (366–384), the doxology that concludes all the psalms (*Gloria Patri et Filio et Spiritui Sancto*); and fourth, a repetition of the antiphon.[2]

In fact, only the Introit always has this structure. In a small number of instances, the Communion chant has also preserved it. But the Offertory chant and nearly all the Communion chants have not preserved, or never had, anything more than an antiphon, with the result that they match exactly their titles: Offertory antiphon, and Communion antiphon.

The Introit is today sung by the cantors or the *schola cantorum* when the clergy have processed to the altar and when the ministers begin their prayers of confession. Even when already sung, it is read silently by the priest in his missal placed on the right of the altar after the censing of the altar. But it remains, strictly speaking, as its name Introit indicates,[3] a chant to accompany a solemn entrance, a chant accompanying those *adventus* (which later became "joyful entries") of the sovereign, his representative, or his portrait, that were so common in Late Antiquity. Strictly speaking, it represents the entrance to the world of Christ foretold by the entire Old Testament: the antiphon (generally) and the verse are sentences from the Old Testament, giving voice to the cries and anticipation of the Jewish people, in its two orders, the patriarchs and the prophets. The *Gloria Patri* is the praise uttered by the last Jewish order, represented by the apostles and the first followers of Jesus, this "small remnant" of the chosen people who greeted the long-awaited Messiah, and who do so

1 The word "antiphon" originally referred to the singing of a psalm antiphonally by two choirs, one replying to the other. The meaning then changed so that the word meant a sentence sung as an introduction to a psalm and then repeated as a refrain at the end of the psalm.

2 The Aspersion antiphon, as we have seen, is composed in the same way: the antiphon *Asperges me*; the first verse of the psalm *Miserere*; the doxology; and then a repetition of the antiphon *Asperges me*.

3 Introit, but also *Ingressa* (the term equivalent to Introit in, for example, the Milanese rite), *Officium* (in the ancient Spanish rites, known as Visigothic, and later, Mozarabic), but also in France until a quite late date, or even antiphon *ad praelegendum*, antiphon for the entrance, according to St Gregory.

here by affirming their faith in the Holy Trinity.[4] The repetition of the antiphon marks the Church's ratification of that which was prefigured by the patriarchs, predicted by the prophets, and preached in its fullness by the apostles in the Gospel.

The priest recites the Introit at the altar, over the missal placed on the left side (that is, on the left-hand side of the cross, or on the right as one looks towards the altar), unlike the bishop, who recites it at his throne or at his faldstool. The missal will not be moved to the other side (on the right-hand side of the cross) except for the Gospel. This left-hand side, still called the "epistle side," because of the principal reading on that side, is symbolically the side of the Old Testament, even if the epistle is often (though not always) a reading from the New Testament (Epistles, Acts of the Apostles, the Apocalypse). Everything that happens on this side of the altar represents what precedes the preaching of the Gospel and prepares for its proper reception.

We will observe that the Introit, the true beginning of the Mass, gives its name to the Mass because of the respect that the ancients had for the *incipit*, the opening word or words of a text:[5] thus we have the Mass of *Quasimodo*, the *Requiem* Mass, the Mass *Spiritus Domini*, etc. As the priest begins the Introit, he makes the sign of the cross, and then reads the text of the antiphon as if it were being proclaimed, in a loud voice.[6]

---

4 Each *Gloria Patri* . . . is accompanied by a bow towards the cross, Christ the Lord, in whose direction all liturgical prayer is virtually oriented. Liturgical bows are, like all other gestures in worship, carefully calibrated: deep bows of the body (for example, that of the *Confiteor*), which represent adoration or penitence; intermediate bows of the body (for example, that of the *Sanctus*), which mark the appropriate reverence; bows of the head alone, which are themselves subdivided into deep bows (for example, at the name of Jesus), intermediate bows (for example, at the name of Mary), and light bows (for example, when one mentions the saint of the day), all of which are bows showing respect. This triple subdivision of the attitude appropriate to prayer reflects also the three stages of the spiritual life (compare St Gregory of Nyssa, Scotus Eriugena, William of St-Thierry): the deep humility of the purgative way, the great reverence of those who are making progress; and the respect within the intimacy of love of the unitive way.

5 The result of this respect for the *incipit* is that papal texts, bulls, encyclicals, or the great documents of the Holy See are still named after their opening words.

6 Liturgically, there are three gradations of volume used in reading: reading in a loud voice (for example, chants, collects, the *Pater noster*);

In some churches, at the great festivals, the Introit is repeated several times by the choir, which gives more time for the censings.

The Introit is as much the victorious entry of Christ, escorted by the Old Testament, as it is the introduction to the service. It has certainly been linked by commentators ancient and modern to the *adventus* of the Incarnation, but also to the ascent of Christ from hell at his Resurrection, escorted by a procession consisting of all the holy souls who had awaited him and who had professed their faith in him before his coming. At root it is the same thing: Christ is accompanied by the Old Testament, but the return ascent from hell is more glorious and a greater victory, and so more liturgical. The triumphal psalm 148, *Laudate Dominum de caelis, laudate eum in excelsis* (Praise ye the Lord from the heavens: praise ye him in the high places), which perhaps for a long time functioned as the Introit for many Masses, at all events provides the exultant and victorious tone of this moment of the Mass, the entry of Christ in order to repeat on the altar his redemptive sacrifice.

This processional entry, even if the actual procession has disappeared from the Mass celebrated by the priest, reminds us of the Roman procession that went from the place of the "collect" of the people to the place of the "station" of the celebration. Leaving aside the return ascent from hell, we can also recall here several different journeys of Christ: his arrival in the womb of the Virgin, his journey from the manger in Bethlehem to the Temple of Jerusalem at the Presentation, or the journey from Bethany to Jerusalem on Palm Sunday, and again the journey from Jerusalem to the Mount of Olives on Maundy Thursday, and then on the Thursday of the Ascension. The entry also represents the march of the Church militant, processing with its Lord and entering with him into its heavenly fatherland, like the People of Israel marching in the desert and entering with Joshua into the Promised Land.

---

reading in a medium voice (for example, the *Sanctus*), and reading in a low or "secret" voice (for example, the Offertory, the Secret, the Canon). The loud voice resembles that of Christ's public prayers, when teaching the *Pater noster* or praying on the Cross; the medium voice represents how the Apostles heard Christ's prayer during the Agony in the Garden; the low voice represents Christ's private prayer in the presence of his Father.

6 THE LITANY OF THE *KYRIE*

Just like the Introit, this is a part of the Mass sung by the choir, although it is also read by the celebrant with his assistants responding. From the historical point of view, it is enough to note that this sung litany belonging to the Mass and the Office derives from an invocation prayer spoken by the deacon or the clergy, with the people picking up the refrain. (The second collect, which appears in the old *Gelasian Sacramentary*, a compilation of the end of the seventh century, bears witness to the insertion into the Roman Mass of the great litaneutical prayer of which the refrain, *Kyrie eleison*, survives: this second collect functioned as the close of the petitions of the litany.) We know from a letter of St Gregory that this invocation, *Kyrie eleison*, took the place of other invocations at Rome at the end of the sixth century.[7] In the Gallican and Hispanic liturgies, the *Kyrie* was preceded by the *Trisagion* (the triple acclamation of the holy God, *Hagios*, "Holy God, Holy Mighty, Holy Immortal, have mercy on us," preserved on Good Friday, in Latin and in Greek, as the refrain of the *Improperia*, the Reproaches, the rebukes uttered by Jesus to his people as they led him to his death).

The triple invocation has retained the Greek language (*Kyrios, Christos, Kyrios, eleeo*, to have mercy), the language that the Roman liturgy used until about the middle of the third century, in fact until the Roman clergy had assimilated the Latin language sufficiently for them to be able to create a suitable translation of the Greek Bible. The texts, the quotations, and the biblical references are in fact the backbone of the liturgy; and the clergy had now sufficiently digested the Latin of public life, of the orators, the rhetors, the officials, for it to be possible for them to render the liturgy in a Latin of adequate nobility. Nevertheless, no one forgot that Greek had been the first language of Christian prayer in Rome (more because it was the language of culture and the Bible than because it was the vernacular). Its retention at this point by the Roman liturgy thus affirms the fundamentally traditional nature of the sacred action: "I have received of the Lord that which also I delivered unto you, that

---

7 St Gregory, *Epistles*, Bk. 9, Ep. 12 (*PL* 77:956).

the Lord Jesus, the same night in which he was betrayed . . ." (1 Cor 11:23).

The reduction in number of these invocations to three times three, with evident reference to the Trinity (*Kyrios*: the Father, *Christos*: the Son, *Kyrios*: the Holy Spirit) occurred in Frankish territory, where all possible implications of the Trinitarian dogma had always been defended with particular force (the addition of the *Filioque*[8] clause to the *Credo* of Constantinople, for example, was the work of Alcuin and Charlemagne).

There is a clear relationship between these invocations, with their origin in a litany, and the numerous Greek litanies and the frequent use of litanies in all the liturgies (various *deprecationes*, particularly in the *ingressa* of the Milanese rite). The repetition of the prayer, recalling "Ask . . . , seek . . . , knock . . . " (Lk 11:9), and prayer to God in the name of Jesus Christ (Jn 16:23–24) impart, without doubt, a penitential tone; all the more so, given that the triple invocation, as the medievals liked to say, recalls the triple nature of the sin for which we must ask for forgiveness: original sin, mortal sin, and venial sin; or again the triple misery of ignorance, fault, and penalty.[9]

But the triple invocation, repeated three times, has here a universalizing aspect: in addition to the Trinity, it also recalls the glory of heaven, with its nine choirs of angels. And then again, it recalls the entire history of humanity, with the three ages of the world according to St Paul: before the Law, under the Law, and under Grace (Rom 5:13); while the use of Greek here affirms the universality of the church and its vocation to gather up the entire world and bring all its peoples together.

So, all things being considered, we must emphasize the victorious implications of this invocation. It consists in the universal proclamation of the triumph of the Cross: which is why Greek, one of the three languages of the *titulus* of the Cross posted on the orders of Pilate—Jesus of Nazareth, the King of the Jews (Jn 19:19–20)—finds a place here. We must not be mistaken: the three invocations certainly make us think of Father, Son, and Holy Spirit, but they are addressed principally to Christ

8 *Qui ex Patre Filioque procedit*, the Holy Spirit "who proceedeth from the Father and the Son."

9 St Thomas Aquinas, *Summa theologiae* IIIa, q83, a4.

the Lord, in all the majesty of his victory over death, which is repeated sacramentally on the altar, true Son of God, whom the Eucharistic liturgy makes present in the strict sense of the term. In the Mass that is starting, he is going to show himself as, and so is already appearing as, a true victim, really present, and sacramentally immolated, but all this in his present state, which is his state of glory. What is being celebrated is his absolute triumph over sin, through the Resurrection, but also and to start with in the very midst of the sacrifice of Calvary: "obedient unto death, even to the death of the cross. For which cause God also hath exalted him" (Phil 2:8–9). We cannot emphasize too highly the fact that always, and right from the start, the sacred action is directed and oriented towards the glorious and victorious Cross, whose representation stands over the altar.

7 THE *GLORIA*

In France, we used joyfully to cry, "Noël, Noël," on every happy political occasion, on the birth of a prince, a royal arrival, implicitly comparing the event to the birth in Bethlehem. That is the meaning of the *Gloria*. To be honest, even if in France we changed to singing the *Te Deum* to honor victories and great events, we must remember that in the Middle Ages on such occasions, people sang the *Gloria*. It was called the Great Doxology, or the Hymn of the Angels, and was a doxology that, like the Introit, followed by the *Kyrie*, was inextricably associated with the entrance of Christ into the world. Strictly speaking, it is the song of the Angels in Bethlehem on Christmas night,[10] recalled by the first two verses, then expanded by acclaiming the Father as "King of Heaven," the Son as "Lamb of God, Son of the Father," and in the last verse the Holy Spirit.

The great doxology thus here celebrates the joyful entry of Christ into his holy city, like those entries of the king or bishop in the Middle Ages, when the use of the *Gloria* was more general. This hymn of the angels makes us think of the *Sanctus*, which comes after the Preface: the heavens open, and the

10 Luke 2:14, where the interpretation of *eudokia* is particularly difficult, meaning either peace to those men to whom God shows his benevolence, or peace to men of good will, as the Vulgate translates it (though this good will presupposes the benevolent gift of grace).

liturgy of heaven is united with that of the earth. The history of salvation, as we must repeat, is reproduced by the celebration of the Mass, but with variations here and there, or differences between different liturgies. This reference to the birth in Bethlehem was replaced in Gaul by the canticle of Zachariah, the *Benedictus*, which greeted the arrival in the world of the Forerunner, St John the Baptist (Lk 1:67–79).

Just as the *Te Deum* is attached to the name of St Ambrose, so the *Gloria* is attached to the name of St Hilary (c. 315–367), bishop of Poitiers. Hilary may have brought it back from the East, where he had been exiled because of his opposition to Arianism. It is piously attributed to him, perhaps, because of the anti-Arian tone of its acclamations of Christ, which the *Te Deum* lacks: *Tu solus sanctus! Tu solus Dominus! Tu solus altissimus, Iesu Christe!*, "Thou only art holy: Thou only art Lord: Thou only, O Jesus Christ, art Most High." The people, as at a coronation, ratifies the anointing of the king by its acclamations. However that may be, the *Gloria* is among the oldest liturgical hymns known, as very properly is the *Te Deum*. Their simple style, somewhat resembling a litany, is also very similar; as is their doxological structure: one part is addressed to the Father, one part to the Son—for the *Te Deum*, in a certain disorder, if one may use the expression: Father, Holy Spirit, Son, with this additional singularity, that the *Te Deum* has at its end verses and responses inspired by the psalms (We beseech thee, therefore, to help thy servants, whom thou hast redeemed with thy precious blood. Make them to be numbered with thy saints in glory everlasting. O Lord, save thy people . . .), perhaps intended to prepare for the prayer that follows.[11] The *Te Deum* and the *Gloria* have in addition all the characteristics of popular chants of acclamation and invocation (rather like the *Christus vincit*).

In reality, the *Gloria* was originally a chant of the Divine Office, assigned to the morning office, which was later called the office of Lauds, as a "hymn of dawn,"[12] along with the *Ben-*

11 We have noticed this liturgical procedure in connection with the prayer *Aufer a nobis*, for which one prepares with a series of verses and responses: "℣. Thou shalt turn again, O God, and quicken us. ℟. And thy people shall rejoice in thee. ℣. Show us, O Lord, thy mercy. ℟. And grant us thy salvation. . . ."

12 The *Gloria*, practically in the form in which it is known today, is

edictus and the *Benedicite*, the Song of the Three Children in the Furnace from the book of Daniel (3:52–66), which one finds at this position in other liturgies, for example in Gaul. We know that at the time of St Caesarius the *Gloria* concluded the office later called Lauds, and that that arrangement lasted for a long time. The *Gloria* is still in this position in the sixteenth century in the Milanese rite. Its incorporation into the Mass is a characteristic of the Roman liturgy and its dependent liturgies. It is tempting to imagine that the transfer took place at Christmas, at the dawn Mass following Lauds, and involved a move from the morning office to the Mass. The fact remains that there has always been movement of the liturgical hymns (such as the *Te Deum* of the Celtic and Gallican liturgies, preceding the Communion) between the Office and the Mass.

These brief observations on the history of the liturgy, which do not directly concern the subject of this work, are intended to underline the link with the morning of the Birth of Christ that the *Gloria* has always represented: the Christ appears in the new morning of the world, foretold by the Old Testament with the Introit, and hailed by the heavenly angels with the *Gloria*. Because the *Gloria* is an angelic hymn, it is also a chant particularly associated with bishops (that is to say, to be sung by the bishop), according to the traditional idea, supported by the first three chapters of the Apocalypse, that the churches are led as much by bishops as by angels. To begin with it was reserved for the pope (that is to say, to be sung by the pope) and only on Christmas night. Pope Symmachus (498–514) extended its use to Masses of martyrs celebrated by a bishop. In the seventh century, ordinary priests were able to sing it, but only at Easter. Finally, in the ninth century, at the time of the definitive formation of the Roman missal, it becomes an integral part of all Masses, except penitential Masses, *Requiem* Masses, or weekday Masses other than at Christmastide and Eastertide (in the thirteenth century, Durandus nevertheless states that the bishop of Bethlehem had the privilege of singing it at all Masses, even Masses for the dead).[13]

---

attested under this title in the fifth century among the psalms recited at the morning office in the Alexandrinus manuscript of the Bible.

13 Durandus, *Rationale*, Bk. 4, ch. xiii, 7.

Liturgically, when the *Gloria* is said at a Mass, the *Te Deum* is also said in the Office (with the exceptions of Maundy Thursday and Holy Saturday). In the same way, on days when one is not said, neither is the other said.

The *Gloria* is therefore a most solemn song of praise, following the entrance of the Lord, taken up by angels and men. This proclamation (that of the *Gloria* by the angel of Bethlehem) follows the pattern of an announcement by a herald, and it reminds us of the popular explosion of joy during coronations at Rheims when the crowd was allowed into the cathedral to see its new king. The celebrant, as he sings the hymn, in a sense, gives the clergy and people the same "good news" that the angel of Bethlehem gave to the shepherds: the news that the heavenly King has appeared among us.

8 THE COLLECT

"Wherefore when he cometh into the world, he saith: Sacrifice and oblation thou wouldest not . . . . Then said I: Behold I come" (Heb 10:5–7). Right from the start, like Christ's life in this world, the Mass is a long prayer of the Son to his Father, which will culminate in the *Fiat voluntas tua* of the *Pater noster*, identical to the "It is finished" of Golgotha.

Here therefore is the first prayer of Christ the priest. When we speak of priestly prayers in the Roman Mass, we think of the three prayers that are today known as the Collect, the Secret, and the Postcommunion, but also of the ensemble formed by the Preface, the Canon (itself formed of a series of prayers, as we shall see) and the *Pater noster* (which, in the Roman Mass, can be thought of as the conclusion of the Canon). The spiritual model of all these priestly prayers is, however, the *Pater noster*, the great prayer that, in the Roman liturgy, the priest recites as Christ's representative. Liturgically, these prayers, after an introductory *Oremus*, "Let us pray," said with a bow of the head to the cross, are said or sung by the celebrant in the attitude of an orant, with hands raised to the level of the shoulders and facing each other, using the royal "we" (for the *Pater noster*, in the introduction, We dare to say . . .). The other prayers of the Mass said by the priest (those of the Confession, and of the Offertory, for example) are more private prayers, in which the priest speaks certainly as a minister, but often (not always) saying "I."

From the stylistic point of view, the priestly prayers (apart of course from the *Pater noster*) are the best example of the liturgical language that the Church of Rome created when Latin was first used in worship. They are typical of the Late Antique rhetoric in which their clerical composers of the fourth century, and above all, of the fifth and sixth centuries, were trained, adapted to the particular artistic prose of the liturgy, with a rhythm, a vocabulary, and a taste that is sober and solemn. The style found in the great liturgical prayers (the orations, the Preface, the Canon) is that of the *elogium*, the panegyric style (the *celebratio*), intended to produce a speech thanking God in the way that one might thank an emperor or a magistrate, or conversely to thank the magistrate and emperor in the way that one might thank God. The Prefaces in their diverse and very numerous forms (those of the Mass; those for the consecration of an object, such as the Paschal candle; of the church; of a person, such as an ordinand, a Father Abbot, a consecrated virgin, the king, etc.) are the incontestable evidence.

For this purpose liturgical prose makes use of different Roman rhetorical registers—the petition, the supplication, the celebration—and of stylistic devices highly valued by the very literate, including antitheses (earthly goods *vis-à-vis* heavenly goods, for example), parallelism and balance, asyndeton (between nouns or adjectives, for example), assonance (repetition of a sound), hyperbaton (separation of a subject from its verb, of a noun from its qualifier), chiasmus, and wordplay with similar-sounding words, paronomasia, etc. The literary success of this renewal of Latin solemnity and of the Roman *gravitas* is the achievement of a Christian Rome that was determined to surpass the ancients in the honor of Christ. The best examples of this style are the Collects, with their rhythm, their concision, their balanced antitheses, their oratorical flow; as also are the Prefaces; and, with its tone at once solemn and well constructed, the unsurpassable masterpiece of Christian Latinity, a sublime piece of poetry in prose: the Roman Canon. This liturgical Latin of Late Antiquity became a mold imparting its shape to a greater or lesser extent to all the subsequent compositions; much as the basilican plan, reinterpreted by Christian worship, remained visible in all the subsequent architectural variations.

Most of these prayers are addressed to the Father. Their conclusion (with assonance in -um: *Per Dominum nostrum Jesum Christum*) repeats what Christ himself said in his Gospel: "I have appointed you . . . that whatsoever you shall ask of the Father in my name, he may give it you" (Jn 15:16).

The prayers are not just extraordinarily rich in doctrine, but they are a real "theological source," that is, a resource from which we can learn the teaching of the Church. The famous saying, *Lex orandi, lex credendi,* "Let us learn what we should believe from the manner in which we pray," or *Legem credendi statuat lex supplicandi,* "Let the rule of prayer dictate the rule of faith," given in the letter to the bishops of Gaul attributed to Pope Celestine I (422–432),[14] concerns precisely the prayers of the Mass treating the subject of grace (for example, the Collect for the Ninth Sunday after Pentecost, "[so] that thou mayst grant [thy servants] their desires, make them to ask what is pleasing to thee"). The same can be said about the Prefaces: one may perhaps think of that of Trinity Sunday, said today on all the Sundays after Epiphany and after Pentecost, which is a real course of positive theological teaching on the subject. The belief of the Roman Church always matches her prayers, and her prayers always match her belief.

The Celebrant's Greeting of the Assistants, Clergy, and People

The Collect is preceded by a greeting of the assistants, the clergy, and the people (as are the Postcommunion and the Secret, although in the latter case the greeting and the prayer are separated by an interval entirely occupied by the Offertory).[15] The ensemble composed of the Preface, the Canon, and the *Pater noster* is similarly preceded by a greeting of the people, the *Dominus vobiscum* that starts the dialogue of the Preface.[16]

---

14 DS 251.

15 Unless the *Dominus vobiscum* of the start of the Offertory was attached to a prayer that later disappeared, and the Secret was preceded by another *Dominus vobiscum* in place of or before the *Orate fratres*.

16 To be precise, we should observe that there are in the course of the Mass seven greetings of this type, corresponding to the seven gifts of the

The greater part of these greetings of the assembled clergy and of all the assistants are preceded by the celebrant kissing the altar (he kisses the consecrated stone, not because it contains relics, but because the five crosses and the anointing with the holy chrism identify it with Christ), just as he kisses the altar before passing on the kiss of peace to the deacon, who will then pass on this kiss of peace to the clergy. It is tempting therefore to compare these general greetings by the celebrant of all those assisting to individual passings on of the peace, which starting from the celebrant who has kissed the altar go from person to person. The individual kiss of peace is accompanied by the formula *Pax tecum*, similar to *Dominus vobiscum*, and even more similar to *Pax vobis*, the greeting given by a bishop at the Collect, while the response of the person who receives the peace individually is exactly the same as that given in response to a collective greeting: *Et cum spiritu tuo*. What is more, the gesture of the celebrant greeting all the assistants and the gesture of the person who passes on the kiss of peace individually are similar, with the hands wide open. This peace, whether collective or individual, seems therefore to represent the "holy kiss" mentioned in the final salutation of the letters of St Paul (Rom 16:16).

"The Lord be with you" is an allusion to the greeting given by Boaz to his harvesters (Ruth 2:4), or again to the greeting of the angel to Gideon (Jdg 6:12). The bishop, who represents the plenitude and perfection of the priestly office, uses before the Collect the same formula as the Lord, *Pax vobis* (Jn 20:20): these were the first words that Christ said to the disciples when he appeared to them after the Resurrection. The clergy and the faithful reply, *Et cum spiritu tuo*, which comes from the end of the letter to Timothy, where St Paul says, "The Lord Jesus Christ be with thy spirit" (2 Tim 4:22). We may note that the bishop says *Pax vobis* – the greeting given by Christ to his disciples in a time of joy and gladness, that of the Resurrection – only when he sings the *Gloria in excelsis*, or to put it more generally, in "joyful" Masses. There is in fact a link between this greeting of

Holy Spirit, according to St Thomas Aquinas (*Summa theologiae* IIIa, q83, aa5–6): before the Collect; before the Gospel; before the Offertory; before the ensemble of the Preface, the Canon, and the *Pater noster*; at the fraction of the host in a specifically Paschal form (*Pax Domini sit semper vobiscum*); before the Postcommunion; and finally, before the dismissal (*Ite missa est*).

the bishop, *Pax vobis*, and the words of the *Gloria*: *Et in terra pax hominibus bonae voluntatis*.

The spiritual significance of this greeting is clear: just like the apostles seeing Christ when he had entered the Upper Room where they were joined together in prayer, the clergy and people, reunited in prayer in the church, receive the same manifestation of the supernatural friendship of Christ. After the response of the faithful, the priest returns to the altar, that is, turns to face East, and in saying *Oremus* he urges the others, those whom he has just greeted, to pray as Christ himself did. When the prayer is finished, they reply *Amen*, a Hebrew word meaning, "May it be done to us as you have asked," or, "May your prayer be favorably received," a word borrowed from the Apocalypse (22:20). *Amen* also has the implication of agreeing: "It is true" (*Amen dico vobis*: Jn 13:16, 20–21).

The Collect Itself

The Collect is the most important of the Mass's prayers or orations or, as some say more loosely, "collects"–that is, the Collect, the Secret, and the Postcommunion. Insofar as the Mass celebrated on a particular day matches the Office of that Day, whether sung or said,[17] this first prayer of the Mass functions also as the prayer of the day: it concludes each of the parts of the day's Office.

Within the Mass, therefore, the *Oratio ad Collectam*, or *collecta*, or yet again the *oratio super populum* (as it is called in Milan) concludes the ceremony of the entrance, which can be thought of as a sort of doublet of the morning section of the Divine Office.

But why is it called the Collect? For two reasons, which perhaps come down to one and the same thing. In Rome this word *collecta* meant the place where people gathered to start the procession that went to the place where the pope was going to say the Mass, the *statio*. Wasn't it rather Gallican usage that gave this prayer the name of Collect, in that in Gothic sacramentaries it is called *collectio*, before subsequently being given the name

17 This is not always the case: one may on certain days say a devotional or votive Mass–a Mass of the Sacred Heart or of the Blessed Virgin, a Nuptial Mass, etc.–although one recites a different office in the breviary.

collecta? It could therefore, or also, reflect the gathering together by the priest of the intentions expressed in the litany, of which only the *Kyrie* survives. The Collect in that case is the prayer collecting the intentions of the people, or (or also) the prayer spoken over the people when they prayed collected together, "collected by prayer," as the Council of Agde put it in 506.[18]

Durandus tells us that in his time, in the late thirteenth century, at Rome, in the cathedral church of the Lateran, this prayer was never said, but that in the Mass, as also in the canonical hours, instead of this prayer the celebrant recited in a loud voice the Lord's Prayer, the *Pater noster*, the first collect of the New Testament.[19] He thought that was the practice of the primitive church.

The priest normally concludes his prayers with the words, *Per Dominum nostrum Jesum Christum*, etc., *in unitate Spiritus Sancti*, etc. In the same way, the Canon finishes with *Per ipsum, et cum ipso, et in ipso est tibi Deo Patri omnipotenti, in unitate Spiritus Sancti, omnis honor et gloria* (By him, and with him, and in him, is to thee, God the Father Almighty, in the unity of the Holy Ghost, all honor and glory), because we must make our requests to the Father in the name of Christ, the one intercessor authorized by God, in order to be certain that our prayer will be acceptable to him (Jn 15:16).

In saying or singing the Collect, as in the case of all the great prayers, the priest raises his hands in the attitude of an orant. This elevation of the hands recalls Moses raising his hands, interceding for his people, in the battle against the Amalekites: when Moses raised his hands towards heaven, Israel had the upper hand, but when he lowered his hands a little, the Amalekites had the upper hand, with the result that Aaron and Hur held his hands up on either side (Ex 17:11–12). We read also that Solomon stood before the altar of the Lord in the presence of the assembly of Israel, and that he "spread forth his hands towards heaven" while praying for his people (3 Kgs 8:22). This attitude of Moses and Solomon was a figure foretelling that of Christ

18 *Conciliorum Galliae, Tam Editorum, Quam Ineditorum, Collectio, Temporum Ordine Digesta &c.*, cong. St Mauri (Paris: Didot, 1789), vol. I, col. 788, Canon 30.
19 Durandus, *Rationale*, Bk. 4, ch. xv, 17.

suspended on the Cross, or again of Christ ascending to heaven at the Ascension with his hands raised. To sum it up, the priest in the Collect, *in persona Christi*, puts into practice the words of the Psalmist, "Let my prayer be directed as incense in thy sight; the lifting up of my hands, as evening sacrifice" (Ps 140:2).

9 THE EPISTLE

We enter here on the office of the readings, of the liturgical proclamation of the Word of God, which will culminate in the reading of the Gospel and in the commentary on the Gospel provided by the homily. This part of the holy mysteries joins two cultic acts: a ritual proclamation of the word of God and a meditation based on a psalm, with the whole having the manner of a solemn ceremonial prayer. As we have seen in the case of the *Gloria*, these proclamations of the sacred texts can just as well remind us of a herald's proclamation. The ritualization of the announcement is part of the message: it is a sacred and mysterious word, passed on and received as such. We can note also in the course of a solemn or pontifical Mass a progression in the dignity of those playing a role: the lector sings any lessons that precede the epistle, the subdeacon sings the epistle, the deacon sings the Gospel, and the bishop, the teacher of his people, pronounces the homily, and if he does not pronounce it himself or is not present, the priest who preaches does so with at least the tacit delegation of the successor of the apostles. The same would be true of a homily preached by a deacon.

If we suppose that this part of the Mass derives in a complex way from the readings that made up the liturgy of the synagogue, the principal difference is that in the Mass the dominant role is played by the apostolic texts, the texts of the New Testament. To be honest, the office of readings of the Mass is, as it were, designed to refute the liturgy of the synagogue, to the extent that its essential theme is to enable the listener to pass spiritually from the preparation provided by the Old Testament to its accomplishment in the New, while passing from the epistle to the Gospel, even if the epistle is in most cases an apostolic text. We pass from Christ foretold to Christ proclaimed, from the type to the realization, from the figure to the accomplishment. This Christic conception of the Old Testament should be enough to put in perspective the connection between this part of the Mass and the office of the synagogue, an office for which the evidence is of later date than the evidence for the earliest Christian liturgy. We would probably do better to talk of imitation and differentiation, with the imitation of Christianity by the Judaism refounded after the suppression of the Jewish revolts in AD 70 and 135 being without doubt as important as the imitation of Judaism by Christianity. If the creation of what one calls the canon of the Hebrew Scriptures by the Jewish rabbis can be attributed in large part to a wish to distinguish their use of Scripture from the Christian use of Scripture, we can imagine that the desire to mark out the distinction between the two played a corresponding role in liturgical development.

A reading from the New Testament other than from the Gospel is always termed an "epistle." From the sixth century, there were never more than two readings in Rome: the epistle and the Gospel. Originally, there were probably more readings (the common practice among the Gallican, Milanese, Visigothic and yet other rites was to have three readings: an Old Testament reading, an epistle, and a Gospel). Even today, in certain Masses during the Ember Days and at certain vigils (Ember Saturdays being regarded as vigils), the epistle can be preceded by up to five readings (or even, before the reforms of the 1950s and 1960s, six or twelve prophecies).[20] Generally, however, the Roman liturgy, like the liturgy of St John Chrysostom, has preserved only one text before the Gospel, often taken from the New Testament, but sometimes from the Old. If there are more than two texts, the order always is: one or more readings taken from the Old Testament, followed by the epistle taken from a text of the New Testament. If there is only one reading, it is always referred to as the "epistle," even if it is not taken from a letter of an apostle (for example, if it is taken from the Apocalypse or the Acts of the Apostles), and even if it is taken from the Old Testament (for example, a text from one of the books of Wisdom).

In the East, this part of the Mass begins with the solemn procession of the Gospel book and is called the Little Entrance

20 At a solemn penitential Mass, these readings preceding the epistle are sung not by the subdeacon, but by a cantor in the centre of the choir, at a music-desk with a missal covered in violet.

(to distinguish it from the Great Entrance of the bread and wine that are going to be consecrated). In Rome, at a pontifical Mass, the Gospel book, into which the papal maniple has been slipped, has already made a solemn appearance in the hands of the subdeacon, at the initial entrance procession. But in the Roman liturgy, the real entrance of the Book of the Word of Christ, corresponding to the Eastern ceremony of the Little Entrance, is the Gospel Procession that we shall discuss shortly.

The word "epistle" comes from the Greek, picked up by the Latin, and means "supplementary mission," *epi-* meaning "in addition," and *stole* meaning "sending." In a solemn Mass, it is therefore the subdeacon, the Christ as proclaimed in the Old Testament, who sings the epistle (in a Mass that is sung but not solemn, the reader could be a lector, as was the case for a long time in Spain and in Gaul both in these Masses and in solemn Masses). Again, even if the text that is read or sung is most frequently taken from the New Testament, it is still considered as a preparation for the preaching of the Gospel. At the altar, the priest reads the epistle on the left-hand side, from the point of view of the cross, the Old Testament side. The subdeacon sings it on the same side, which is of course the right-hand side from the point of view of the faithful, and he sings it at the foot of the altar steps, or at the corresponding *ambo*, or from the right-hand half of the rood or chancel screen, the large and high screen closing off the choir, from the top of which the readings of the Divine Office were read, preceded by the reader's request to the celebrant: *Jube, Domine, benedicere*, "I beg you, Father, bless me," from where the screen derived its French name of the *jubé*.[21] Since this reading is the final preparation for the Gospel of Christ, this announcement is identified with that of St John the Baptist, the last of the prophets (Mt 11:9),[22] who sums up in himself the entire Old Testament. It is sung facing the altar, that is, facing east, in other words towards the Christ who will return "as lightning cometh out of the east, and appeareth even into the west" (Mt 24:27).

---

21 This follows the method of pronouncing Latin used in France until the start of the twentieth century, giving *jubé*, rather than the Roman *yubé*.
22 Durandus, *Rationale*, Bk. 4, ch. xvi, 2–5.

The faithful sit down to listen to the epistle, on the church floor if necessary, as probably happened in the Middle Ages, because this teaching must be heard in a restful silence. Durandus notes one medieval curiosity: soldiers had the privilege of standing upright during the reading of the epistles of St Paul, since he was a soldier of the Gospel and is often portrayed armed with the sword of the Word of God (Eph 6:17).

It will be seen that after reading the epistle the subdeacon kneels before the celebrant, in order first to kiss his hand, as a sign of peace, and then to receive his blessing; unlike the deacon, who after reading the Gospel comes to the celebrant to kiss his hand and to receive his blessing, but does not kneel. That reflects the fact that the prophets, though certainly joined to the power of Christ the Word of God, did not enjoy an intimate relationship with him until much later, when he descended to hell. The apostles, by contrast, who are represented by the deacon, received Christ's peace and blessing at his Resurrection, by the virtue of his death, receiving therefore the power to preach and to announce the Gospel of the Word of God.

10 THE SINGING OF THE PSALM

Between the epistle and the Gospel lies an interval in which a psalm is sung in responsorial mode (that is, sung alternately by a soloist and the choir, or by one part of the choir followed by the other part). The principle, according to which a reading is followed by the singing of psalm verses, is the same as that according to which, in the Divine Office, at Matins, or at Vigil Masses, which are very close to the office of Matins, readings are followed by a responsory or a responsorial psalm (a few verses of a psalm, sometimes of another text). It is one of those moments (along with the Introit, the hymn of the *Gloria*, the litany of the Kyrie, and the singing of the *Pater noster*) where the Mass and the Divine Office are seen at their closest. It is also an occasion for the singers to display their virtuosity, a time for listening and meditating, a moment when the allegorical tradition thinks particularly of the listening and meditating undertaken by the apostles, who had received the word of the Lord and were praying with him as they recited the psalm verses that foretold his coming.

This meditation, which precedes the proclamation of the Gospel, takes several forms.

First comes the Gradual, or gradual psalm. This takes its name from the *gradus*, or steps, of the altar, because on feast days, it would be sung, along with the Alleluia, from the altar or ambo steps, and spiritually it takes its name from the steps or degrees of virtue by which the apostles climbed the mountain of the Gospel, whether the Mount of the Beatitudes or the Mount of the Transfiguration.[23] The Gradual is a follow-up to the epistle: the Alleluia is an introduction to the Gospel.

Second comes the Alleluia and its occasional companion, the Sequence. The Alleluia itself (a Hebrew word, meaning "praise the Lord") is a particularly joyful fragment made out of ornate alleluia chants that frame one or two verses of a psalm. The end of the word alleluia provides a long exercise in vocalization called the *jubilus*. From being used at Eastertide, the Alleluia has now, perhaps since the time of St Gregory, become used throughout the year, except in Lent, in the season of Septuagesima, on penitential weekdays, and of course it is not used in a *Requiem* Mass. It follows the Gradual, or in Eastertide even replaces it, and has generally extended beyond the use of a single verse (except at Easter, when the Church uses the particularly joyful ancient Alleluia, *Haec dies quam fecit Dominus*, "This is the day which the Lord hath made, let us exult and be glad").[24] The Alleluia expresses the joy in the hearts of the apostles in response to the promises of Christ concerning the spread of his message and of the miracles worked by him or in his name: "Jesus . . . manifested his glory; and his disciples believed in him" (Jn 2:11).

The Sequence (or Prose – the word "Sequence" derives from the Germanic world) is a piece of poetry which, as its name suggests, generally follows the Alleluia, which it prolongs and to which it is attached (but not always: consider the *Dies Irae* in *Requiem* Masses). It is a bit like a *neuma* or *pneuma*, a breath, a

---

23 In the same way, St Thomas Aquinas says that the Gradual reflects progress, the *profectum vitae* (*Summa theologiae* IIIa, q83, a4).

24 There is a similar composition in the responses for Matins on Christmas Day; and there is also a similarity to an Introit of very ancient form, *Gaudeamus omnes in Domino, diem festum celebrantes, in honore . . .* "Let us rejoice together in the Lord while celebrating this festive day, in honor of . . ." See, for example, the Introit for All Saints, for St Anne, for St Agatha.

glide, a doubling of the last note of the Alleluia, but it becomes an independent text. It is an ecclesiastical composition but, unlike most of the hymns integral to the Divine Office, it does not try to follow the comparatively flexible rules of classical Latin versification. It often follows an accentual meter, or one based on the number of syllables, and it sometimes rhymes, for example in the form AAB, CCB, etc. It recalls the processions of the Middle Ages, or indeed sometimes the dialogues of liturgical drama (*Dic nobis, Maria, quid vidisti in via?* asks the Easter sequence *Victimae Paschali Laudes*, "Tell us, Mary Magdalen, what did you see on the road?" *Sepulcrum Christi viventis*, she replies, *et gloriam resurgentis*, "The tomb of the Living Christ, and the glory of his resurrection"). The repertoire of Latin sequences is immense, and their composition, like that of the hymns, was until the seventeenth and eighteenth centuries one of the outstanding areas of learned liturgical composition, or indeed of compositions designed for popular use. We have here a literary genre, or rather a musical genre, similar to that of the "tropes," supplementary phrases and word groups added to fill out the long neumes (melodies based on the vocalization of a word, of the close of the Alleluia, or of certain antiphons), or yet again to expound (people also spoke of "farsing" or "farcing") the liturgical or musical phrase in order to add a pious comment.[25] The editors of the missal of St Pius V considered the number of these sequences outside of Rome excessive, and retained five of the best of them: *Victimae Paschali Laudes*, for Easter and its octave; *Veni Sancte Spiritus*, for Pentecost and its octave; St Thomas Aquinas's *Lauda Sion*, for Corpus Christi (and, until 1962, its octave); *Stabat Mater*, for the Mass (celebrated twice) of the Sorrows of the Holy Virgin; and *Dies Irae*, for *Requiem* Masses.[26] The sequence prolongs and expands on the cry of joy

25 Sometimes the tropes used even to function as a translation of sung Epistles or Gospels: the Latin text was "troped" with comments in old French sung to an identical melody. Thus, in the so-called Mass of Eleanor of Aquitaine, of the thirteenth century, or again at Aix, on the feast of St Stephen, a narrative of the martyrdom of the saint based on that described by the Acts of the Apostles was sung in the old Provençal language.

26 *Dies Irae* has the peculiarity that it does not follow the Alleluia; and since it is not therefore strictly a "sequence," its legitimacy in the *Requiem Mass* has been disputed. That is why in French liturgies of the seventeenth or eighteenth centuries – which contain, moreover, many other

of the Alleluia, and expresses the unending praise of the disciples of Christ, who derive life from his mysteries. "How often," said St Augustine, "have I wept while listening to your hymns and canticles, deeply moved by the voices of the sweet sounds of your Church!"[27]

Both in the Alleluia and in the sequences, there is a spiritual mounting of the steps towards the Upper Chamber, where the apostles "were persevering with one mind in prayer" (Acts 1:14), while preparing themselves for the descent of the Holy Spirit and for the preaching of the Gospel; or yet again a spiritual ascent of the Mount of the Ascension.

Third and last comes the tract, *tractus*, which replaces the Alleluia when it is omitted for penitential reasons. The tract was originally an entire psalm sung solo, without repetition, in a drawn-out style or *tractim*, from which it gets its name. It is found fully developed on the first Sunday in Lent, on Palm Sunday and again on Good Friday, before the singing of the Passion Narrative. On this occasion it is the Mount of Olives, the mount of watching and of prayer, which we climb step by step: "And going out, he went, according to his custom, to the mount of Olives. And his disciples also followed him. And when he was come to the place, he said to them: Pray, lest ye enter into temptation" (Lk 22:39–40). Or again it is the Mount of Golgotha that we ascend in company with Jesus Christ.

11 THE GOSPEL

The ceremonial of a low Mass, and even more of a solemn Mass, shows that, with the Gospel, we enter one of the great moments of the celebration. Up until that point, everything has effectively taken place on the left-hand side of the altar cross, the "epistle side," representing the Old Testament. Now, the altar missal moves to the right-hand side of the altar cross, the "Gospel side," representing the New Testament.

In a solemn Mass, the minister of the Gospel (that is, the deacon) undergoes a double preparation, like an apostle of Christ.

---

sequences – it is not included in *Requiem* Masses! Thus, for instance, it is absent from the *Requiem* Mass settings of Gilles or Campra, to mention the best known, even though it is present in Mozart's *Requiem*, and, after the return of the Roman rite to France, in that of Fauré.

27 St Augustine, *Confessions*, Bk. IX, ch. 14.

First, at the altar, on his knees on the highest step of the altar on which he has placed the Gospel book, he asks God for a purification similar to that undergone by Isaiah in the Temple at his calling (Is 6:6–7): *Munda cor meum ac labia mea*... (Cleanse my heart and my lips, O God almighty, who didst cleanse the lips of the prophet Isaias with a live coal: vouchsafe, of thy gracious mercy, so to cleanse me, that I may worthily proclaim thy holy Gospel).

Then, in front of the celebrant, the deacon, holding the Gospel book against his breast, comes to ask the blessing of the celebrant (Pray, sir, a blessing. The Lord be in thy heart, and on thy lips . . .). After the deacon has been blessed by the celebrant, the celebrant places his right hand on the Gospel book and presents it to the deacon to be kissed as an indication that Christ confers his power and his virtue on his apostles, giving them the gifts of his spirit that flow out from him, especially from his hand, the source of good works. Christ passes on to him in particular the gifts of languages, of speech, and of the voice, with the hand of the celebrant touching the purified mouth of the deacon and the purified mouth of the deacon kissing the consecrated hand of the celebrant. From then on, the Lord's right hand passes on his Spirit, which alone can give an understanding of the mysteries, uncovering what is hidden within them, can give the grace necessary to talk of them, and can communicate the power to make them heard. This kiss is a kiss of respect, but it is even more designed to plumb the depths of the divine force of Jesus Christ's holy humanity, and in particular the force of his humano-divine speech.

The triumphal procession that escorts the Gospel is a real entrance of Christ in the form of his Word. It moves forward thus: the thurifer walks at the head, his censer smoking with the incense that burns on the fiery heart of Christ and that spreads abroad the sweet fragrance of the virtues of the Lord, breathing out the prayer that rises perpetually from his holy humanity;[28] the two acolytes follow, with their candles representing the light of Jesus Christ expressed in his Word, spread by the apostles, the

28 When the incense is blessed, the thurifer as a mark of respect holds the censer in his right hand: that is what he does here. The rest of the time, he holds it in his left hand.

bishops, and the doctors (or again by the two Testaments, the Old containing Christ in figures, the New containing Christ unveiled).

When the procession arrives at the place from which the Gospel is to be proclaimed, the Gospel book, representing Christ, is censed three times in the same way as the celebrant or the Holy Sacrament. The book is supported by the subdeacon, who functions as a sort of living lectern (if the book is laid on a lectern, the subdeacon stands behind it and places his hands on it).[29] The subdeacon represents the Old Testament, which supports the New Testament that it foretells. Often old Gospel lecterns have the form of an eagle with wings outstretched, representing the most mystical of the Gospels, that of St John, and recalling also the psalm that talks about the word of God, "flying upon the wings of the winds" (Ps 17:11). The lectern is covered with a silk cloth in the liturgical color of the day, just as the altar missal, in accordance with the recommendations of the liturgists, is placed on a cushion of silk of the color of the day, with the cloth and the cushion symbolizing the tenderness of Christian hearts receiving the word of God: "And I will give you a new heart, and put a new spirit within you: and I will take away the stony heart out of your flesh, and will give you a heart of flesh" (Ezek 36:26).[30]

The Gospel is sung facing north, that is, towards the icy land of the infidels, which is going to be enveloped in the fire of the preaching of the apostles (in the same way that the altar missal is placed, for the reading of the Gospel, at an angle on the north corner of the altar: it was because of this practice of reading the Gospel facing north, and the mystical explanation lying behind it, that ever since the ninth century the missal has been moved to this side now, rather than, as previously, at the Offertory).

The deacon then proceeds to carry out one of the oldest liturgical acts. He makes the sign of the cross on the *incipit*, the

29 When the Gospel was sung from an *ambo* or the rood screen, the custom of certain churches (including that of the Church of Rome) was that if there were two sets of stairs, the subdeacon and the deacon, the Old and the New Testaments, should each mount by his own set of stairs.

30 One should really cover the binding of missals and Gospel books with a silk cover of the colour of the day, at least for solemn offices, unless their binding is already highly ornamented. Thus, when people see them from a distance, they will observe the honor and respect that the most sacred objects are shown when they are covered as with a heavenly vestment (that is, a cope).

start, of the Gospel text that he is going to sing. He makes a sign of the cross on his forehead, an action that his assistants then repeat, because he must not be ashamed of the Gospel (the forehead is where he was signed with the cross at confirmation and where he is marked with ashes on Ash Wednesday). He makes a sign of the cross on his mouth because he must testify to the cross. Finally he makes a sign of the cross on his heart because that is where the cross must be imprinted.

All his assistants, all the members of the choir, all the ministers, including the celebrant, face towards the Gospel book, which during the singing of the Gospel extract becomes the axis around which the entire church revolves; for this Gospel book, held up, illuminated, censed, is nothing other than the representation of Christ speaking through the mouth of his apostles and the voice of his Church.

This then remains the situation until the celebrant has respectfully kissed the Gospel on the *incipit*: the subdeacon brings the book back to him for him to do this, without any genuflection or other form of greeting, as if he were carrying the Blessed Sacrament itself. This kiss of respect and love given to the start of the text is accompanied by a short *apologia* recited by the celebrant (By the words of the Gospel may our sins be blotted out), which shows that the Gospel has the power of a sacramental to wipe out venial sins.[31] In Paris, the subdeacon used also to take the Gospel book to the choir for them to kiss, accompanied by the verbal exchange, *Haec sunt verba sancta – Credo et confiteor* (Here are the holy words – I believe and confess them).

The clergy and people unite in a final act of homage with *Laus tibi Christe* (Praise be to thee, O Christ), which, along with other salutations such as *Gloria tibi, Domine* (Glory be to thee, O Lord), derive from old Gallican practice. The faithful used also to make a sign of the cross at the end of the Gospel, a custom that has often reappeared at the end of the homily.

All hear the Gospel standing to show their hope in the resurrection, like the elect in heaven who are "standing before the throne and before the Lamb" (Rev 7:9); their determination to

31 The placing on the head of a "canon" of the Last Gospel (one of the three small framed texts, or altar canons, used in the traditional Mass, displaying in this case the start of the Gospel according to St John) has sometimes even been used as a rite of exorcism.

complete the virtual pilgrimage undertaken by the Gospel, like the Hebrews who ate the Paschal Lamb standing, their loins girt, sandals on their feet, and their staff in hand (Ex 12:11); their readiness to undertake combat in the service of Christ; and an Apostolic readiness to set out at once to preach the gospel. In some churches, everyone held lighted candles aloft during the singing of the Gospel, as is always done at Candlemass on February 2nd.

Finally, after the Christ-book has been kissed by the celebrant, Christ the Priest, he is censed three times: the same honor is thus shown to the image of Christ in the form of the altar cross, the word of Christ in the form of the Gospel book, and Christ in the person of his minister, in the form of the celebrant, as will be shown to Christ when he is really present at the Elevation.

12 THE HOMILY

The homily or sermon is also a liturgical action, which follows the Gospel and is normally applied to commenting on the Gospel, like the teaching of the Fathers.[32] It is even an action that is properly episcopal, the responsibility of the doctor of the faith in the person of the bishop. We must always remember that priests preach in virtue of at least tacit delegation from the bishop. That is why the priest (the most senior of the ministers, the priest assisting), if he is preaching in the presence of the bishop during a pontifical Mass, asks for a blessing from the bishop before beginning his homily.[33] The *Caeremoniale Episcoporum* surrounds the preaching of the bishop, doctor of his people, with great solemnity: he preaches in cross and miter, wearing cope or chasuble, vestments that mark him out as presiding over a pontifical Mass, and normally preaches seated at his episcopal throne or at the armchair or faldstool.[34] The episcopal

32 Other types of preaching, such as the proclamation of a jubilee or a funeral oration (doubtless because it is often a eulogy of the deceased), should be given, not after the Gospel, but after the Mass (for *Requiem* Masses, they should be given before the absolution and *in nigris*, that is, without priestly vestments). The informal address given at a marriage, in advance of the Mass and preliminary to the exchange of consents, and the address before Communion that can occur in certain circumstances, are closer to the warnings that the Ritual advises pastors to give before the administration of a sacrament.

33 *Caerimoniale Episcoporum*, Bk. 1, ch. xxii, 2.

34 *Caerimoniale Episcoporum*, Bk. 2, ch. viii, 48.

throne is in fact the special location, the *cathedra*, of the homily by the preacher to whom the homily is most naturally assigned, the bishop in his diocese. The priest can give his homily from the pulpit or from the altar step, or in some entirely different but suitable place. The bishop's throne, the pulpit,[35] or the altar step thus represents the divine summit from which divine wisdom flows down over the people. The medievals, like St Thomas Aquinas, used to apply to a doctor's preaching the verse, "Thou waterest the hills from thy upper rooms: the earth shall be filled with the fruit of thy works" (Ps 103:13).[36]

When we speak of "prayers after the homily,"[37] which could precede or follow the homily at a Sunday high Mass, we must recall the dismissal of the catechumens that, in antiquity, took place after the Gospel and before the Offertory. The catechumens, and public penitents, were dismissed by the deacon, with, for example, the formula "Holy things for holy people: let those unworthy retire." All left, apart from those who could assist at the holy mysteries starting with the Offertory, or, putting it differently, who could remain present at the part of the Office that unfolds between this *missa catechumenorum* and the *missa fidelium*, the final dismissal of the faithful. This deeply Roman term *missa*, meaning dismissal, would become the name of the celebration of the holy mysteries that started at this solemn dismissal of the catechumens, and would by extension become the name of the whole of the celebration.[38]

---

35 The French word *chaire*, meaning chair or *cathedra*, a raised seat used for speaking or lecturing, covers both the bishop's throne, which is permanently fixed in his cathedral church, and the pulpit, which replaced the *ambo* towards the thirteenth century and is formed of a chamber or box joined to the floor by a pillar, and often surmounted by a sounding-board. The pulpit combines the honor paid to the word of God with practical acoustic considerations that obtained in the days before the introduction of microphones and speakers.

36 St Thomas Aquinas, "In Praise of Holy Scripture." For an English translation, see "Inaugural Lecture," in Simon Tugwell, ed. and trans., *Albert and Thomas* (New York: Paulist Press, 1988), 355–60; or "The Inaugural Sermons," in Ralph McInerny, ed. and trans., *Thomas Aquinas, Selected Writings* (London: Penguin, 1998), 5–17.

37 This phrase covers the entirety of announcements of every sort made at a Sunday high Mass.

38 The act of dismissal, because of its importance, here gives its name to the ceremony that it concludes. Nevertheless, speaking more generally, it is possible that a ceremonial unit, with or without what is properly

Now, the dismissal of the catechumens was usually linked to a litany. The deacon would pronounce the prayers expressing the intentions of the Church, and the people would reply, *Kyrie eleison*, or *Miserere nobis*, or would alternate between the two. The Latin liturgy has preserved this type of invitation, once a year, in the Catholic or Universal Prayers of Good Friday, and, as we have seen, in retaining the *Kyrie*, though without specific named intentions, at the beginning of each Mass. These prayers reflecting the principal intentions of the Church used to be part of the daily Mass, and St Augustine often concludes his sermons with what seems to be an invitation to take part in these invocations: *Conversi ad Dominum!* (Let us turn to the Lord!) The intention is that the people should return, redirect themselves to, the altar cross.

Prayers after the homily, with the same purpose of invocations for all sorts of intentions and situated practically at the same moment, namely at the dividing line between the office to which the catechumens were admitted and the office at which only the faithful assisted, existed from the High Middle Ages up until fairly recent times, led by the preacher from the pulpit, before, or sometimes after, the homily, particularly for the recently deceased, for this or that need of the Christian people, for prisoners, for the conversion of sinners, for travelers, etc. These prayers after the homily survived here and there almost until our own time. Often, a general confession, that is a recitation of the *Confiteor*, was added to these prayers, recalling the occasions when a recital of the *Confiteor* accompanied blessings from the bishop and indulgences given after the homily.[39]

"Let us turn towards the Lord!" So the homily, just as much as what precedes and surrounds it, is an invitation to a conversion of heart, as a final act of preparation before entering the Holy of Holies in the mysterious sacrifice of the altar.

---

termed a dismissal, could have been described as a *missa*: thus hymns and similar compositions (antiphons, psalms, hymns) within the vigils of the night office or at the end of the night, which later came to be called Matins, were referred to, in Gaul for example, as *missae*.

39 *Caerimoniale Episcoporum*, Bk. 1, ch. xxv, 1: it is the deacon who sings the *Confiteor* before the publication of the indulgence that has been granted and of the associated blessing.

PART 2

The Mass Properly So-called

THE EUCHARISTIC SACRIFICE

I *The Offertory*

EXTENDING FROM THE *CREDO* TO THE SECRET

13 THE *CREDO* AND THE BLESSING OF THE BREAD

The Credo

The *Credo* sums up the whole of Christian doctrine.[1] Strictly speaking, it is not a part of the Offertory, but is an addition of Eastern origin, and is curiously quite similar to the *Gloria*,[2] which is a hymn rather than a creed, but which, like the *Credo*, has very much the feel of an antiphonal composition. Clearly, the purpose of the recitation of the *Credo* was to affirm the Christological faith (Christ's divinity, the differences between and union of his two natures, and – by the addition of the *Filioque* clause – the procession of the Holy Spirit).[3] The practice of including the *Credo* in the Mass had been adopted in Spain towards the end of the sixth century, when the Visigoths abandoned Arianism with its denial of the divinity of Christ. But whereas the Greeks sang the *Credo* immediately before the Preface, the Spanish placed it after the Consecration and before the *Pater noster*, on the grounds that

---

1 We have to distinguish between several Creeds, each more or less complete. The Apostles' Creed is the oldest; the Nicene Creed extends the section relating to the Son; the Niceno-Constantinopolitan Creed of 381 adds clauses relating to the Holy Spirit, to which the Franks under Charlemagne added a final refinement, the *Filioque* clause. This Creed, which is recited at this point in the Mass, is the most complete of the ancient Creeds.

2 The gestures accompanying the recitation are, moreover, exactly the same (hands extended, lifted up, joined again, a bowing of the head at the *Deum*), and similar to those at the start of the solemn prayers.

3 The introduction of the *Filioque* clause into the *Credo* was required by Charlemagne at the Council of Aix-la-Chapelle or Aachen in 809, basing himself on a Spanish practice.

it was a ceremonial preparation for communion, rather like a baptismal rite, an arrangement that has been preserved in the Mozarabic rite.

Rome, on the other hand, knew nothing about reciting the *Credo* during the Mass: no doubt the *Mater et Magistra*, the Mother and Teacher of the Faith, considered that she did not need to prove her adherence to a faith that she had never abandoned. What is more, the doctrinal purity of the Canon, of the one Eucharistic prayer that was used in the Roman liturgy, was sufficient to affirm the one true Catholic faith. The *Credo* was included by Rome at a rather late date, in the eleventh century, when the Roman rite that had been adopted in Gaul returned to Rome enriched by local Gallican usages; and it was definitively accepted by Rome only at the coronation of the Emperor Henry II in 1014. That is why in certain particularly solemn Masses, such as those of Maundy Thursday and the Paschal Vigil, which have preserved an older format, the *Credo* is not recited.

We will discover that the tropes or organ pieces that formerly developed in great numbers around the *Kyrie*, the *Gloria*, the *Sanctus*, the *Agnus Dei*, and the *Ite Missa est*, either never developed around the *Credo*, or were forbidden. In truth, it was impossible to expand on the terms of the profession of faith since they were already complete in themselves. A common practice, to underline the unanimous acceptance of the Roman faith, was for two choirs to sing the *Credo* in unison, unlike the *Gloria*, which was often sung in responsorial fashion (with one part of the choir, or at least the cantors, or the *schola cantorum*, singing one verse and the rest of the choir, or the whole choir, singing the following verse).

In order to enter into a spiritual understanding of this recitation or singing of the *Credo*, we must remember that originally the proclamation of the *Credo*—its "passing on" by the person to whom it had been "entrusted"—was a baptismal rite.[4] It is to the baptized, and only to them, that the *Credo* has been entrusted, for they are going to enter truly into the holy mysteries: this recitation forms a threshold that they cross, just

4 Catechumens used to be entrusted with the *Credo* in what was termed the *traditio symboli*; they learnt it and then had to "pass it on" by reciting it before the baptism, an action which was termed the *redditio symboli*.

like the catechumens who were led to the baptistery in order for them to receive there, by reciting the *Credo*, the sacrament that would allow them to communicate. The *Credo* is therefore a preliminary "illumination" by the Faith, like that found at baptism, which the clergy and faithful receive as they pronounce its phrases.

That is also why recitation of the *Credo* by the baptized is reserved for Mass on Sunday, the Paschal Day, and so the day appropriate for baptisms (the day also for which, as we have seen, aspersion is reserved, a ceremony that recalls baptism), as well as for Masses on the most important feasts, that is to say, First Class Feasts, Feasts of Our Lord of the Second Class, and Feasts of Our Lady and of the Apostles, who are witnesses to the Faith (and also, until the reforms of 1962, for Feasts of the Doctors of the Church, and for the Feast of St Mary Magdalen, who was given the task of announcing the Resurrection to the apostles, and thereby earned the title of "apostle to the apostles").

The Blessing of the Bread

A practice that survived in certain areas almost to our own time was to bless bread at the start of the Offertory with the prayer of blessing from the Roman Ritual, *Domine Iesu Christe, Panis Angelorum* . . . "Bread of Angels . . . ," which alludes to the pre-Eucharistic miracle of the multiplication of the loaves. In this connection we will see later on that the prayer *Per quem haec omnia* . . . (Through whom, O Lord, thou dost create, hallow, quicken, and bless these thine ever-bountiful gifts and give them to us), towards the conclusion of the Canon, may refer to products of the earth (oil, grapes, beans, honey and milk) that in Late Antiquity were brought to the altar to receive a blessing there. The blessing of loaves that will not be subsequently consecrated is a traditional practice. The priest can thus bless loaves at the start of the Offertory of the parish high Mass on Sundays (Durandus knows of this blessing, but places it after the final blessing),[5] and the loaves are distributed to the faithful towards the end of the Mass, with each recipient eating the portion that he is given after signing himself with it on

5 Durandus, *Rationale*, Bk. 4, chs. liii, 3; lix, 10.

the forehead, on the stomach, and on the shoulders, and after kissing it. These pieces of blessed bread used sometimes to be called "eulogies." French authors in the old days either saw this pious custom as a substitute for the communion of the faithful, which was much less frequent than it is today (and was almost impossible at the Sunday high Mass celebrated at a late hour of the morning, since communicants had to keep a full Eucharistic fast, with food, drink, and even water prohibited from midnight); or they saw it as a relic of the offering of the faithful, since these loaves for blessing were offered each Sunday by designated donors and were often brought up by them at the moment of the Offertory. At the Mass of Holy Saturday, in certain places, this moment saw the blessing of the Paschal Lamb, which people would then eat, since with the arrival of Easter Day the Lenten Fast had come to an end.[6]

14 THE *DOMINUS VOBISCUM* AND THE *OREMUS*

It would be easy to suppose that the greeting and the *Oremus* at the start of the Offertory are linked to the Secret, which will be said at the end of the Offertory (before which there is effectively, at any rate today, neither a greeting nor an *Oremus*). But it has also been suggested that they were linked to the litany that could occur at this point; or yet again, that they used to precede another prayer, no longer to be found in the Roman rite, separate from the Secret, the *Oratio super Sindonem*, a prayer spoken at the solemn unveiling of the oblations, which is preserved in the *Gelasian Sacramentary* and in the Milanese rite, but not in the *Gregorian Sacramentary* (dated to the end of the seventh century).[7]

Here we enter the Offertory, strictly speaking, a term that must be understood in the strong sense of a "sacrifice." The

6 For example, in the abbey of Ligugé: see Joris Karl Huysmans, *L'Oblat*, 5th ed. (Paris: P.-V. Stock, 1903), 286.

7 In the Roman Mass as described by Durandus in the thirteenth century, there used to be another *Dominus vobiscum*, inserted in the prayers of the Offertory, which had the particular feature that it was said, like the others, in a low voice, and which preceded the final invitation of the Offertory, *Orate fratres*. . . (Durandus, *Rationale*, Bk. 4, ch. xxxii, 3). This Secret *Dominus vobiscum* was perhaps linked with the Secret which follows. Its insertion appears to confirm that the *Dominus vobiscum* which is said before the Offertory chant is not linked to the Secret.

oblations that will shortly be consecrated are brought to the altar and unveiled. All the Christian liturgies, in a spiritual pedagogy married to the very rhythm of the Incarnation—"when he cometh into the world, he saith: Sacrifice and oblation thou wouldest not: but a body thou hast fitted to me .... Then said I: Behold I come: in the head of the book it is written of me: that I should do thy will, O God" (Heb 10:5–7)—proceed to a sort of pre-consecration. At once, the liturgical sequence is upset: the Offertory anticipates the act that is going to reproduce the sacrifice of the Cross, just as Christ anticipated the offering of Passion.

Allegorically, this moment of the Mass therefore recalls those moments in Christ's life in which more than elsewhere he offers himself in an anticipation of his Passion: the offering of Christ to the Father, as we have just seen, when he came into the world and entered the womb of Mary; the offering of Christ in the Temple, at the Presentation; and the offering during the Agony in the Garden of Gethsemane, which is recalled particularly when the priest invites the ministers to pray (*Orate fratres ...*), an invitation like that of Gethsemane (Lk 22:40), and when the priest prays in silence, recalling the solitary prayer of Christ on the Mount of Olives.

At this point we must emphasize the traditional comparison of the Offertory of the Mass with the Presentation of Jesus in the Temple. Surely that Presentation was above all a liturgical action? This rite applied to firstborn males, forty days after their birth.[8] It was when parents really repurchased their male firstborn, for whom in substitution they gave the animals offered in sacrifice. The rite reflected the preservation of the firstborn of the Hebrews during the tenth of the plagues of Egypt, and the sacrifice of Isaac demanded of Abraham his father. Firstborn male children and Abraham's firstborn son are both figures of Christ, the sacrificed Son of God: figures that were not yet fully realized, since the firstborn of the Hebrews had been spared, as had Abraham's only son.

8 "And after the days of her purification, according to the law of Moses, were accomplished, they carried him to Jerusalem, to present him to the Lord: As it is written in the law of the Lord: Every male opening the womb shall be called holy to the Lord: And to offer a sacrifice, according as it is written in the law of the Lord, a pair of turtledoves, or two young pigeons" (Lk 2:22–24).

By this act Jesus showed what he had come into the world to accomplish: his self-offering on the Cross and for eternity. He did this first on the altar and in the temple formed by the womb of his mother. He next demonstrated it on the day of the Presentation in the Temple at Jerusalem. He finally repeated it in the Garden of Gethsemane.[9] The twin mysteries of his death and Resurrection, the ultimate focus of the offering of the Presentation in the Temple, were represented by these two pigeons (Lk 12:8) brought by Joseph, the sacrificial offering of the poor (in substitution for a lamb and a turtle dove), the one offered in sacrifice for sin, to represent the death and sacrificial slaughter of Jesus Christ on the Cross, the other offered as a holocaust–that is to say, thrown into the fire and wholly consumed–to represent the Resurrection of Jesus Christ consumed by the fire of his divinity.

Simeon announced to the Holy Virgin that her soul would one day be pierced by the sword of sorrow (Lk 2:35). In this way she started to feel the pain of the sacrifice of Christ in the Temple on the day when he was as it were publicly marked out for death: she is already the Mother of Pity. French spiritual writers, from whom this account of the Presentation or Offertory is taken, liked to underline the almost priestly role of Mary, who offered Jesus Christ when he was in her womb, then again in the Temple on the fortieth day, and finally on the Cross on Good Friday, and who, ever since her Assumption, offers him for all eternity in heaven. For since she had given birth to him, Jesus Christ still belonged to her even when he had left the flesh. He could not be presented except with the consent of, and by the hands of, his most holy Mother. At the Presentation Mary offered her Son in advance as a sacrifice as she would one day have to offer him to God on Calvary, in the manner of a priest who, at the Mass, offers in advance the oblations that he is again going to offer (in the sacrificial sense of the word) at the consecration.

Mary also lifted up Jesus in her hands to put him in the hands of Simeon, who represents the eternal Father, in the same way that the priest lifts up a little above the altar the host

9 "And going a little further, he fell upon his face, praying, and saying: My Father, if it be possible, let this chalice pass from me. Nevertheless not as I will, but as thou wilt" (Mt 26:39).

and the chalice that he offers. By this offering in the Temple, Jesus Christ was made ready to be offered in his entirety, in the same way that the oblations are prepared for the perfect offering that takes place at the consecration.

15 THE OFFERTORY CHANT

The Offertory chant is, as already explained, one of the three processional chants or antiphons of the Mass, along with the Introit chant and the Communion chant. It corresponds above all to one of the three entrances of the Lord Christ (the other two being the entrance of the celebrant at the start of the Mass, and the entrance of the Gospel). According to St Isidore of Seville, whose *Etymologies*, which are more mystical than scientific (in the modern sense of the term), had so much influence on medieval commentators, the Offertory takes its name from the *ferta*, offerings brought to the altar and consecrated by the priests: "offertory" thus means roughly that which is presented in advance, or *praefertum*.[10]

Even if it is more obvious during the Great Entrance of the Eastern liturgies, the Offertory chant of the Roman rite, accompanied by the unveiling of the chalice and paten and followed by the censing of the oblations, nevertheless recalls the joy, the cries, the music, and the chants of the Old Testament that accompanied holy offerings (Prov 22:8, recalled in 2 Cor 9:7): the sounding of trumpets in the Temple; the solemn presentation of the offerings of Solomon at the dedication of the Temple and the altar; the people who ran with offerings to meet Moses when he came down from the mountain; and the joy of the people of Israel when they offered gifts for the construction of the Tabernacle. It is an exceptional joy, since the offering leads to the sacrifice, and can be compared to the entry of Christ into Jerusalem, hailed by the Hebrews holding palm branches (Mk 11:1–10). The commentators, when they come to the Offertory chant, also recall with similar gladness the cry of the woman of the Apocalypse – who represents the Church and the Virgin Mary – clothed with the sun (that is to say, with Christ), having the moon beneath her feet (that is to say, trampling underfoot all that changes), and on her head

10 St Isidore, *Etymologiae*, Bk. 6, ch. xix, 24.

a crown of twelve stars (that is to say, the choir of the twelve apostles), and who cries out in the pain and labor of childbirth (Rev 12:1–2).[11]

Traces of the offerings of the faithful survived in certain churches (in the rite of Lyon, in the offering of bread and wine by two priests on various Lenten weekdays) or, in certain areas, in a ceremonial offering of a candle accompanied by a kiss of peace using a pax tablet.[12] More generally, the offering of the faithful survives in the substitute form of the Collection in its various guises (coins, offerings for votive candles, Mass fees, offerings for the construction of churches or the purchase of sacred vessels, offerings following the fulfilment of a vow): "Honor the Lord with thy substance, and give him of the first of all thy fruits" (Prov 3:9). All these gifts are already sacrificial offerings: thus Judas Maccabaeus offered 12,000 silver drachms as a sacrifice for the sins of the departed (2 Mc 12:43). The medieval rite expected the person making the offering to kiss the hand of the priest receiving the offering, in the same way that the ordinand kisses the hand of the bishop when being given his candle, a gesture showing that charity and worship are linked with good works. It was also expected that the priest would touch with his hand the offerings that were being made: "He shall put his hand upon the head of the victim, and it shall be acceptable, and help to its expiation" (Lev 1:4).

We have already spoken of the loaves offered to be blessed and then distributed as a survival of the offering of the faithful. This ceremony of the offering of loaves was particularly special at Christmas (either because they were prepared in a special way, or because on this occasion the loaves were offered to the priests), perhaps because of the spiritual link between Christmas and the Eucharist (until the reform of 1962, the Preface for

11 The reference, in the case of the Virgin Mary, is to the painful childbirth at Golgotha and not to the painless birth in Bethlehem.

12 The pax tablet, pax-board, or *osculatorium* is a metal plaque bearing an engraving of a scene portraying an aspect of the Christian faith. It was given to clerics or civil dignitaries for them to kiss, or indeed to lay people, who would approach the choir screen for this purpose at the moment of the Offertory, in areas where this sort of Offertory procession had been preserved—including Offertories at *Requiem* Masses, where the kiss of peace was excluded in principle.

Corpus Christi in the Roman rite was the Preface of the Nativity; what is more, the etymology of Bethlehem as "House of Bread" is recalled by a lesson for Matins on Christmas Day drawn from St Gregory).[13]

16 THE ROMAN OFFERTORY

The Sacred Veils

The veiling and unveiling of the oblations had great importance in the ancient forms of the liturgy. In the present state of the Roman rite, we will note that at this moment of the celebration, the chalice and the paten, on which the host to be consecrated has already been placed, are unveiled (like the candles that are to be blessed during the feast of the Purification or the ashes of Ash Wednesday). Are the oblations or the sacred vessels, veiled until this point in the ceremony, sacred? Yes, assuredly, in both cases, according to the liturgical principle of respect for certain sacred objects or items that are consecrated or need to be consecrated, which are covered or only touched by means of veils. These veils, when extended, become humeral veils, a sort of shawl. We should also think of the veil that falls across the door in the iconostasis in the Eastern liturgies when the Eucharistic prayer starts. That is why the chalice is covered by a veil, namely by a piece of silk of the color of the day, at the start and the end of Mass. This chalice veil is accompanied by a secondary item, the burse, a cardboard case covered in silk of the same color that carefully protects the corporal, the linen cloth on which the oblations will be placed. During a solemn Mass, the subdeacon, standing at the foot of the altar, holds the veiled paten from the Offertory through to the Fraction preceding the Communion by means of the humeral veil, or shawl, a silk rectangle that is worn over the shoulders and attached across the chest with a clasp or ribbons, and covers the hands.[14]

---

13 Seventh lesson for Christmas Day Matins in the Roman Breviary.

14 There are three sorts of liturgical shawls: (1) the light silk *vimpa* of clergy who carry the pontifical regalia of the bishop or of the prelate whom they are assisting; (2) the subdeacon's shawl, made of silk of the colour of the day, which is based on the chalice veil; and (3) the humeral veil of white silk (it is of white silk in the current Roman rite, but was previously of red silk for the feasts of Corpus Christi and Maundy Thursday, as it still is in the Milanese rite) which the officiant or the deacon uses to

The spotless corporal, made of linen or hemp, is unfolded on the altar at this moment in a solemn Mass (or a little before, at the end of the *Credo*). The name "corporal" is linked to the fact that the oblations that will become the body (or *Corpus*) and Blood of Christ are laid on the corporal. In Latin it is called the *palla* (or in medieval Latin, the *palla corporalis*). It therefore has the same name as the "pall," a square of starched linen or hemp (or even board covered in linen), which covers the chalice and is in fact an extension of the corporal. In certain Latin rites such as the rite of Lyon or the customs of the Premonstratensians, the old usage is preserved in which use is made of a very large corporal allowing the chalice to be covered by one of its corners that is then folded back on the chalice. In the Roman rite, the pall is a separate item. Corporal and pall thus recall the linen burial cloths that received and covered the Body of the Lord, just as those linen burial cloths were prefigured by the swaddling clothes of the Manger.

The "Apologiae"

The actions of the Offertory – the elevation of the paten, the elevation of the chalice, and the actions that accompany them, the preparation of the chalice, the censing, and the washing of hands – are accompanied by "personal" or "private" prayers of the minister, all of which clearly underline, through their sacrificial content, that the bloodless sacramental offering renewing the bloody offering of Calvary has already started.

It is well known that these sacrificial prayers of the Roman Offertory have been the principal victims of the reform that followed Vatican II, on the grounds that they formed "doublets" of the prayers of consecration, something that is the result of the anticipation involved in the ceremonies surrounding the preparation and offering of the oblations in all the Catholic liturgies. For the most part, these ceremonies fall under the heading of *apologiae*, or *apologiae sacerdotis* (as we saw above,

---

transport the Blessed Sacrament (in procession, transport, or benediction) and which is based on the silk fabric covering the tabernacle, sometimes known as the *conopaeum*, or on the silk fabric covering the *ciborium*. By analogy, when a relic of the True Cross is used to give a blessing, it is carried by means of a shawl of red silk.

people also used to speak of them as *excusationes*, accusations, for example at the ministers' confession in front of the altar).[15]

These *apologiae* can already be found in sacramentaries from the seventh century (such as the *Missale Gothicum*): they multiplied from the Carolingian period onwards and underwent their greatest development in the tenth and eleventh centuries. A manuscript of the second half of the ninth century, the *Sacramentary of Amiens*, is the first to integrate a succession of prayers of this sort into the body of the Mass: vesting prayers, prayers for the ascent to the altar, prayers to accompany censing, Offertory prayers, five possible alternative forms for the *Suscipe sancta Trinitas* concluding the Offertory, the *Orate fratres*, prayers to be said during the *Sanctus*, other prayers to accompany the Fraction of the Host, prayers preceding the Communion, the prayer *Placeat* that follows the priestly blessing (and that today precedes it), and finally prayers to accompany the removal of the vestments.

The fact that the Offertory and the Roman Canon are both read in a low voice underlines the links between them. Nevertheless, the silence of the Offertory does not have the same sacred character as that of the Canon: the prayers of the Offertory are silent because they are personal prayers by the minister carrying out the actions of the Offertory. Mystically, they represent the solitary prayer of Christ at Gethsemane. They are generally prayers in which the speaker refers to himself as "I,"[16] and are thus distinct from the great priestly prayers (the Collect, the Secret, and the Postcommunion, and the entire structure

15 They do not all fall under this heading, which is in any case flexible: the prayer accompanying the infusion of water into the wine, *Deus qui humanae substantiae. . . .*, is a prayer for the feast of Christmas from the Roman sacramentaries, as has been mentioned in the Introduction.

16 But not always. Compare the prayer *In spiritu humilitatis* . . . (In a humble spirit . . .), and the last prayer of the Offertory, *Suscipe, sancta Trinitas* . . . (Receive, O holy Trinity, this offering, which we make to thee, in remembrance of the Passion, Ascension, and Resurrection of our Lord Jesus Christ . . .). Conversely, among ancient witnesses to the prayer *Hanc igitur*—in the Canon, the priestly prayer *par excellence*, preceding the consecration—instead of *Hanc igitur oblationem servitutis nostrae* (We therefore beseech thee, O Lord . . . to receive this offering of our bounden duty), we find *servitutis meae* (of *my* bounden duty). That makes us think of the *apologia* of the final benediction, *Placeat tibi, sancta Trinitas, obsequium servitutis meae* . . . (May the homage of my service be pleasing to thee, O holy Trinity . . .).

Preface-Canon-*Pater noster*), all of them prayers in which the speaker uses the royal "we." A certain number of them are addressed to Jesus Christ, whereas all the great priestly prayers, except for certain Collects, Secrets or Postcommunions, are addressed to the Father.

The links between Offertory and Canon are clear from the themes of the prayers, with the earlier prayers forming "doubles" of the later.

The *Suscipe, sancte Pater, hanc immaculatam hostiam* . . . (Receive, O holy Father, almighty, eternal God, this spotless host, which I, thine unworthy servant, do offer unto thee, my living and true God, for mine own countless sins, offences, and negligences, and for all here present; as also for all faithful Christians, living and dead, that it may avail for my own and for their salvation unto life eternal) corresponds to the *Hanc igitur* . . . (We therefore beseech thee, O Lord, to be appeased, and to receive this offering of our bounden duty, as also of thy whole household; order our days in thy peace; grant that we may be rescued from eternal damnation, and counted within the fold of thine elect) of the Canon and to the consecration of the Host (This is my Body). This *Suscipe* is particularly important for the development of the ultimate propitiatory purpose of the Mass: an oblation for the sins of the living and the dead with a view to their salvation.

The *Deus qui humanae* . . . (O God, who in creating human nature didst marvelously ennoble it, and hast still more marvelously reformed it; grant that, by the mystery of this water and wine, we may be made partakers of his divinity who vouchsafed to become partaker of our humanity, Jesus Christ, thy Son, our Lord) and the *Offerimus, tibi, Domine, calicem salutaris* . . . (We offer unto thee, O Lord, the chalice of salvation, beseeching thy clemency, that it may rise up in the sight of thy divine majesty, as a savor of sweetness, for our salvation, and for that of the whole world) correspond to the consecration of the wine (This is the chalice of my blood). *Deus, qui Humanae substantiae* . . . is, as we have seen, an ancient prayer assigned by the sacramentaries to the feast of Christmas. It refers to the representation, by the admixture of the water to the wine, of the union of the faithful with Christ. It does no more than take up an allegory of the patristic period to which reference has already been made ("When the wine in the chalice is mixed with the water, the people is being united with Christ," says St Cyprian),[17] which in its turn depends for its authority at least on scriptural symbolism: "The waters that you saw... are peoples, and nations, and tongues" (Rev 17:15). Attention is thus focused on the humanity of Christ and of the faithful united with him. The text has not given an *a posteriori* allegorical explanation to the action, the admixture: on the contrary, it is a clear example of the allegorical meaning of the action explaining the choice of accompanying texts. In fact, the admixture is of immense theological importance. The decree of the Council of Florence (1438–1445) relating to the Armenians, who only acknowledged the one divine nature in Christ and who consecrated only wine, without the water that symbolizes Christ's humanity, refers to the extreme appropriateness of the admixture, citing Rev 17:15.[18] To tell the truth, the allegory is double: in the Milanese and Carthusian rites the prayer also alludes to the water that issued from Christ's side.[19] In fact it is a triple allegory, if we take account of St Thomas Aquinas,[20] who in addition to a historical reason[21] gives three mystical reasons for the mixing of wine and water in the chalice, of which the first two have just been mentioned: as a representation of the Passion, with the water and the Blood flowing from Christ's open side (in the Carthusian Offertory, the priest says, "From the side of Our Lord Jesus Christ flowed Blood and water for the redemption of the world"); as a symbol of the union of the people with Christ; but also, as a demonstration of the effect of the sacrament, namely entry into eternal life, represented by the water that quenches every thirst (Jn 4:13–14).

The prayer using the royal "we," *In spiritu humilitatis...* (In a humble spirit, and a contrite heart, may we be received by thee,

---

17 St Cyprian, Epistle 63 (*PL* 4:384).

18 DS 1320.

19 The decree of the Council of Florence relating to the Armenians also recalls the water that issued from Christ's side.

20 St Thomas Aquinas, *Summa theologiae* IIIa, q74, a6.

21 Namely, the historical fact that Christ mixed water with the wine at the Last Supper, which is proved, according to St Thomas Aquinas, by the prophecy "drink the wine which I have mingled for you" (Prov 9:5).

O Lord; and may our sacrifice so be offered up in thy sight this day that it may be pleasing to thee, O Lord God) and the invocation *Veni, sanctificator* . . . (Come, O thou who makest holy, almighty, eternal God and bless this sacrifice, prepared for thy holy name), which derive from Gallican missals, correspond to the *epiklesis, Supplices te rogamus* . . . (We most humbly beseech thee, Almighty God, to command that these things be borne by the hands of thy holy angel to thine altar on high, in the sight of thy divine majesty, that as many of us as, at this altar, shall partake of and receive the most holy Body and Blood of thy Son, may be filled with every heavenly blessing and grace). For all that, it does not seem that the *sanctificator* invoked here is specifically intended as the Person of the Holy Spirit. Moreover, contrary to the usual opinion, the notion of an *epiklesis* (a request, accompanied by a deep bow, that the power of God may descend or that the sacrifice may be raised up to him) does not necessarily imply an entreaty to the Holy Spirit.

Psalm 25:6–12, *Lavabo* . . . (I wash my hands among the innocent . . . Destroy not my soul with the wicked, O God: nor my life with men of blood. In whose hands are iniquities: their right hand is filled with gifts. But I have walked in mine innocence . . . My foot hath stood in the straight way: in the churches I will bless thee, O Lord), which accompanies the washing of his hands by the celebrant, and has given its name to the action, prepares us for the *Nobis quoque peccatoribus* . . . (To us sinners, also, thy servants, hoping in the multitude of thy mercies, vouchsafe to grant some part and fellowship with the holy apostles and martyrs . . . into whose company we pray thee admit us, not considering our merit, but of thine own free pardon). "Wash yourselves, be clean," says Isaiah (1:16). According to liturgical historians, this washing of hands may have been mystical from the very beginning. If not, it could be more plausibly linked to the solemn censing than to the ancient oblation of the people: St Cyril of Jerusalem (c. 315–386) had already noted that those who had to wash their hands had not had a share in the receiving of the oblations. This washing of the hands, it seems, was already present in the pontifical Mass of the fifth and sixth centuries, and was at the same point in the Mass as it is today. The priest who is going to offer the sacrifice washes his hands, symbolizing his deeds,[22] to indicate that he must wash and purify his conscience of evil deeds with the tears of penitence and compunction, according to the verse, "Every night I will wash my bed: I will water my couch with my tears" (Ps 6:7).[23]

The last great prayer of the Offertory, *Suscipe, sancta Trinitas, . . . ob memoriam passionis, resurrectionis, et ascensionis . . .* (Receive, O Holy Trinity, this offering, which we make to thee, in remembrance of the Passion, Resurrection, and Ascension of our Lord Jesus Christ, and in honor of blessed Mary ever virgin, of blessed John the Baptist, of the holy apostles Peter and Paul, of these and of all the saints: that it may avail to their honor and our salvation: and may they vouchsafe to intercede for us in heaven, whose memory we celebrate on earth) highlights the finality of the sacrifice. It is an *anamnesis* (remembrance, recollection), like that in the Canon, *Unde et memores . . .* (Wherefore, O Lord, we thy servants, as also thy holy people, calling to mind the blessed passion of the same Christ thy Son our Lord, and also his rising up from hell, and his glorious ascension into heaven, do offer unto thy most excellent majesty, of thine own gifts bestowed upon us . . .). But the prayer also recalls the *Communicantes* with its roll call of the saints (Communicating, and reverencing the memory, first, of the glorious Mary, ever a Virgin, Mother of our Lord Jesus Christ; likewise of thy blessed apostles and martyrs, Peter and Paul, Andrew, James . . . and of all thy saints; by whose merits and prayers grant that in all things we may be guarded by thy protecting help). It is a prayer addressed to the Holy Trinity, even though the Canon, like every Eucharistic prayer, is addressed to the Father. Latinists will note that in the oldest missals the more classical form *in honore* with the ablative was used (*beatae Mariae semper Virginis et . . .*) rather than *in honorem* with the

22 Because the hand is the "instrument of instruments," as Aristotle says (*De Anima* 3.8, 432a1–2), all of a man's works are attributed to his hands. That is why in Ps 25 it is said, "I wash my hands in innocence" (St Thomas Aquinas, *Summa theologiae* IIIa, q83, a5, ad 1).

23 The current pontifical Mass preserves two handwashings at the Offertory: one, seated, after the reading of the Offertory chant (a washing with a wholly mystical meaning, since the bishop takes off his gloves to perform it), the other, at the altar, after the censing with bare hands of the oblations, of the cross, and of the altar.

accusative, an effect heightened by the fact that an *ad honorem* (*ut illis proficiat ad honorem*) follows. *In honore* is equivalent to *in veneratione, in honore sanctorum*, and makes us think of the "*in honore deorum*," the feast day of the gods in old Latin. We may also note that the progression *illis ad honorem . . . nobis ad salutem . . . ; intercedere in caelis . . . quorum memoriam agimus in terris* is an interesting imitation in the Latin of the High Middle Ages of the measured parallelisms of the Latin of Late Antiquity.

The *Orate, fratres* . . . (Brethren, pray that my sacrifice and yours may be acceptable to God the Father Almighty. May the Lord receive the sacrifice at thy hands, to the praise and glory of his name, to our benefit, and to that of all his holy church) recalls the prayer *Quam oblationem* . . . (Which offering do thou, O God, vouchsafe in all things, to bless, consecrate, approve, make reasonable and acceptable) of the Canon: *fiat acceptabile–facere acceptabilem*, that the sacrifice that is offered may be judged acceptable by God himself so that he can receive it. The theology is admirable, and again reveals the rigorous precision of Rome's *lex orandi*. But this *Orate, fratres* is above all a greeting, like *Dominus vobiscum*: the priest kisses the altar and extends his hands as a sign of peace. It can thus be a sort of blessing by the priest who is going to offer the sacrifice: we will note, in fact, that the double idea of an acceptable sacrifice and of an offering by the celebrant on behalf of those in whose name he is making the offering reappears in *Placeat tibi, sancta Trinitas* . . . (May the homage of my service be pleasing to thee, O holy Trinity; and grant that the sacrifice which I, though unworthy, have offered in the sight of thy majesty, may be acceptable to thee: and through thy mercy win forgiveness for me and for all those for whom I have offered it), the other *apologia* that precedes the final blessing. Now, for the *Orate, fratres* the celebrant turns round in a complete circle, in a movement that is identical to that of the final blessing. Finally, we must remember that at the end of the silent prayer of the Offertory (representing the silent prayer of Christ in the Garden of Gethsemane) the priest's invitation to the ministers to pray before entering on the sacrifice echoes that of Christ to his disciples at Gethsemane: "Pray, lest ye enter into temptation" (Lk 22:40).

17 THE CENSING OF THE OBLATIONS

The censing of the Offertory takes place between the prayer *Veni, Sanctificator* and the *Lavabo*. It has become the most solemn censing of the Mass, but in the Roman rite it is not as old as the first censing. It was imported from Frankish practice. On the other hand, it did exist among the Greeks, and took place at the Great Entrance. If we link it to the unveiling of the chalice and paten that has just taken place, we can say that it forms a more restrained equivalent of the Byzantine Great Entrance. We have already mentioned the criticism that the Offertory is a mere "doublet," which has been levelled against it ever since the publication of Josef Andreas Jungmann's *Missarum Sollemnia* in 1952. At the time of the reform of the late 1960s, this became the great justification for the suppression of the Offertory. However, one can with equal justification draw attention to another formal "doublet" (among many others, for imitative repetition is a characteristic of the rhythm of a liturgy): just as in the Byzantine rite, the Great Entrance of the oblations is a more imposing doublet of the Little Entrance of the Gospel Book, which is transferred solemnly and placed on the altar before the chant of the *Trisagion*, so in the Roman rite, the honors paid to the oblations are a doublet of those paid previously to the Gospel.

This censing, unlike the previous one, is all-embracing: the oblations are incensed first, followed by the altar cross, the altar, the ministers, and the clergy and the faithful, just as at the censing of the *Magnificat* at Vespers (with this slight difference, that in the Mass only the high altar is incensed, and not the other altars, images, and statues, as could happen at Vespers).

As the celebrant places incense in the censer, an action that he carries out three times, and as he blesses the censer with his hand, he prays, *Per intercessionem beati Michaelis Archangeli...* (Through the intercession of blessed Michael the Archangel standing at the right of the altar of incense, and of all his elect, may the Lord vouchsafe to bless this incense, and to receive it for a sweet savor).

The incense, according to St Thomas Aquinas, who expands on the classic commentary of Pseudo-Dionysius cited in the Introduction, thus represents the "sweet savor" of the grace of

Christ, the *gratia capitis*, the grace of the Head, which spreads from Christ to the faithful by the work of His ministers.[24]

The celebrant then censes the oblations with the censer, moving it in cruciform and circular movements. So he traces three crosses over the bread and wine, to indicate that Christ's death, symbolized in an unbloody way on the altar, was offered in honor of the most holy Trinity. While tracing these crosses, the priest says, *Incensum istud a te benedictum, ascendat ad te, Domine*... (May this incense that thou hast blessed, O Lord, rise up before thee...): the incense is the expression of the "evening sacrifice," the sacrifice of Golgotha, in the course of which Christ "lifted up his hands" (Ps 140:2) on the cross, and from which the savor of prayer rises up to God. This most traditional of the censings, even if it is not necessarily the most ancient, underlines the link between the sacrificial prayer of the censing and the act of Calvary.[25]

The priest then traces three circles with the smoking censer around the offerings consisting of the bread and the chalice, while saying, *Et descendat super nos misericordia tua*... (and may thy mercy come down upon us) in order to show that this host and this sacrifice are surrounded by the merits of Jesus Christ. This good savor of the merits and prayers of Christ, which fills the entire house (Jn 12:3), also recalls the gesture of Mary Magdalen. We will therefore note that this triple censing recalls the three occasions when she anointed Christ (or, in the case of the last, the anointing prepared for the tomb and which she wished to carry out on Easter morning, the occasion when she *wanted* to anoint Christ, since the intention is as good as the action): the first being when she anointed Jesus's feet in the house of Simon the Pharisee (Lk 7:36–38); the second being when she spread perfume on his hair (Mt 26:6–7) and his feet (Jn 12:3) in the house of Simon the leper; and the third being when she bought aromatic spices to go and anoint Jesus when he had been laid in the tomb (Mk 16:1). The spread of the

24 St Thomas Aquinas, *Summa theologiae* IIIa, q83, a5, ad 2.

25 Just like the censing *par excellence* of evening prayer, that of Vespers, which is sung at the time of the *lucernarium*, when the lights are lit because the night is falling, in the same way that night fell on Golgotha at the time of the Sacrifice: "Let my prayer be directed as incense in thy sight; the lifting up of my hands, as evening sacrifice" (Ps 140:2).

incense, like that of the perfume spread by Mary Magdalen's vase, signifies that this action, which heralds the meritorious death of Christ, shines out over all the church: "Amen I say to you, wheresoever this gospel shall be preached in the whole world, that also which she hath done, shall be told for a memory of her" (Mt 26:13).

Then the priest censes the altar cross three times, just as the Blessed Sacrament, the celebrant, or the Gospel-book are incensed, while saying, "Let my prayer, O Lord, be directed as incense in thy sight . . ." He continues by censing the altar (. . . let the lifting up of my hands be directed as the evening sacrifice. Set a watch, O Lord, before my mouth, and a door round about my lips; that my heart incline not to evil words, to make excuses in sins). We must remember that after the censing of the altar cross, the rite presumes the censing successively of the relics placed to the right of the cross, then of those placed to the left of the cross, if there are any, and then of the altar-table itself (at the foot close to the altar step, above the altar-table, at the sides of the altar, and in front of the altar).

This is followed by the censing of the celebrant,[26] the assistants, the clergy who are present, and then the whole people, carefully respecting the hierarchical order: the *ordo sacerdotum et Levitarum*, the ranking of the priests and Levites in classes for the prescribed tasks of service, which imitates the *ordo creationis*, with which God regulated the onward movement of the world, the celestial hierarchies, the movements of the stars, and the various classes of beings to be found below the vault of heaven. The word *ordo* and its embodiment in the disposition of the personnel in the choir of the church, the carefully organized format of processions, and the sequence of the censings, has additionally become one of the most characteristic words describing the sacred *actio*, the priestly and Christic ceremonial, of which the cult of the Temple was the figure.

Of course, the offering of incense at the altar also symbolizes the Angel who stood beside the altar of the Temple, holding in his hand the censer from which the smoke of the incense rose in the presence of the Lord (Rev 8:3–4). This angel is compared

26 He hands over the censer, saying, "May the Lord enkindle in us the fire of his love, and the flame of everlasting charity."

to St Michael,[27] but above all reflects Christ, the Angel of Great Counsel,[28] offering his own immaculate flesh, full of the fire of the Holy Spirit, to the Lord on our behalf on the altar of the Cross, in the odor of sweetness. The smoke of the incense gives material expression, in some way, along with the prayer of Christ, to the prayers of his saints.

From this is derived the moral sense: we must burn the incense of devotion in the censer of our heart with the fire of charity, so that it may release its odor of sweet virtue; our offering, and we ourselves, must be an agreeable savor in the presence of God: "to execute the office of the priesthood, and to have praise, and to glorify his people in his name . . . to offer sacrifice to God, incense, and a good savor" (Sirach 45:19-20).

Are we not a royal people of priests (Rev 1:6, 5:10, 20:6)? This incense, through the priest who takes it and censes the sacrifice and the altar, is the Christ who takes it on himself in his sacerdotal prayer. It is therefore normal for the clergy and all the people to be censed, to show that they all have their own share in the action of the priest.

The equivalence between censing and sacrifice has always provided some proof of this. Regarding the second censing in the Mass, Durandus recalls a quotation from Burchard, reporting a decision of the Council of Rouen: "We have decreed that while the Gospel is being read, and immediately after the reading has finished, the next action is to be censing above the oblation, in memory of the death of our Redeemer."[29]

After this, the priest, now purified of evil works, with his hands symbolizing his works, must no longer use for any other purpose the fingers that are going to touch the Blessed Sacrament, until after the communion (after the consecration, he will join together the fingers that have touched the Blessed Sacrament, the thumb and index finger of each hand, to prevent any particles of the host that have become attached to them from falling off).

---

27 This is the origin of the prayer for the blessing of incense mentioned earlier.

28 A title taken from the Introit for the Mass of Christmas Day.

29 Durandus, *Rationale*, Bk. 4, ch. xxxi, 4. Burchard, *Decretum*, III, 227 (*PL* 115:722). Burchard (d. 1023) was a German lawyer and canonist, and bishop of Worms; author of a collection of Canons, *Magnum Volumen Canonum*, in twenty books, compiled 1012-1023, and printed in Cologne in 1548.

18 THE SECRET AND THE SILENCE OF THE GREAT PRAYER

As things stand, the Secret that concludes the Offertory is the second great priestly prayer of the Roman Mass. It is possible that its name of *oratio super oblata*, prayer over the oblations, which was given to it by the *Gregorian Sacramentary*, is of Gallican origin. It is "secret" because at Rome the custom was adopted of saying it in a low voice, like the Canon to which it is the prelude, with the voice raised in between the two for the Preface. That is the origin of the name *Secreta* in the *Gelasian Sacramentary*, which is testimony to silence, at least at this point in the Mass. The great moment of the Passion is approaching. In praying in a low voice, the Roman priest is a figure of the prayer that Christ made after moving away from the disciples, "My Father, if it is possible, let this cup pass from me; yet not what I will but what you will" (Matthew 26:39). The *Orate, fratres* that precedes it is also, as we have seen, comparable to Jesus's invitation to the disciples in the Garden of Gethsemane, "Watch ye, and pray that ye enter not into temptation. The spirit indeed is willing, but the flesh weak" (Mt 26:41).

Of course, we must remember that the silence of the Offertory that precedes the Secret has a different sacred character from that of the Secret and the Canon: the prayers of the Offertory are silent because they are the personal prayers of the minister who is carrying out the action of oblation; the great priestly prayers of the Secret and the Canon are silent because of the mystery wrapped up within them. This prayer also, unlike the Collect, is not linked to the liturgical year. It is focused on the oblations and the sacrifice. The conclusion of the prayer, for which the priest raises his voice, forms a link to the Preface, which is said out loud.[30]

This silence recalls, not just the prayer in the Garden of Gethsemane that Christ offered on his own (*secreta*) without any witnesses (Mt 26:36), but also Christ's practice, on numerous occasions after his ceremonial entrance into Jerusalem and before his death, of going apart to pray (Jn 12:36). In the First Book of Samuel, Hannah, who is a type of the church, obtained

---

30 We have noted above that in the time of Durandus, in the thirteenth century, the Secret was preceded by a *Dominus vobiscum*, which was itself "Secret" (and, in fact, the first stage of the invitation, *Orate, fratres . . .*).

the granting of her request, the birth of a male child, Samuel, not by a noisy demand, but by silent devotion: "Now Anna spoke in her heart, and only her lips moved, but her voice was not heard at all" (1 Sam 1:13). "The Lord said to Moses: Why criest thou to me?" (Ex 14:15); and the Psalmist says, "The things you say in your hearts, be sorry for them upon your beds" (Ps 4:5).

To tell the truth, the Canon, or *Actio*, was itself for a long time termed the "Secret," while the prayer that precedes it was then called the "Little Secret" or *Secretella*. The silence of the Roman liturgy in general and of its Canon in particular, which in the old days was sometimes called the "sanctuary," constitutes the very "flesh" of the liturgical action, to borrow a phrase from the historian of the sacred, Alphonse Dupront.[31] It has often been remarked, with regard to the recitation of the prayers of the Canon at Rome in a low voice, that what the East accomplished in the sanctuary closed off by the iconostasis, the West wrapped soberly in silence (in the same way that the Roman Offertory was the simpler equivalent of the majestic sacralization of the offerings of the Great Entrance in the East). In the East, the sacredness of the Secret was preserved by the partition of stone or wood that separated the sanctuary from the nave, and over the door of which hung a curtain; in the West, in the Roman rite, the sacredness of the Secret was preserved by the low voice in which the priest recited the Canon.[32]

We must be more precise on this point. The silent recitation of the Canon, according to the historians, is fully attested for the ninth century, representing the fullest development of the idea that the celebrant "entered alone" into the Canon. This dating is important. We should remember, as a matter of fact, that until the sixteenth century, canonical and pontifical ceremonies were practically invisible to the people, because the chancels or choirs of cathedrals and collegiate churches were

31 Alphonse Dupront, *Du Sacré: croisades et pèlerinages, images et langages* (Paris: Gallimard, 1987), 510.

32 But Durandus speaks of "the drawing of curtains" in front of the altar "in certain churches" when the Canon was said (*Rationale*, Bk. 4, ch. xxxix, 1). He refers here not to the practice of Greek churches, but to a custom that was in use for a long time in certain churches and cathedrals in France.

hidden behind rood or chancel screens, many of which were to disappear in the pre- and post-Tridentine period. But at the junction of the Merovingian and Carolingian periods, when the shape of the Roman Mass was definitively fixed, the multiplication of private Masses enabled the people to assist, sometimes in close proximity, as is shown by later illustrations, at numerous low Masses. These Masses were therefore very visible, and celebrated without any screen to mask them from sight. This led to a physical proximity unknown in the East, where the only form of the Divine Liturgy was the sung liturgy, in which the people listened from some way off to the chanting taking place behind the iconostasis. The result, naturally, was that in areas following Roman practice, the Secret of the sacred action joined those aspects that, in the absence of chancel screen or iconostasis, the Mass has shrouded in secrecy. The "Secret" of the Canon is, truth be told, one of the essential features of our liturgy: it is the image of Christ praying in silence as he approaches his own sacrifice, which is going to be renewed sacramentally by the approaching consecration.

II *The Canon, or the Roman Eucharistic Prayer*

EXTENDING FROM THE PREFACE TO THE *PATER NOSTER*

19 THE PREFACE

Sursum corda: the priest invites the people to lift up their hearts, or to raise them to the Lord, following the exhortation of the Apostle, who said, "Seek the things that are above . . . not the things that are upon the earth" (Col 3:1–2). The saints in heaven and the holy ones on the earth join the angels in singing the same songs of praise: "And they sang as it were a new canticle, before the throne, and before the four living creatures, and the ancients; and no man could say the canticle, but those hundred and forty-four thousand, who were purchased from the earth" (Rev 14:3).

Initially the Preface and the Canon formed a single whole. The celebrant starts each of these great prayers by lifting up his hands and then bringing them together, bowing towards the altar cross (a deep bow for the beginning of the Canon, coinciding with its first words: *Te igitur, clementissime Pater . . .*): he does this as he says *Oremus* for the Collects and the *Pater noster*, and as he says *Gratias agamus Domino Deo nostro* (Let us give thanks to the Lord our God) for the Preface. All these prayers are recited (in the case of the Secret and the Canon) or sung (in the case of the Preface and the *Pater noster*) with the hands raised in the attitude of an orant and using the royal "we."

In the *Apostolic Constitutions*, a compilation dating approximately from the fourth century and containing instructions for Christian living and liturgical practice, we find elements of *praefationes* (that is, of what we term the Preface and the Eucharistic prayer).

The Preface therefore becomes the first movement of the Eucharistic prayer, the *praefatio*, an expression of gratitude (It is truly meet and just, . . . that . . . we give thanks to thee . . .) imparting its own tone to all the following action, that is to say, to the *Eucharist*, or, in other words, the giving of thanks.

The Preface is followed by the three major parts of the Canon, namely an intercession (accompanied by a *commendatio*, an entrusting to God of the church on earth united with the church in heaven), into the middle of which is added the recitation of the Institution; the most important part, the *petitio*, the request that God approve the sacrifice (Upon which do thou vouchsafe to look with a propitious and serene countenance . . . We most humbly beseech thee to command that these things be borne . . . to thine altar on high, in the sight of thy divine majesty . . .), and a final intercession.

Be that as it may, the term *praefatio*, used to designate this introductory section, is very ancient (from the fourth century). Durandus would also call it a "Preparation" or a "Hymn of the Angels," since it closes by evoking the praise of the spirits in heaven.[1] *Praefatio* is a technical term of the Roman liturgy, and of the closely linked African liturgy. The Mozarabic liturgies speak of *illatio, immolatio*; the Gallican liturgies of *contestatio*, a very Roman term for this solemn discourse. These introductions to the Eucharistic prayer, of which there are very many in all the Latin liturgies[2] (and which in the Gallican and Hispanic liturgies, and generally in all the "Gothic" liturgies, are expressed at much greater length than in the Roman liturgy, at least if one regards the common Preface as a template), tended in the Roman liturgy to diminish in number in the course of Late Antiquity, although without arriving at a single form as exemplified by the Canon. Strictly speaking, the Roman missal does not really contain different Prefaces, but one prayer of which the beginning and end are virtually fixed, but which has a section written for the appropriate feast inserted in between, an "embolism," or variable insertion.[3]

---

1 Durandus, *Rationale*, Bk. 4, ch. xxxiii, 3–4.

2 For example, the Gallican Preface for the Holy Innocents.

3 This practice of composing what seems to be an improvisation (in reality, a changeable central part placed within a fixed framework) is exactly

Today the Roman liturgy has eleven ancient Prefaces, or rather eleven variations (the common Preface, and the Prefaces for Christmas, Epiphany, Lent, Holy Cross, Easter, Ascension, Pentecost, Trinity Sunday,[4] the Apostles, and the Virgin Mary, the last of which was added in the eleventh century), to which there have been added more recently, on different occasions, five other variations, namely the Prefaces for Masses for the dead, for St Joseph, for the Sacred Heart, for Christ the King, and for the Chrism Mass (without counting the Prefaces that are proper to specific dioceses: Prefaces for saints, for Maundy Thursday and/or *Corpus Christi*, for a Patron Saint, for a Dedication Feast, and for Advent).

Just like the Canon, which the Preface introduces (and just like, also, most collects, in the general sense of orations, and *a fortiori* like the *Pater noster*), the Preface is a prayer to the Father through the Son. Every Preface comprises two parts that are virtually fixed, the two parts of the common Preface: the first continues the preceding dialogue, developing "Let us give thanks to the Lord our God / It is meet and just" into "It is truly meet and just, right and availing unto our salvation . . ."; the second prepares for the hymn of the *Sanctus* that will follow: "Through whom," i.e., through Christ, "the angels praise thy majesty, the dominions worship it . . ." It is also possible that the dialogue of praise that precedes the Preface is, like the *Sanctus*, the remains of an ancient hymn.

Between these two parts, which are practically unvarying and are drawn from the common Preface, the other Prefaces introduce a changeable portion linked to the relevant feast (the Virgin Mary, the Apostles, the Trinity, etc.). This prayer is called the Preface because it precedes the principal sacrifice. It is really a sort of preamble to all the prayers that will follow, from

---

the same for the two other prayers which have preserved modifications appropriate to the feast being celebrated, namely the *Communicantes* (with modifications for Christmas, Epiphany, Easter, Ascension, Pentecost) and the *Hanc igitur* (with similar modifications for Easter and Pentecost): the variable part is inserted between the two fixed elements, with the result that we cannot really speak of different prayers.

4 A Preface used since the fourteenth century for each Sunday which does not have its own proper Preface. It was universally mandated in the Roman rite in 1759 by Clement XIII.

the *Te igitur* to the *Pater noster*, and which will form one single giving of thanks, a thanksgiving or "eucharist" in the course of which Christ will renew his "eucharist," the thanksgiving that he offered on Golgotha. All that, *gratias agere*, giving thanks, is the preeminent duty of the Church, which Christian Latinity expresses in perhaps the most solemn tones of its entire repertoire: *dignum et justum* . . . *aequum et salutare* . . . *semper et ubique* . . . (truly meet and just, right and availing unto salvation . . . at all times and at all places . . .).

The heavens opened during the *Gloria*. During the Preface, we enter in, and those praying on the earth take their place alongside the saints and the angels who are rapt in the contemplation of the beauty of God. *Cum quibus et nostras voces ut admitti jubeas deprecamur supplici confessione dicentes* . . . (With these we pray thee join our own voices also, while we say with lowly praise . . .) in order to sing this eternal song of all the blessed, *Sanctus, Sanctus, Sanctus* . . .

This moment of the Mass corresponds to the prayer of praise at the completion of the Last Supper, in which we find perhaps echoes of the most ancient Eucharistic themes: "These things Jesus spoke, and lifting up his eyes to heaven, he said: Father, the hour is come, glorify thy Son, that thy Son may glorify thee. As thou hast given him power over all flesh, that he may give eternal life to all whom thou hast given him" (Jn 17:1–2).[5]

20 THE *SANCTUS*

The Canon opens with the expression, *supplices rogamus*, "we humbly pray," which echoes the end of the common preface, *supplici confessione dicentes*, "while we say with lowly praise." Into the break between these two phrases, that is to say, into

---

5 See also John 17:17–19. John 17 is a prayer contemporary with the Eucharistic rites of the first century. It gives us an insight into the earliest stages of what will in Rome much later be called a Preface, a *Vere dignum*. This is echoed in the *Didache*, a text hardly later than St John's Gospel: "We thank thee, our Father, for the life and knowledge which thou madest known to us through Jesus thy Son. Glory be to thee for ever" (*Didache* 9:3). Jesus, the celebrant, speaks to his Father. The tone of this prayer in St John's Gospel is one of thanksgiving: Jesus speaks of his departure to the Father and of his glorification; he asks for his disciples to be sanctified and unified, in the manner of a single communion, "that the love wherewith thou hast loved me, may be in them, and I in them" (Jn 17:26).

the break between the Preface and the Eucharistic prayer – the latter following naturally on from the former – the *Sanctus* was inserted, initially in the East, and then, in the fourth century, in the West. The *Sanctus* is an ancient hymn inspired by Isaiah: St Clement and Tertullian allude to it, and it has been inserted in the Mass in the same way as the *Gloria* has.

The text is drawn from Isaiah's vision of the Seraphim (6:3): "And they cried one to another, and said: Holy, holy, holy, the Lord God of hosts, all the earth is full of his glory." (The text of the Vulgate says, *plena est terra*, "the earth is full," while the *Sanctus* of the Roman Mass says, *pleni sunt caeli et terra*, "the heavens and the earth are full." The text of the Vulgate recalls the *Deus exercituum*, "the Lord of Hosts," while the *Sanctus* of the Mass recalls the *Deus Sabaoth* (the Hebrew equivalent), which shows that the hymn is older than St Jerome's translation of the Bible, which was carried out in the fourth century.) Moreover, it is not only the Seraphim who sang the song beneath the sublime throne of God, but according to the Apocalypse, the four animals also sang day and night, in a corresponding vision, "Holy, holy, holy, Lord God Almighty" (Rev 4:8).

When we say that God is holy, we mean not that he himself has been sanctified, but that he sanctifies others, from which follows, "be holy because I am holy" (Lev 11:44). Did not Christ's "Eucharistic prayer" in St John, which we have just recalled, say, "Sanctify them in truth . . . . And for them do I sanctify myself, that they also may be sanctified in truth" (Jn 17:17–19)?

The verse *Benedictus qui venit in nomine Domini*, "Blessed is the one who comes in the name of the Lord," taken from the Messianic Psalm 117, as well as the *Hosanna*, "help us," "save us," could perhaps be a little later in origin.

Like the *Gloria*, and like the *Credo* later, the *Sanctus* was originally chanted by the celebrant (the gesture of opening his hands wide for the Preface and then bringing them together again with a bow in order to start the *Sanctus* is quite similar in all three cases).

This hymn is therefore formed partly of the speech of angels and partly of the speech of men: it starts with the seraphim praising God, as seen and heard by Isaiah, and ends with men praising Christ.[6] The context is that of the acclamation of Jesus as he descends towards the Holy City for his sacrifice on Palm Sunday: "And the multitudes that went before and that followed, cried, saying: Hosanna to the son of David: Blessed is he that cometh in the name of the Lord: Hosanna in the highest" (Mt 21:9).[7]

The angels and the men repeat the word *Sanctus* three times to honor the Trinity, and they say *Dominus Deus* once to express God's essential unity. The text of Isaiah describes a vision that came to the prophet in the Temple, when he saw God. Here then, the priest bows in order to recite the *Sanctus* and in doing so represents Christ, who is about to complete his own sacrifice. The priest is joined by the deacon and the subdeacon, the New Testament and the Old Testament, who have mounted the altar steps with him and bow with him. The three of them together represent the heavenly church and the earthly church united in Christ as they contemplate the holiness of God in himself, the essence of the beatific vision.

The *Sanctus* therefore represents this blissful fulfilment of Christ's soul in the very depths of the Passion, in the Upper Room, in the Garden of Gethsemane, and right through to Golgotha. The vision that Christ had in his human soul, from the first moment of his conception, endures in the time of the Passion. This blessed fulfilment consisting in his vision of God was preserved in the upper part of his soul, in its "summit," without overflowing onto his other powers nor onto his body, all of which suffered in the bloody sacrifice.[8]

But we must not forget that the Christ who makes himself present on the altar and who there renews his sacrifice is the Christ who is in his state of glory, something demonstrated equally by the *Sanctus*: the humanity that is going to be offered sacramentally on the altar is that which is united with the thrice-holy God, which is seated at the right hand of the Father, and which rejoices for ever in its vision in a blaze of glory.

---

6 Praise for the divinity of Christ is followed by praise for his humanity (St Thomas Aquinas, *Summa theologiae* IIIa, q83, a4).

7 This text is part of the Gospel reading for the blessing of the palms on Palm Sunday. See also Mk 11:9–10.

8 St Thomas Aquinas, *Summa theologiae* IIIa, q46, a8.

21 THE CANON, THE EUCHARISTIC ACTION

This is not the place to describe the history of the Roman Canon, which is without doubt the most ancient of the Eucharistic prayers currently in use,[9] first attested in the *De Sacramentis* attributed to St Ambrose (end of the fourth century: towards 390).[10]

We must nevertheless recall that St Gregory speaks of a *scholasticus* as the editor of the Canon.[11] It is possible that the editors used the Greek elements of a preexisting *anaphora* (a Greek Eucharistic prayer), but they created a composition that is totally Roman. This Latin composition might date to the first stage of the Latinization of the Roman church, that is to say, to the time of Pope Cornelius (251–53), the period when Latin became the liturgical language of Rome (evidenced by the fact that Cornelius is the last pope to be named in the *Communicantes*).

Structural similarities have been observed between the Roman Canon and the text of the "Strasbourg papyrus," which contains what could be an early version of the *anaphora* of St Mark. However, this papyrus is not earlier than the fourth or fifth century (in other words, it is contemporary with St Ambrose's *De Sacramentis*). If we supposed that the Strasbourg papyrus was a witness to a text at least a century older, we could say, with Enrico Mazza, that the oldest anaphora of St Mark and

9 It is worth recalling that the reconstruction of an anaphora on the basis of the famous *Apostolic Tradition*, attributed by some to Hippolytus (is this an Eastern writer of the third century, later confused with a contemporary Roman priest, the first antipope, and later martyred?), is highly disputable. The Greek original is lost, but part of the text has been recovered from the *Egyptian Church Order*, preserved in Coptic, Arabic, and Ethiopic translations, and in an old Latin version of the fifth century. The principal specialist behind this ingenious reconstruction was Dom Bernard Botte. In fact, the establishment of an original text from fragments and edited translations is an extremely complex and highly uncertain procedure. There is moreover no parallel with the later Roman liturgy (except in the second Eucharistic prayer of the missal of Paul VI, itself based on this hazardous reconstruction): echoes are found, on the other hand, in the East, for example in the consecration of bishops (compare a later edition, the *Epitome*, which may reproduce the Greek original for the ordination of a bishop) and in the formula for the consecration of bishops in the *Pontifical* of Paul VI.

10 St Ambrose, *De Sacramentis*, Bk. 4, chs. 5, 21–6, 29.

11 St Gregory, *Epistles*, Bk. 9, Ep. 26 (*PL*, 77:964–65).

the Roman Canon derive from a common ancestor.[12] It would follow that the Roman Canon is in fact the oldest Eucharistic prayer preserved to this day (setting aside the reconstruction of the anaphora drawn from the *Apostolic Tradition* attributed to St Hippolytus, c. 170–c. 236).[13]

---

12 Enrico Mazza, *L'Action Eucharistique: origine, développement, interprétation* (Paris: Cerf, 1999).

13 Mention of the famous Strasbourg papyrus provides an opportunity to discuss some suggested accounts of the introduction of the narrative of the Institution at the Last Supper into the Eucharistic prayer. The Strasbourg papyrus contains an ancient Christian prayer, probably an *anaphora*, intended to form the first part of the Coptic liturgy of St Mark (also known later as the Divine Liturgy of St Cyril). The papyrus was probably written in the fourth or fifth century, but could represent an older text, and so could have been a complete *anaphora*. The papyrus starts with a blessing of God like that of Neh 9:6, continues with a reference to Jesus Christ the Saviour, followed by an offering of a reasonable (in Greek, *logiken*) sacrifice and of bloodless worship (compare Rom 12:1) with a quotation of Mal 1:11. The second part starts with an address to the incense and the Offertory, followed by a prayer of intercession for the church, the army, the princes, the souls of those who have fallen asleep, the Fathers and the bishops. The text concludes with a doxology.

Because of the absence of a narrative of the Institution, this possible witness to a very ancient anaphora is grist to the mill of those who think that a narrative of the Institution did not exist in the most ancient anaphoras (because it was spoken aloud, or merely because it was not written down?). It should be said that a text of the Pontifical Council for the Promotion of Christian Unity on this topic, *Guidelines for Admission to the Eucharist between the Chaldean Church and the Assyrian Church of the East* (*La Documentation Catholique*, March 3, 2002, 213–14), has provoked considerable concern. The document concerns the usage of the *Anaphora* of the Apostles Addai and Mari in the separated Assyrian Church. This Eucharistic prayer, one of three used by this Church, has the distinctive feature of not containing a narrative of the Institution. The words of the Saviour, "This is my Body" and "This is the chalice of my Blood," which constitute, according to the Council of Florence, the *form* of the sacrament, do not appear there. On the other hand, the *anaphora* contains clear allusions to the Body and Blood of Christ present on the altar and offered in sacrifice for the remission of sins. The manuscripts of this *anaphora* are late, but the geographical and ecclesiastical isolation of the region (eastern Syria) and the strong Jewish influence suggest that some parts of the *anaphora* could be very old, although its age does not affect the global priority of the Roman Canon.

It remains a fact that the *De Sacramentis*, at the end of the fourth century, reports the words of the Institution. Its purpose, moreover, in recalling the words of the Canon, is to state that "before the consecration, the offerings are bread, but after the words of Christ have been uttered, they are the Body of Christ" (St Ambrose, *De Sacramentis*, Bk. 4, ch. 5, 23).

The language in which the Roman liturgy is couched, and which is so characteristic, was formed precisely between the composition of the Canon in Latin and the following centuries—that is, between the third and seventh centuries, passing through the epoch of Constantine in the fourth century and the golden age of the sixth century. Roman tradition prevailed not only in the incorruptible doctrine of the *Mater et Magistra*, but also in a corresponding literary style, a specifically Roman ecclesiastical style. The period was also the golden age of the other Latin liturgies, the Merovingian in Gaul and the Visigothic in Spain, which would ultimately give way to the Roman liturgy, with the Gallic liturgy merging with the Roman. The sixth century also saw Justinian I (483–565), who rebuilt Hagia Sophia and gave the Byzantine rite its characteristic "imperial" style. However, the noble and hieratic style of the city that was the mistress of the world saw itself, in its sacred language and in its ceremonial, as equally "imperial," and most particularly in the "theology of victory" that the Roman Mass expresses.

It must be emphasized that the principal characteristic of the Roman Eucharistic liturgy is the unique position of its Eucharistic prayer, already attested at the beginning of the fifth century. The very name itself, *Canon actionis*, unchangeable "action," given to this unique Eucharistic prayer brings out the specific character of the rite that is being celebrated (in this case, the Roman Mass) and its immutability (the same is true of other immutable liturgical Canons, such as the central part of Matins, the *orthros*, in the Byzantine rite, an invariable Canon formed of nine poetic odes). In this case, the term *Canon missae* therefore reminds us of its uniqueness, of its invariable nature, of the immutable rule of the faith, since Rome asserts that she is completely free from all error, including, and above all, in the heart of hearts of the sacramental life: let us not forget that Rome was slow to introduce into the Mass the *Credo*, of which, from the Christological and sacramental point of view, the Canon was already the living expression. There is therefore nothing more characteristically Roman than its unique

---

Even if we make the unproven assertion that the words of the Institution were not spoken aloud or referred to in the second century, their introduction, validated by the usage of Rome, was undoubtedly a dogmatic advance.

Eucharistic prayer, its *Canon missae*, which is a veritable and venerable statement of belief regarding the Eucharistic sacrifice.

St Gregory therefore said that it had been composed by a *scholasticus*. At the time of this statement,[14] while the sixth century was drawing to its close, Late Antique Rome, conscious of its cultural inheritance, had completed the work of developing its liturgy. The Preface and the Canon were the most Roman of all the elements of this liturgy, with their own language, their own rhythm, their sobriety, their balanced contrasts. If we do not find in the Canon the inspired prayers of the Prefaces, we nevertheless find unfolding the lapidary style of a Roman public proclamation. Consequently, even if we suppose that it makes use of Greek precedents, it Romanizes them completely: even on this supposition, which is by no means implausible, we cannot speak correctly of a translation.

It is hardly worthwhile to get involved in the countless discussions over the subdivision of the Canon, except to note that the Canon sets up, in the classical manner, a sequence of priestly prayers each ending with a "Through Christ our Lord. Amen" into the midst of which is inserted the narrative of the Institution of the Eucharist. The Canon thus breaks down into three great prayers, one of which ends with the *Communicantes . . . Per eumdem Christum Dominum nostrum. Amen*, the second of which ends with the *Supplices te rogamus . . . Per eumdem Christum Dominum nostrum. Amen*, and the last of which ends with the Little Elevation: *Per ipsum, et cum ipso*, etc., *per omnia saecula saeculorum*, while these three prayers contain within their midst the narrative of the Institution and the surrounding prayers, which means that the entire discourse is composed of four parts: three prayers (the intercession, the petition, and the final intercession) and the narrative of the Institution.[15] If we suppose what is by no means certain,

---

14 Which relates to a text witnessed to two centuries earlier, which reduces the evidential value of the statement, but which, unlike other Roman traditions about this or that aspect of the liturgy, does not piously attribute the Canon to the Apostles, and so constitutes a tradition that is much more credible so far as the "quality of the product" is concerned: the Canon is regarded as the work of a literary specialist.

15 The *Hanc igitur* (which ends with *Per Christum Dominum nostrum. Amen*) might be an originally independent prayer, added to form a unit

namely that the Canon as attested by the *De Sacramentis* of (or attributed to) St Ambrose gives a full account of all its prayers, then it came to an end with the *Supplices*.[16] At once it follows that the *Hanc igitur* and the *Quam Oblationem* were two later additions, together with their doxologies. On this assumption, then, one can say that the ancient Canon ended with the *Supplices* and that a second ending was added later, the ending that introduces the Little Elevation.

Whatever the truth of the matter, the Canon in its final form is a completely coherent unity, constituting an "Offertory," that is to say, a sacrificial offering by the Son to the Father, with at its heart the central narrative of the Institution of the Eucharist, which identifies the consecrated oblations sacramentally and offers them in sacrifice.

The celebrant starts the Canon by raising his hands and by bowing, just as at the start of the hymns and of the Preface, except that here, at this particularly solemn moment, he bows in a deep bow that he completes by kissing the altar. More so than all the other solemn embraces of the sacred stone, this kiss, given at the entry into the sanctuary of the Canon, embodies

---

with the *Quam oblationem*, which prolongs the final words of the *Hanc igitur* in order to establish a link with the narrative of the Institution; and the *Memento* of the dead (which ends with *Per eumdem Christum Dominum nostrum. Amen*) may have been added to form a pendant to the prayer for the living.

16 According to St Ambrose (*De Sacramentis*, Bk. 4), the priest prays as follows: "(5, 21) Make for us this oblation approved, ratified, reasonable, acceptable, seeing that it is the figure of the body and blood of our Lord Jesus Christ, who the day before he suffered took bread in his holy hands, and looked up to heaven to thee, holy Father, almighty, everlasting God, and giving thanks, he blessed, brake, and having broken, delivered it to his Apostles and to his disciples, saying, Take, and eat ye all of this; for this is my body, which shall be broken for many. (5, 22) Likewise also after supper, the day before he suffered, he took the cup, looked up to heaven to thee, holy Father, almighty, everlasting God, and giving thanks, blessed it and delivered it to his Apostles and to his disciples, saying, Take, and drink ye all of this; for this is my blood . . . (6, 27) Therefore having in remembrance his most glorious passion and resurrection from the dead and ascension into heaven, we offer to thee this spotless offering, reasonable offering, unbloody offering, this holy bread and cup of eternal life: and we ask and pray that thou wouldst receive this oblation on thy altar on high by the hands of thy angels, as thou didst vouchsafe to receive the presents of thy righteous servant Abel, and the sacrifice of our patriarch Abraham, and that which the high priest Melchizedek offered to thee."

the symbolism of which we have already spoken: it is the kiss of the most holy marriage of humanity and divinity in the Son of God incarnate and it is the kiss of the Christ, who at the Ascension, glorious and victorious over death, returns in his humanity to his Father. The celebrant again extends his hands in the attitude of the orant, since the Canon continues the great priestly prayers that began with the Preface and was interrupted by the triumphal insertion of the *Sanctus*. More than at any other moment, the celebrant, an *alter Christus*, is in the position of Moses, interceding for his people at the battle against the Amalekites (Ex 17:11–12).

Let us look therefore in succession at these three parts and the inserted narrative: first, the prayers of intercession; second, the enclosed narrative of the Institution; third, the petition; and fourth, the prayers of intercession.

Prayers of Intercession

Three very ancient prayers, from the *Te igitur* to the *Communicantes*, make up a single prayer culminating in *Per Christum Dominum nostrum. Amen.*

Te igitur: a prayer that the sacrifice may be approved (Wherefore, O most merciful Father, we humbly pray and beseech thee, through Jesus Christ thy Son our Lord, that thou wouldst vouchsafe to receive and bless these ✠ gifts, these ✠ offerings, this ✠ holy and unblemished sacrifice, which in the first place we offer thee for thy holy Catholic Church, that it may please thee to grant her peace: as also to protect, unite, and govern her throughout the world, together with thy servant *N.*, our pope, *N.*, our bishop, as also all orthodox believers who keep the Catholic and Apostolic faith). It is offered to the Father, by the Son, for the Church. The offerings consist of *dona* (gifts that come from God), which are at the same time *munera* (offerings made by men) and become *sacrificia* (oblations accepted by God). Partly because of the mention of the Church, the pope, the bishop, the faithful, and, in the old days, the king or the emperor,[17] and

17 Reference to the king was maintained in France until the end of the Second Empire, and was repeated, at the end of the Sunday high Mass, by a triple supplication: *Domine, salvum fac regem/imperatorem* N., *et exaudi nos*. . . "Lord, save King/Emperor *N.*, and hear us. . . ," which in some

partly because God is asked *adunare*, to bring the Church together in a spirit of union, people have seen in this passage of the Canon a survival from the Catholic prayers developed in the Good Friday Prayer. The three signs of the cross over the newly designated victim recall the thirty pieces of silver for which the victim was betrayed, according to St Thomas Aquinas[18] and Durandus.[19] So far as concerns the numerous signs of the cross made during the Canon, if one agrees that the first of the *Ordines Romani*, "*Ordo I*" (a *ceremoniale*, or book of rites and ceremonies, for the Papal Mass on Easter morning, dating to the eighth century), is evidence of a Roman ritual tradition several centuries older, then its attestation of the repetition of these gestures during the Canon would confirm that they originated in the Late Antique period.[20]

The *Memento* (Be mindful, O Lord, of thy servants and handmaids, *N.* and *N.*, and of all here present, whose faith and devotion are known unto thee; for whom we offer, or who offer up to thee this sacrifice of praise for themselves and theirs, for the redeeming of their souls, for the hope of their safety and salvation, and who pay their vows to thee, the eternal, living, and true God) is otherwise known as the reading of the diptychs, the tablets containing the names of the benefactors and those who were making the offerings. There has been much discussion of the placing of this *Memento* and of the *Hanc igitur*, whose conclusion seems to indicate that it is an independent piece. The *Memento* affirms in a very particular and concrete way the salvific finality of the sacrifice offered. Corresponding to the priest's intention, which he names in silence, is the offering of the *honoraria* by the faithful who have asked for a Mass with a particular intention, to which we can compare the gifts of natural produce that have already been brought forward at the Offertory. The

---

areas continued to be sung as *Domine, salvam fac rempublicam, et exaudi nos*... until the separation of Church and State.

18 St Thomas Aquinas, *Summa theologiae* IIIa, q83, a5, ad 3.

19 Durandus, *Rationale*, Bk. 4, ch. xxxvi, 8.

20 These signs of the cross have been criticised for "designating" the host. In practice, that is what they do, as does the entirety of the Canon and preceding Offertory, the purpose of which is to "designate" the offerings as such, first as offerings which are going to be consecrated and then as offerings which have been consecrated. The narrative of the Institution is surely the ultimate consecration-designation: "This is my Body..."; "This is the chalice of my Blood..."

action of the faithful in offering matter for the sacrifice (the surplus being an *honorarium* for the clergy), or today in offering *honoraria*, corresponds to the action of the young boy who offered the five loaves and the two fishes that were used for the Feeding of the Five Thousand (Jn 6:5–13). Moreover, the intention of the Mass that the donor has requested does not imply an exclusive narrowing of Christ's total sacrifice to this purpose or that purpose, but simply marks a relative priority.[21]

The *Communicantes* has become a commemoration of the saints (Communicating, and reverencing the memory, first, of the glorious Mary, ever a Virgin, Mother of our God and Lord Jesus Christ; of blessed Joseph, spouse of the same virgin; likewise of thy blessed apostles and martyrs, Peter and Paul, Andrew, James, John, Thomas, James, Philip, Bartholomew, Matthew, Simon and Thaddeus; of Linus, Cletus, Clement, Xystus, Cornelius, Cyprian, Lawrence, Chrysogonus, John and Paul, Cosmas and Damian, and of all thy saints; by whose merits and prayers grant that in all things we may be guarded by thy protecting help. Through the same Christ our Lord. Amen). The saints were ordered with particular care: Mary (*semper virgo, genetrix Dei*, "ever Virgin, Mother of God," with "Mother of God" referring to the title recognized at the Council of Ephesus in 431,[22] but with the very Roman word *genetrix*); St Joseph, following the addition made by Pope John XXIII (1958–1963);[23] then the other saints (the text, starting with St Thomas, follows the order of the festivals in Rome, as do the litanies of Roman saints), that is to say, six pontiffs and six non-pontiffs, all venerated in Rome. The complete ordering may be due to St Gregory. The *Communicantes*, whose ancient title was *infra actionem* (one also finds *infra Canonem*) varies somewhat according to the feast. In the Tridentine missal,

21 Pope Pius VI (1775–1799) condemned those who denied that any special benefit followed from the application of the sacrifice in accordance with the intention of those offering the sacrifice (*Auctorem Fidei*, DS 2630).

22 DS 251.

23 This addition features in the last *editio post typica* of the 1962 missal, the one issued by Pope Paul VI in 1964. *En passant* it is worth noting that the last traditional *Missale Romanum* is also, in a way, a missal of Paul VI: those who currently use the traditional form of the Roman rite are said to follow "the missal of Pope John XXIII" when, in fact, they are equally following one of the missals of Pope Paul VI.

there are seven different versions of the *Communicantes*, for Christmas, Epiphany, Maundy Thursday, Holy Saturday, Easter, Ascension and Pentecost. For Easter and Pentecost the ensuing *Hanc igitur* also varies. The *Communicantes* are the members of the ecclesial communion who are celebrating the victorious death of Christ: the prayer specifies the solemn feast that they are celebrating by using the formula *celebrantes diem sacratissimum* (celebrating this most holy day). The list of the saints of the *Communicantes* is in fact joined to the preceding *Memento* of the living (Be mindful, O Lord, of thy servants and handmaids . . . and of all here present . . .), just as, later on, the list of the *Nobis quoque peccatoribus* is joined to the preceding *Memento* of the dead (Be mindful, O Lord, of thy servants and handmaids . . . who are gone before us . . . and sleep in the sleep of peace). The conclusion that closes the *Communicantes* indicates the end of a complete section, since the rubric requires the celebrant to bring his hands together without a final bow and to place them vertically above the oblations (in reality, over the chalice) for the *Hanc igitur*.

The Institution Narrative and the Double Consecration of the Body and Blood of Christ

This part, which is formed of elements making up a single whole, is – apart from the *Hanc igitur* – that which is quoted by St Ambrose.

The *Hanc Igitur* (We therefore beseech thee, O Lord, to be appeased, and to receive this offering of our bounden duty, as also of thy whole household; order our days in thy peace; grant that we be rescued from eternal damnation, and counted within the fold of thine elect) returns to the theme of the offering. As with the *Communicantes*, the central section can change (currently, it changes for Easter and Pentecost and their octaves). It finishes with a conclusion, which would imply that it is an independent unit. However, in certain ancient versions, it does not have the doxology: the *Hanc igitur* in this case is joined to the *Quam oblationem*, which would seem quite normal (*oblationem servitutis . . . quam oblationem . . .* this offering of our bounden duty . . . which offering . . .). But this is not necessarily the original placing, since the *quam* (which offering) in the following prayer does not exist in the *De Sacramentis* and seems to have been added because of the current placing. There is also an instance where the *Hanc igitur* is joined to the *Memento*. The words *diesque nostros in tua pace disponas* (order our days in thy peace) are attributed to St Gregory (to whom are attributed numerous Collects asking for peace for the Roman church, given the dramatic times through which he lived). It is not until towards 1500 that we find rubrics indicating that the priest should stretch out his hands over the chalice. In the thirteenth century, according to Durandus, the priest in certain churches used to make a deep bow.[24] The stretching out of the hands recalled a similar gesture made over the victims by the priests of the Old Testament. This gesture, says Olier, marks the fact that God is taking possession of the victim and also of us, as his elect.[25] The purpose is well indicated by *oblationem servitutis nostrae, sed et cunctae familiae tuae*, a dutiful offering made by all of us, both the priest and those assisting at the Mass.

Quam oblationem insists on the sacrificial symbolism of the oblations (Which offering do thou, O God, vouchsafe in all things to bless ✠, consecrate ✠, approve ✠, make reasonable and acceptable, that it may become for us the Body ✠ and Blood ✠ of thy most beloved Son our Lord Jesus Christ). The *De Sacramentis* said: *hanc oblationem . . . quod figura est corporis et sanguinis Jesu Christi . . .* (this oblation . . . which is a figure of the body and blood of our Lord Jesus Christ . . .). Later, greater precision was imparted to the text: *Quam oblationem . . . ut nobis corpus et sanguis fiat dilectissimi filii tui Domini nostri Jesu Christi* (Which offering . . . that it may become for us the Body and Blood of thy most beloved Son Our Lord Jesus Christ). We can see here, with this precise definition, the clarity of dogmatic detail sought by the Roman Canon.[26] Furthermore, the quality of the oblation is carefully specified: God is asked to bless it, to receive it (*adscribere*, that is assign it to the credit of a particular person), to ratify it, to make it perfect (for the phrase *rationabile*, compare the *rationabile obsequium* of Rom 12:1, that is to

---

24 Durandus, *Rationale*, *Bk.* 4, ch. xxxix, 1.

25 Olier, *L'esprit des cérémonies*, Bk. 7, ch. i.

26 We can see this even more clearly from the explanations given by St Gregory for the position of the *Pater noster*, noted above, p. 8.

say, appropriate to the divine reason)[27] and agreeable to him. All these qualities required by God can come only from him.

Qui pridie: this is the narrative of the Institution, the central moment of the Canon[28] (even if the petition that follows, beginning with the prayer *Unde et memores* and ending with the *epiklesis, Supplices te rogamus*, is the climax of the Eucharistic prayer). According to St Thomas Aquinas, the saying *mysterium fidei*, "mystery of the faith," as well as the adjective *aeterni*, "eternal" (*novi et aeterni testamenti*, of the new and eternal covenant), which cannot be found in the narratives of the New Testament, derive from oral tradition.[29] The interpolation *mysterium fidei* would imply that the Eucharist contains all the mysteries of Christ: "the whole mystery of our salvation is comprised in this sacrament."[30] It is "the mystery of faith," the "sacrament par *excellence*." The elevation of the host, which follows its consecration, dates from the twelfth century, that of the chalice is a little later.[31] This double elevation underlines the force of the symbol of the sacrificial death of Christ represented by the separate elements.[32] Each elevation is preceded and followed by a genuflection.[33] The elevation is also a

27 Compare the "reasonable sacrifice" of the Strasbourg papyrus, mentioned above.

28 We must not forget that there are four accounts of the Institution of the Holy Eucharist in the New Testament (Mt 26:26–9; Mk 14:22–5; Lk 22:19–20; 1 Cor 11:23–5) and more than eighty liturgical accounts, which differ from each other only in minor particulars.

29 St Thomas Aquinas, *Summa theologiae* IIIa, q78, a3, ad 9. Innocent III mentions this as a possibility, but does not assert its truth (he does, however, say that these words should not suggest that the sacrament contains only a symbol; quite the contrary). See DS 782.

30 St Thomas Aquinas, *Summa theologiae* IIIa, q83, a4.

31 What prompted the elevation of the chalice, among other things, was the necessity of combating opinions such as those of the Parisian doctor Peter the chanter (d. 1197), who imagined that at the consecration of the bread only the bloodless Body of Christ was present.

32 St Thomas Aquinas, *Summa theologiae* IIIa q74, a1 and q78, a3, ad 2 & 7, and *Summa contra gentiles*, Bk. 4, ch. 61; Pius XII, *Mediator Dei* (DS 3848). Of course, even if the elements are separate, yet the blood, soul, and divinity of Christ accompany his body, just as the body, soul, and divinity of Christ accompany his blood (St Thomas Aquinas, *Summa contra gentiles*, Bk. 4, ch. 64).

33 The practice of genuflecting before the consecrated host is said to have started with Maurice of Sully, bishop of Paris from 1160 to 1196. We must remember that it was general practice for the high altar to carry a

response to the desire of those assisting at Mass to "see God," to see the host and adore it, a practice that gave birth to the display of the Blessed Sacrament, in a manner similar to that in which the bodily remains of saints had been displayed in reliquaries (the Eucharistic monstrances and the monstrances in which relics were displayed were originally very similar). The bell is rung, as the silver trumpets had been rung at sacrifice time. We should note finally that the elevation recalls the Ascension and the completion of the sacrifice: for Charles de Condren (1588–1641) and for Olier, Christ's Ascension was a sort of passage through fire that completed his sacrifice, as in ancient sacrifices, consuming it entirely (or consummating it, as they would say) and completing its transfer to the world of the divine, as a piece of wood is transformed by flames. In the same way, in the sacrifices of the Old Law, "the victim was raised to heaven in the flames," with the result that Christ's Ascension (of which the essential symbolic moment was his final farewell) is symbolized also by the elevation of his Body and Blood, which thus also symbolize the completion of his sacrifice in the glory of the Resurrection. The picture that Olier commissioned to illustrate his explanation of the high Mass on Sunday portrays this precise moment of the elevation, a moment that was for him highly symbolic of the completion of the holocaust.[34] According to the rubrics, the priest's fingers, thumb and forefinger, which have touched and are going to touch the consecrated bread, must from this point remain

---

tabernacle only from the period of the Counter-Reformation (it was one of the issues on which St Charles Borromeo campaigned). Previously, the blessed elements were preserved for the sick and for prisoners either in a niche carved in the walls of the apse or sanctuary (an *armarium*), or in a separate Eucharistic tower, or in a receptacle in the shape of a dove, suspended in the centre of the *ciborium* or hanging on a bracket (sometimes the dove was itself encased in a tower). If the Blessed Sacrament is not present where Mass is being said, the genuflections (or deep bows, whether of the celebrant or of dignitaries) at solemn Masses are made to the altar cross.

34 This painting portrays a Sunday Mass, with green vestments, and shows the altar surrounded by the members of the Church Militant, the Suffering Church, and the Church Triumphant. An engraving, with an explanation of the painting's iconography, can be found in Étienne Michel Faillon, *Vie de M. Olier, Fondateur du Séminaire de S. Sulpice* (Paris: Poussielgue-Rusand; Le Mans: C. Richelet, 1841), Part III, Book ii, note 2.

joined together, to ensure that no particles adhering to them can be lost. The complete range of actions honoring the Blessed Sacrament–namely the torches carried by the torchbearers at the start of the Canon to celebrate the consecration, the candle beside the altar, lit after the consecration, and the censings that accompany the elevations and genuflections of which we have recently spoken–date from the twelfth and thirteenth centuries and were introduced into the Roman liturgy following the practice in France (including northern France and Burgundy), and are some of the manifestations of the very strong movement for adoration of the Body and Blood of Christ that developed at this period in France, Flanders, Artois, and Brabant.[35] These torches, which the torchbearers carry, from two to six in number according to the solemnity of the festival, normally have four wicks each, giving a strong flame that symbolizes the Burning Bush (Ex 3:2), which is itself a symbol of the furnace of love constituted by the Eucharist, which burns without ever being consumed.

The Petition: Culmination of the Eucharistic Prayer

Unde et memores (Wherefore, O Lord, we thy servants, as also thy holy people, calling to mind the blessed passion of the same Christ thy Son our Lord, and also his rising up from hell, and his glorious ascension into heaven, do offer unto thy most excellent majesty, of thine own gifts bestowed upon us, a pure ✠ victim, a holy ✠ victim, a spotless ✠ victim, the holy ✠ Bread of eternal life, and the chalice ✠ of everlasting salvation): this is an *anamnesis*, a "remembrance," a "recollection," which enlarges upon the words of the Institution, "Do this in memory of me." It is because of that Institution that we are *memores*, that we are

35 This movement was responsible for the spread of processions of the Blessed Sacrament and the composition of the Office of *Corpus Christi*, whose attribution to St Thomas Aquinas is no longer in doubt. At a high Mass, when the torchbearers bring up the torches and all the members of the clergy in the choir kneel, these two actions go together, since they are linked honors paid to the Blessed Sacrament at the moment when it becomes present. If there is no communion of the faithful, the torches are removed after the elevation and the members of the choir stand up again (except on penitential days, when the choir stays on its knees until the priest has received communion, and the torches similarly remain in position in front of the altar).

engaged in remembering. St Isidore used to speak of a *confirmatio sacramenti* (many prayers, which started with *post pridie*, *post mysteria*, and were pages of beautiful theology, used to be inserted in practice into the Latin Visigothic rites after the consecration). The admirable theological precision of Roman prayer can be seen in the *nec non*, "and also." The Mass is essentially and in practice an efficacious but unbloody recollection of the Passion. However, as the theologians say, the Resurrection and the Ascension also have an exemplary and efficacious power. The Resurrection is what enables our future resurrection, just as the Ascension enables our future entry into heaven. That is why, when we recall the Passion, we "also" recall the Resurrection and the Ascension, as the *anamnesis* says. We see the same oratorical rhythm as in the *Hanc igitur: nos servi tui, sed et plebs tua sancta.* (It would be better to translate it as "We, your servant . . . ," since it is the celebrant who speaks, using the royal "we," rather than "We, your servants . . . ") In the *Unde et memores*, after the consecration, the priest makes five signs of the cross, just as he did in the *Quam oblationem* before the consecration. The first three signs of the cross are no longer over the oblations, as they were before the consecration, but are now over the consecrated *hostia*. These are general signs of the cross, made over the chalice and the bread, which designate "the pure victim, the holy victim, the spotless victim." Two other signs of the cross, which follow, over the bread and over the chalice, have a particular theological role and designate the victim in the two separate forms: "the holy Bread of eternal life, and the chalice of everlasting salvation."[36] We can observe a sort of theological *chiasmus*: before the consecration, in the *Quam oblationem*, the last two signs of the cross over the bread and the wine proclaimed that these oblations were going to become *corpus* and *sanguis*, "Body" and "Blood"; after the consecration, the two signs of the cross mark out the "bread" and the "chalice": *panem sanctum vitae aeternae et calicem salutis perpetuae*, "the holy Bread of eternal life, and the chalice of everlasting salvation."

36 These five signs of the cross in total recall the five identical signs of the cross in the *Quam oblationem*, before the consecration, and represent the five wounds of Christ (St Thomas Aquinas, *Summa theologiae* IIIa, q83, a5, ad 3).

The *Supra quae* (Upon which do thou vouchsafe to look with a propitious and serene countenance, and to accept them, as thou wert graciously pleased to accept the gifts of thy just servant Abel, and the sacrifice of our patriarch Abraham, and that which thy high priest Melchisedech offered to thee, a holy sacrifice, a spotless victim),[37] which is said over the holy bread and the chalice of eternal salvation, continues the idea of a sacrificial offering. It is a preparation for the *epiklesis,* which will bring the Canon to its first endpoint. May God look favorably upon the offerings that have been given in gratitude! Here we encounter reference to a triple typology of sacrifices accepted by God: that of Abel, that of Abraham, that of Melchisedech. The words *Sanctum sacrificium, immaculatam hostiam,* "a holy sacrifice, a spotless victim," are attributed to Pope St Leo the Great (440-461). The addition seems to refer grammatically and spiritually to the most "typical" offering of the three listed, that of the bread and wine of Melchisedech, which corresponds best to the elements, the bread and the wine on the altar, over which, *supra quae,* the prayer is said. Certainly, the principal "figure" is the immolated Lamb.[38] The rubrics dictate that at the

37 Grammatically the relative pronoun *quae,* in the accusative plural, relates not to the generic *hostiam,* but to *panem* and *calicem,* which specify the form in which the victim is present. The difficulty is that *quae* is neuter, while the two antecedents are masculine. In reality, the Christian rhetors followed an old rule, not often observed, which assigns a neuter adjective or pronoun to subjects or antecedents which may be masculine or feminine but are not living. For corroboration, see Alfred Ernout and François Thomas, *Syntaxe Latine* (Paris: Klincksieck, 1964), 129; Albert Blaise, *Manuel du Latin Chrétien* (Turnhout: Brepols, 1955), §202. In the same way, in the psalm of prayers of confession, called "prayers at the foot of the altar," *ipsa,* a neuter demonstrative fulfilling the role of a relative, has two feminine antecedents (*Emitte lucem tuam, et veritatem tuam: ipsa me deduxerunt . . .*).

38 Compare St Thomas Aquinas who observes, regarding the three elements of the sacrament, that the *sacramentum,* the sacramental sign, is prefigured particularly by Melchisedech's sacrifice of bread and wine; that the *res et sacramentum,* the Christ really present in the form of the Passion but without the shedding of blood, is prefigured by the rite of Atonement in the Temple; and that the *res,* the grace accorded by sacramental communion, is particularly represented by the heavenly manna. Aquinas adds, however, that the paschal Lamb prefigured all three aspects of the sacrament: eaten with unleavened bread and sacrificed for the Passover, its blood, smeared on the doorposts, protected the children of Israel (*Summa theologiae* IIIa, q73, a6).

end of this prayer the celebrant brings his hands together in preparation for the deep bow, with his hands on the altar, of the great *petitio* that is yet to follow.

The *Supplices te rogamus* (We most humbly beseech thee, almighty God, to command that these things be borne by the hands of thy holy angel to thine altar on high, in the sight of thy divine majesty, that as many of us as, at this altar, shall partake of and receive the most holy Body ✠ and ✠ Blood of thy Son may be filled with every heavenly blessing and grace) thus causes this part of the Canon to close (*Per Dominum nostrum Jesum Christum. Amen*) with the idea of oblation. This is the first ending of the Roman Canon. This prayer is, moreover, the real equivalent of the Eastern *epiklesis*: "Command that these things be borne by the hands of thy holy angel to thine altar on high." The liturgists speak of a "communion *epiklesis*," that is an invocation aimed at uniting the earthly altar and the heavenly altar, distinct from the "consecration *epiklesis*" of the Eastern liturgies, where God is asked to descend on the sacred elements by the power of his Spirit. According to Durandus, the priest in the thirteenth century used to rest his crossed hands on his breast and make a very deep bow.[39]

There have been many discussions of the identity of the "Angel." Durandus wrote, "He is the Angel of Great Counsel, the Counsellor on whose advice the Father created and recreated the world," otherwise known as Christ-Wisdom, the Word incarnate. [40] But he adds that the altar on high in the presence of God is also the crucified Christ sitting in glory at the right hand of the Father. The Angel brings these "sacraments" to this altar, revealing his wounds, and interceding for us, who bring the sacraments to fulfilment on earth. Olier and Pierre Lebrun take a similar view.[41] It is worth noting that the *De Sacramentis* refers to angels in the plural (*per manus angelorum tuorum*) rather than the singular, which would not contradict the idea of a "communion *epiklesis*," but would prevent identification of

---

39 Durandus, *Rationale*, Bk. 4, ch. xliv, 4.
40 Durandus, *Rationale*, Bk. 4, ch. xliv, 9.
41 Pierre Lebrun, *Explication litérale, historique et dogmatique des prières et des cérémonies de la Messe, suivant les anciens auteurs et les monumens de toutes les églises du monde chrétien, avec les dissertations et des notes sur les endroits difficiles & sur l'origine des rits* (Tours: Forts dans la Foi, 1976), 404.

the angels with Christ. St Thomas Aquinas, who thinks that the Angel can be compared to Christ, derives the following mystical etymology: the Mass, *missa*, takes its name from the fact that, through the Angel, the priest sends (*mittit*) his prayers to God, or again because Christ is the approved victim sent (*missa*) to us.[42] All of which underlines that the meaning of the prayer *Supplices te rogamus* is at the heart of this oblation of the holy victim, which we know as the Canon, and is therefore also at the heart of the whole celebration.

New Prayers of Intercession and a New Conclusion

After this first conclusion, the Canon nevertheless continues, a bit like the Gospel of St John that, after a first conclusion at the end of Chapter 20, adds a last chapter, Chapter 21, containing a new conclusion.

The *Memento* of the dead (Be mindful, O Lord, of thy servants and handmaids *N.* and *N.*, who are gone before us with the sign of faith, and sleep in the sleep of peace. To these, O Lord, and to all that rest in Christ, we beseech thee, grant a place of refreshment, light, and peace. Through the same Christ our Lord) originated in private Masses and has undoubtedly been placed here to form a counterpart of the *Memento* of the living. To tell the truth, we do not know what its initial position was, but the practice of praying for the dead at Mass is very ancient. Perhaps prayer for the dead was included in a litany or in the heart of a prayer with wider "catholic" intentions (we have examples of some *Memento*-type prayers that also refer to travelers, to prisoners, etc.). This Memento is particularly important as testifying to the rule of faith: "If anyone says that the sacrifice of the Mass is merely one of praise and of the giving of thanks, or is a simple commemoration of the sacrifice that took place on the cross, and is not propitiatory, or that it profits only the person receiving, and that it should not be offered for the living and the dead for their sins, penalties, satisfactions and other necessities, let him be anathema."[43]

The language of the prayer is particularly poetic, with its description of the paradise to which admission of these

42 St Thomas Aquinas, *Summa theologiae* IIIa, q83, a4, ad 9.
43 Council of Trent, Session 22, canon 3: DS 1753.

souls is requested as a *locum refrigerii, lucis et pacis* (a place of refreshment, light, and peace). Even though the name of Jesus, which requires an inclination of the head, is not included in the conclusion (*per Christum Dominum nostrum. Amen*) the celebrant bows nevertheless because of the importance of the request.

Nobis quoque peccatoribus (To us sinners, also, thy servants, hoping in the multitude of thy mercies, vouchsafe to grant some part and fellowship with thy holy apostles and martyrs: with John, Stephen, Matthias, Barnabas, Ignatius, Alexander, Marcellinus, Peter, Felicity, Perpetua, Agatha, Lucy, Agnes, Cecily, Anastasia, and with all the saints, into whose company we pray thee admit us, not considering our merit, but of thine own free pardon) – "To us sinners also," says the celebrant, raising his voice a little and striking his breast, all out of humility. He asks to be given some part and fellowship with the saints, of which a new list is here given, with this prayer becoming a sequel (*quoque*, "also") to the recalling of those who died "marked with the sign of faith" of the *Memento*. The *Per Christum Dominum nostrum* conclusive of the prayer repeats that of the *Memento* and will in its turn be repeated by that of the *Per quem haec omnia*. The first saint to be named is St John the Baptist, who is traditionally named after the consecration in Eastern liturgies, but who is above all the titular (jointly with St John the Evangelist) of the cathedral of Rome, the basilica of St John Lateran, which is the name commonly given to the church that is Mother and Teacher (originally, the Basilica of Saint Savior). The other saints (Stephen, Matthias, Barnabas . . . Agatha, Lucy, Cecily, Anastasia), are the objects of particular veneration in Rome. Twentieth-century authors have tended to attach the *Nobis quoque peccatoribus* to the *Supplices* in the Canon, though without universal agreement.[44] However they seem to agree that, if the first list of saints in the Canon in fact belonged to the *Memento* of the living, then the second would belong to the *Memento* of the dead, and would help to perfect the symmetry between the sections of the Canon preceding and following the Institution Narrative.

44 Compare Enrico Mazza, *L'Anafora eucaristica: studi sulle origine* (Roma: Edizione liturgiche, 2007), 267.

The celebrant's slight raising of the voice was known from the *Ordo I*, which would have left Rome for the territories of Pepin the Short around 750 or a little later. As with all the details in this *Ordo*, it may give an indication of Roman usage or it may have been added during the book's travel into Frankish territory. In a practical sense, the raising of the voice was a sign for the subdeacons, who had been bowed since the start of the Canon, to stand upright, to reply *Amen*, and to go and get the paten for the Fraction. As for the intention of the prayer, Mazza thinks that it was a prayer connected with the *Memento* of the dead, in imitation of a prayer found in the Alexandrian anaphora, which contains this intention for the celebrating clergy (*nobis . . . famulis*).[45] The proof of this would lie in the word *societatem*, which would be a translation of the word *kleron* in the Alexandrian anaphora, and would therefore refer to the clerical order. However, even supposing that that were so, the distinction that the celebrant would be making at this point, separating out the clergy in whose name particularly he would be appealing to the mercy of God, no longer applies in the Canon regarded as a whole, where the "we" of the great priestly prayers is always the royal "we." In the "us sinners, also," as always elsewhere, the celebrant is speaking in the name of all, as the representative of the *Senatus Populusque Romanus Christianus*.

The conclusion of the Canon: the start of the following prayer, *Per quem haec omnia* (Through Christ our Lord; through whom, O Lord, thou dost create, hal✠low, quick✠en, and ble✠ss these thine ever-bountiful gifts and give them to us. By ✠ him and with ✠ him and in ✠ him, is to thee, God the Father ✠ Almighty, in the unity of the Holy ✠ Ghost, all honor and glory. For ever and ever), could, with the phrase *haec omnia bona*, recall the fruits of the earth (oil, grapes, beans, honey, and milk), which would be receiving a blessing and would have nothing to do with the matter for sacrifice brought up during the Offertory, and so nothing to do with the consecrated oblations. Lebrun does not believe this at all;[46] but nevertheless Durandus reports the existence of this usage in the High Middle Ages:

45 Mazza, 294.
46 Lebrun, *Explication litérale*, 420.

> It is at this moment that grapes are blessed, as we will explain in Part Six relating to Maundy Thursday, in the Office of the Day. In the *Canon of the Apostles* we read, "It should not be allowed to offer at the altar, that is for a blessing, anything other than new ears of grain, grapes, oil for the lamps, beans, perfumes and incense, and that at the moment when the Holy Sacrament is celebrated."[47]

Despite all that, Durandus applies the *haec bona* only to the consecrated bread and wine, at the cost of having to explain *omnia*, "all these good things," thus:

> There follows *Per quem haec omnia*. It says *omnia*, because all things were created through the Son, as St John says, *Omnia per ipsum facta sunt et sine ipso factum est nihil* (John 1:3), and Genesis says, "God saw everything that he had made, and indeed, it was very good" (Genesis 1:31). *Creas* refers to the act of forming nature; *sanctificas*, to the consecration of matter; *vivificas*, to the transubstantiation of the creature; *benedicis*, to the accumulation of grace. *Haec omnia* has simply the value of a demonstrative pronoun, although the tense of the verb is a general present, which goes beyond the accepted meaning of the immediate present. The sense is therefore: *haec omnia*, that is to say, the bread, the wine and the water; *semper bona creas*, you always make them good in accordance with the original regular causes; *sanctificas*, according to the sacramental causes; *vivificas*, so that they may become flesh and blood; *et benedicis*, so that they may preserve unity and charity.[48]

Then comes the Great Doxology that completes the Canon, unless one thinks, with St Gregory, that it is the *Pater noster* that really completes the Roman Canon. St Justin, in his *First Apology*, written towards 152, is the first to testify that at the end of the Eucharistic prayer, the bishop offers praise and glory to the Father through the Son and the Holy Spirit, and the people respond, "Amen."[49] The final "Little Elevation" that

47 Durandus, *Rationale*, Bk. 4, ch. xlvi, 8.
48 Durandus, *Rationale*, Bk. 4, ch. xlvi, 9.
49 Justin, *First Apology*, chs. 85–87.

accompanies this doxology is particularly expressive of the offering to the Father of the sacrifice of the Body and of the Blood that has been shed.[50] The sacrifice is complete: we can join the medievals in saying that the three signs of the cross that the celebrant makes before this "Little Elevation," with his hand over the host and the chalice, which the celebrant then repeats with the host itself above the chalice, remind us that at the third hour on Good Friday Christ was crucified by being condemned by the Jews (Mk 15:24), at the sixth hour he was crucified by the hands of the pagans (Jn 9:14), and at the ninth hour "bowing his head, he gave up the ghost." (Jn 19:30). Then, to highlight the separation of the Savior's body and soul in death, as St Thomas Aquinas explains, the celebrant makes two signs of the cross with the host in front of the chalice of the Blood.[51]

If we suppose that the *Per quem* could have been a prayer focused on the "fruits of the earth" that had been brought forward and that received a blessing at this moment, we must nevertheless not forget that the Canon has become a single whole, in which the *Per quem* today is focused on the oblations, since they are directly indicated by three signs of the cross: "thou dost create, hal✠low, quick✠en, and ble✠ss these thine ever-bountiful gifts." When explaining the Bible, while not ignoring our interest in a diachronic explanation of the sacred text, which tries to understand the successive states of the text and the original meaning of each part, we must nevertheless insist on the overriding importance of the synchronic interpretation, which takes the text as the entity that it has become in the Canon of Scripture. Everything else being equal, without rejecting (indeed, quite the contrary) the necessity of uncovering the successive states and the original meaning of each part of the Canon, we must give priority to the meaning of the whole text that has developed, in the form in which the Church presents it to our faith and our prayer; more especially because it is part of the very principle of the Canon's development that we should insist that it represents a complete whole (and what is more, a unique

50 It was not necessarily the only "Little Elevation": in a fair number of places, a second "Little Elevation" was to be found in the medieval period during the *Pater noster*.

51 St Thomas Aquinas, *Summa theologiae* IIIa, q83, a5, ad 3.

whole, in that it is the only Roman Eucharistic prayer). That is confirmed by the famous remark of St Gregory, who attributes its composition to a *scholasticus*, as if it had been composed at a single sitting by a single author, who (in reality, we mean the group of men who) could not be said to be *inspired*, in the sense that the authors of Holy Scripture were inspired, but who must theologically be considered to have been *assisted*, to the extent that he, under the authority of the pope, created the Eucharistic prayer, the very heart of the incorruptible *lex orandi* of the Church of Peter.

22 THE LORD'S PRAYER

The *Pater noster* is the priestly prayer *par excellence*, the prayer of the compassionate High Priest, which is brought forward to the heart of the Mass, to the moment when all "is consummated" (Jn 19:30). The recitation of the *Pater noster* is one of the important parts of the rite of baptism. The *Pater noster* has always, according to the most ancient sources, had a place in the Divine Office. It was present, we can be absolutely sure, in the Roman Mass at the end of the fourth century. Among the Greeks it was, strictly speaking, a communion prayer, placed after the Fraction. In Rome, in Milan, in Spain, it was reserved for the priest.

The rhetorical royal "we" of the great priestly prayers finds its way into the brief and very ancient introduction (Let us pray. Taught by the precepts of salvation, and following the divine commandment, we make bold to say . . .). Known to St Jerome, quoted by St Cyprian almost word for word (*audemus dicere*), this introduction's theme reminds us of that of the *Apostolic Constitutions*: holding fast to the practice of the apostles. The *Pater noster* itself is sung or recited by the celebrant with his hands extended: it is the prayer *par excellence*, the prayer of the Lord, which was "handed on" to the catechumens, like the *Credo*.

St Gregory, in a letter to John of Syracuse, confirms that the authentic Roman practice was for the *Pater noster* to be sung by the priest alone, unlike the practice of the Greeks.[52] St Gregory

---

52 "The Lord's Prayer, among the Greeks, is said by all the people; among us, by the priest alone." St Gregory, *Epistles*, Bk. 9, Ep. 26 (*PL* 77:964–65).

seems to confirm a tendency (guaranteed by St Augustine[53] and observable in Milan and Spain) to make the prayer a priestly prayer, a tendency that he heightens by noting that the prayer concludes the Eucharistic prayer: the priest then moves away from the altar, and the Fraction follows.

St Gregory shows in the same letter that in the ancient Roman rite the *Pater noster* came immediately after the Canon and before the Fraction. Among the Greeks, in Gaul,[54] in Africa, in Spain, and in Milan, the *Pater noster* is by contrast inserted after the breaking of the bread. The same is true in the Eastern rites (except in Byzantium, where it is in the same place as in Rome, but sung by all the assistants, or more precisely, by a lector, while the priest and people recite it in silence). In Rome, consequently, the *Pater noster* served as the final completion of the Canon. The priest, as in the Canon, kept his hands extended. The faithful conclude the prayer in the same way as they conclude the Eucharistic prayer, either by saying *Amen*, or in Rome by singing the final petition.

We can, nevertheless, following the *De Sacramentis*, consider the *Pater noster* as a prayer that heralds the communion,[55] especially since with the fourth petition, for the forgiveness of sins, the prayer constitutes the necessary cleansing of the heart before communicants go up to the altar (Mt 5:23–24).

Durandus observes that "the *Pater noster* contains seven petitions, after the *captatio benevolentiae* (*Pater noster, qui es in caelis*), which correspond, though not in the same order, to the seven words of Christ on the Cross."[56] The first of these words is "Father, forgive them" (Lk 23:34); the second, "Woman, Behold thy Son" (Jn 19:26); the third, "Behold thy mother" (Jn 19:27); the fourth, "This day thou shalt be with me in paradise" (Lk 23:43); the fifth, "Eli, Eli . . ." (Mk 15:34, Mt 27:46);

53 "In the church, this prayer of our Lord, to which the faithful listen, is recited every day at the altar of God." St Augustine, Sermon 68, ch. xiii, 12 (*PL* 38:399).

54 Philippe Bernard, *Transitions liturgiques en Gaule carolingienne: une traduction commentée des deux "lettres" faussement attribuées à l'évêque Germain de Paris* (Paris: Hora Decima, 2008), 309ff.

55 That is the basis on which St Ambrose comments on the prayer (though with the observation that the *Pater noster* follows immediately on the consecration): *De Sacramentis*, Bk. 5, chs. 4, 18–30.

56 Durandus, *Rationale*, Bk. 4, ch. xlvii, 7.

the sixth, "Father, into thy hands . . ." (Lk 23:46); and the seventh, "It is consummated" (Jn 19:30). Or yet again, the seven petitions correspond to the seven sayings associated with the Virgin, reported by the Gospels, of which the first is "How shall this be done?" (Lk 1:34); the second, "Behold the handmaid of the Lord; be it done to me according to thy word" (Lk 1:38); the third, "As soon as the voice of thy salutation sounded in my ears, the infant in my womb leaped for joy" (Lk 1:44);[57] the fourth, "My soul doth magnify the Lord" (Luke 1:46); the fifth, "They have no wine" (Jn 2:3); the sixth, "Whatsoever he shall say to you, do ye" (Jn 2:5); and the seventh, "Son, why hast thou done so to us?" (Lk 2:48).

The prayer "Deliver us, we beseech thee, from all evils," which follows the *Pater noster*, is an extension of the final petition, and has developed into an attached prayer, a sort of very ancient *apologia*.[58] It is described as an "embolism" in the *Pater noster*, because it was a possible variation, or insertion (in Greek, an *embolisma*, from *emballein*, to insert, to burst into) after the final petition. The prayer is recited in a low voice. It invokes St Peter, St Paul, and St Andrew (the last, as a brother of St Peter, and possibly under the influence of Constantinople). The doxology, said out loud, which brings the prayer to a close, serves as a frame for the following Fraction and the Commixture.

The *Pater noster* is thus the moment of the Mass that represents the entombment of Christ after he has been sacrificed (the Canon) and before his Resurrection (the Commixture, as we shall see). The hallowing of God's name and the accomplishment of his will on heaven and on earth are fully achieved when all "is finished" and when Christ, brought down from the Cross and entrusted to his mother, is placed in the tomb.

---

57 These words are not those of the Virgin, but are addressed to her by her cousin Elizabeth. Nevertheless, "the sound of your greeting" is like an echo of unrecorded words of the Virgin.

58 In the *De Sacramentis*, it is recorded that after the *Pater noster* the priest says, "Through our Lord Jesus Christ, in whom you possess honor, praise, glory, majesty, power, with the Holy Spirit, from the beginning, now, and for ever world without end. Amen" (St Ambrose, *De Sacramentis*, Bk. 6, ch. 5, 24). This prayer is very close to the current conclusion of the Canon: "By him, and with him, and in him, is to thee, God the Father Almighty, in the unity of the Holy Ghost, all honor and glory. For ever and ever. Amen."

The place that St Gregory either assigns to the *Pater noster* or, if the prayer was already in that position, confirms for it, and the reason that he gives for this placing, are particularly important if we are to understand the theological and mystical implications of this prayer in the Roman rite: it would not be fitting, says St Gregory, for us to say a prayer that was of merely human composition, the Canon, over the sacrificed oblation (the Body and the Blood, consecrated separately and not yet brought together in the Commixture, which is to follow), and not to say the Lord's own prayer over the symbols of his sacramental sacrifice.[59] With the *Pater noster*, the sacramental oblation is completed, and its fruits are ready to be distributed in the communion.

The Mass, in the strict sense of the word, comes to an end here, as St Caesarius observed:

> The Mass does not take place when the holy scriptures are read in the church, but when the gifts are offered and the Body and Blood of the Lord are consecrated. For you can just as well read the lessons at home, whether they are taken from a prophet, from the Apostle, or from the Gospel, or you can listen to other people reading them; but you can hear and watch the consecration of the Body and Blood of Christ only in the house of God. That is why anyone who wants to participate in the entire Mass and benefit his soul thereby must stay in the church, in a humble posture and with a contrite heart, until the moment when the Lord's Prayer is said and the blessing is given to the people.[60]

This prayer, which is as it were a Roman addition to the Eucharistic prayer, constitutes a quite remarkable dogmatic refinement in the *lex orandi* of the Church who is the Mother and Teacher. Certainly, it is an excellent preparation for communion, but first and foremost it announces the completion of the sacramental sacrifice that has just been presented on the altar.

---

59 If we did not say the *Pater noster*, St Gregory explains, "we would, over the oblation, say a prayer composed by a scholar, and over our Lord's actual Body and Blood, we would *not* say the traditional prayer that he handed down to us!" St Gregory, *Epistles*, Bk. 9, Ep. 26 (*PL* 77:964–65).

60 St Caesarius of Arles, Sermon 73, 2. The blessing to which St Caesarius refers is the blessing preceding the Communion.

III *The Communion,* WHICH IS CENTERED ON THE RESURRECTION

23 THE FRACTION, THE COMMIXTURE

We pass from the period of the sacrificial death, symbolized by the separate holy elements of the Body and the Blood, to the period of the Resurrection, symbolized by the bringing together of the Body and the Blood in the ceremony of the Commixture (the mixing of a fragment of the consecrated bread with the consecrated wine). That is why the rites of the Fraction of the host and of the Commixture, which precede the distribution in the communion, were transferred in Rome and among the Byzantines to after the *Pater noster*. Bishops, priests, and deacons used to break the bread with a view to the communion of the faithful while the *Agnus Dei* was sung, or indeed another chant for the Fraction, such as can be found in most liturgies. In Rome today, the Fraction takes place during the doxology (Through the same Jesus Christ thy son our Lord, who liveth and reigneth with thee in the unity of the holy Ghost, one God, forever and ever, Amen) attached to the embolism in the *Pater noster* (Deliver us, we beseech thee, O Lord . . .), while the Commixture takes place during the greeting that follows (The peace of the Lord be always with you). The Fraction therefore takes place before the chant that is proper to it, that is, the *Agnus Dei* (much as, at the beginning of the Mass, the actual entry of the ministers into the sanctuary precedes the chant that is proper to it, that is, the Introit).

After having broken the large host into two, and then after having removed a portion of one of the two halves, the celebrant makes three signs of the cross over the chalice with this portion, while saying: *Pax Domini sit semper vobiscum* (The peace of the

Lord be always with you). Then he drops this portion of the consecrated host into chalice of consecrated wine, saying the corresponding *apologia* in a low voice (May this mingling and hallowing of the Body and Blood of our Lord Jesus Christ avail us that receive it unto life everlasting).

We should note that these three signs of the cross existed in *Ordo I*. In reality, however, there were two commixtures in the papal Mass.

The first commixture was made after the *Pax Domini*, using a fragment from an earlier consecration. This was linked with the rite of the *sancta*, of the consecrated "holy elements," or the rite of the *fermentum*, of the "leaven" or "yeast." When the bishop of Rome advanced towards the altar, an acolyte presented him with a box containing the *sancta*, the Eucharistic elements remaining from the previous celebration. At the Fraction, this bread, consecrated at an earlier Eucharist, was placed in the chalice so that the bishop could consume it together with the consecrated wine. That was the first commixture. In addition, it was a counterpart to the preparation of parallel commixtures that were about to take place in the other churches of Rome and its environs: fragments were taken from the *sancta* of the Sunday Mass to be sent by the pope to the priests of the various *tituli* (Roman parishes) where the pope was not due to celebrate, so that these priests could say Mass in the pope's name, place a fragment of the papal *fermentum* in their chalice, and demonstrate thereby their shared communion with the bishop of Rome.

The second Commixture took place as follows: when the pontiff made his communion, he bit off a piece of the consecrated bread, and placed what was left in the consecrated wine. This was really what we know as the Commixture, which allows the celebrant, after communicating with the Body of Christ, to communicate in both Body and Blood at the same time. Thus, St Thomas Aquinas, in his hymn for Lauds on *Corpus Christi*, wrote:

Carnem dedit et sanguinem,	He gave his Flesh and Blood,
Ut duplicis substantiae	that He might feed the whole man
Totum cibaret hominem	made up of twofold substance.[1]

1 St Thomas Aquinas, *Verbum supernum prodiens.* English translation from Paul Murray OP, *Aquinas at Prayer: The Bible, Mysticism and Poetry* (London: Bloomsbury Continuum, 2013), 215.

The fact that this second Commixture, which has become the only Commixture, has been brought forward to the moment of the *Pax Domini*, replacing the earlier Commixture, remains as a trace of the ancient rite of the *fermentum*, which disappeared in the Carolingian period (and in any case made no sense outside Rome).

This last and sole Commixture represents the bringing together of the Body and Blood, and so represents the Resurrection. In fact, to interpret the symbolism of this mixture correctly, we must always remember that Leviticus describes the blood as the location of the soul, in the same way that the heart is thought to be the location of feelings of love: "the life of all flesh is in the blood" (Lev 17:14).[2] The Commixture of the Body and Blood of Christ thus represents the reunion of his soul, which had come back up out of hell, and his Body, which had stayed in the tomb: in other words, it represents the Resurrection. We move from the sadness of the Passion on the Friday evening to the joy of the Resurrection on the Sunday morning: "In the evening weeping shall have place, and in the morning gladness" (Ps 29:6).

Moreover, the greeting and what follows represent the visits that Christ then paid to his disciples. In fact, with *Pax Domini sit semper vobiscum*, the priest recalls that on the first day of the week, after his Resurrection from the dead, Jesus, standing in the midst of his disciples, said to them: "Peace be to you." He would repeat his greeting, "Peace be to you" (Jn 20:19–21).

The breaking of the host itself, which precedes the Commixture, also recalls the Resurrection of the Lord, in that it reminds us of his breaking of bread for the disciples in Emmaus (Lk 24:30). Or again, it recalls the visits by the holy women to the tomb. Durandus gives more details:

> The subdeacon, while the choir responds *Sed libera nos a malo*, approaches the deacon, and hands over to him the veiled paten: the deacon receives it, and unveils it. He presents it, and hands it over uncovered to the priest, while kissing his hand or his right shoulder. The priest makes the sign of the cross over his face with the paten, and then kisses it. The deacon and subdeacon represent,

2 Aristotle, similarly, mentions the belief that the blood is the seat of the soul (*De Anima*, Bk. 1, ch. 2, 21, 405b7).

> both in their number and in the duty that they perform, those holy women, of whom the Gospel-writer Matthew says: "And in the end of the sabbath, when it began to dawn towards the first day of the week, came Mary Magdalen and the other Mary, to see the sepulcher" (Mt 28:1).[3]

And a little later,

> the three signs of the cross represent the period of three days during which Christ lay in the tomb, or the fact that three women went to look for Christ at the mouth of the tomb, giving rise to the saying, "Why seek you the living with the dead?" (Lk 24:5).[4]

It is particularly important to note that between the *Pater noster* and the communion, St Augustine attests the existence of a blessing.[5] St Caesarius in the sixth century[6] and St Gregory of Tours[7] say that the faithful should stay for this blessing. Did there exist, in Gaul and elsewhere (and earlier, in Rome) a third dismissal? In other words, in addition to the *missa catechumenorum*, before the Offertory, and the *missa fidelium*, at the end of the ceremony, was there an intermediary *missa* for those who were not *communicantes*, who were not going to take communion? Or, quite simply, did this blessing indicate that the Mass strictly speaking, the sacrificial offering that had started after the dismissal of the catechumens and the public penitents, was now finished?

It is certain that in Gaul this blessing by the bishop (then also by the priest) was of great solemnity.[8] Now, at the end of the thirteenth century it had not totally disappeared (for the bishops, at any rate) in the dioceses of the old Carolingian empire, as is shown by Durandus,[9] who nevertheless in principle follows the order of the Roman Mass:

---

3 Durandus, *Rationale*, Bk. 4, ch. l, 1.
4 Durandus, *Rationale*, Bk. 4, ch. li, 15.
5 St Augustine, Ep. 149 (*PL* vol. 23:637).
6 St Caesarius of Arles, Sermon 73, 2.
7 St Gregory of Tours, *De Miraculis Sancti Martini*, Bk. 2, ch. 48 (*PL* 71:963). St Gregory notes that when this blessing has been given, *expletis missis*, with the Mass finished, the people start to communicate.
8 Philippe Bernard, *Transitions liturgiques en Gaule carolingienne*, 330ff.
9 The first version of his *Rationale* was completed in 1286, and a second version towards 1296.

> In certain churches, while the priest says the *Pater noster*, his hands are held up by the deacon, and when the bishop gives the solemn blessing after the *Pater noster*, his hands are held up by the deacon and the priest, both of which represent Hur and Aaron holding up the hands of Moses while he was praying, as has been mentioned in the section *About the Collect*.[10]

While it survived, was this episcopal blessing before the communion moved little by little to the end of the celebration, in the course of the Middle Ages, thus being brought into line with Roman usage, as Durandus seems to indicate?[11]

The mystical justification for a pontifical blessing right at the end of the Mass is particularly interesting: in the same way that on the evening of Easter Day Jesus said *Pax vobis* to his disciples twice (Jn 20: 19–21), so it is fitting that the bishop should bless his clergy and people twice. In other words, the final blessing, a repetition of the blessing after the Fraction and the Commixture, which eventually became the only blessing, finds its allegorical explanation in a certain parallelism between this final part of the Mass and the final part of Our Savior's life on earth, namely his Resurrection. This entire section of the Mass, consisting of the ceremonies of the Fraction and the Commixture (with or without a solemn blessing), the Communion, and then all the ceremonies that follow, envelops the celebrants and their assistants in the spiritual climate experienced by the apostles and the first Christians between the first Easter and the Ascension.

24 THE *AGNUS DEI* AND THE KISS OF PEACE

The *Agnus Dei* was therefore a "Fraction chant," a *confractorium* (in the liturgies of Lyon and of the Carthusians, it was performed before the Commixture). This song should have been variable, but seems to have been fixed in its current state in Rome in the papacy of Sergius I (687–701), who had come from

10 Durandus, *Rationale*, Bk. 4, ch. li, 15.

11 "And although this (i.e., the bishop's blessing after the Fraction) is a solemn blessing, it does not prevent certain others from giving a new solemn blessing at the end of the Mass . . . . However, at a Mass for the Dead, the pontiff does not give a solemn blessing, because all solemnity at such a Mass is excluded." Durandus, *Rationale*, Bk. 4, ch. li, 23–24.

the Syrian East. Its Johannine invocation of the Lamb of God (Jn 1:29, 36; Rev 5:6, and 13:8) suggests the influence of the liturgy of St James. It was perhaps sung by the priest, like the *Sanctus*, since it is copied in sacramentaries (unlike the *Kyrie*, which was to be found only in the antiphonary).

The triple invocation at the end of the ceremony parallels the triple invocation of the *Kyrie* at the beginning. The meanings of the two chants are close: the Lamb was sent through the benevolence of the Trinity; he was immolated because of the three sorts of sins for which forgiveness is asked (thoughts, words, actions; original sin, venial sin, mortal sin); or again because of the triple misery of ignorance, fault, and punishment.

Some prayers whose theme is peace form an introduction to the ceremony of the Kiss of Peace: the *Da propitius pacem*, within the embolism in the *Pater noster* (Mercifully grant peace); the *Pax Domini* (The peace of the Lord be always with you) of the Commixture; the *Da nobis pacem* (Grant us peace) of the final petition of the *Agnus Dei*; and the first *apologia* that follows the *Agnus Dei*, *Domine Jesu Christe, qui dixisti apostolis tuis* . . . (O Lord Jesus Christ, who didst say to thy apostles: Peace I leave with you, my peace I grant unto you; look not upon my sins, but upon the faith of thy Church; and vouchsafe to her that peace and unity which is agreeable to thy will . . .). It is worth noting that this *apologia*, which explains and prepares immediately for the Kiss of Peace, is also an echo of the *Te igitur*, which asks for the peace and unity of the church, . . . *in primis quae tibi offerimus pro Ecclesia tua sancta catholica: quam pacificare, custodire, adunare et regere digneris* . . . (which in the first place we offer thee for thy holy Catholic Church, that it may please thee to grant her peace: as also to protect, unite, and govern her throughout the world . . .).

This *apologia, Domine Jesu Christe, qui dixisti Apostolis tuis* . . . , and the request for peace of the last *Agnus Dei* (*dona nobis pacem*) are omitted in *Requiem* Masses, in the Mass on Maundy Thursday, and at the first Mass of Easter, none of which has the ceremony of the Peace.

In reality, it is the greeting *Pax Domini* accompanying the (first) Commixture that led principally to the Kiss of Peace. The Kiss was exchanged before the Fraction. Elsewhere, in the

Gallican and Mozarabic liturgies and the ancient Milanese liturgy, the Kiss of Peace was exchanged at the Offertory, after the reading of the diptychs. That is roughly the place that it occupies in the Eastern liturgies, before the Eucharistic prayer.

The Peace, which in the old days was shared with all the faithful present (who were, without doubt, those staying to communicate), and then from the thirteenth century onwards with the clergy alone (whose members had in fact for a long time been the only ones to communicate), proceeds from the altar: the celebrant, who has kissed the altar at the same time as the deacon (in some areas, it was the host, or the chalice, which was kissed), transmits the peace to the deacon; this last takes it to the subdeacon, who takes it to the choir. The Peace can nevertheless be taken to the faithful, or to some of them, if that is the custom, by using the pax tablet (which was discussed under the Offertory, p. 80).

This Kiss of Peace is a kiss of communion, though close also to a kiss of veneration. We have noted that the *Dominus vobiscum* that follows the kiss of the altar used to belong to the Kiss of Peace. There were in the Middle Ages other moments also when the Peace was shared: at the start of the Mass, when the pontiff was approaching the altar, and again at the bringing of the paten, and then again also at the final blessing (in the form, by preference, of a kiss on the shoulder). In all these cases, the purpose was to express or prepare for sacramental communion, in the spirit of the fourth petition of the *Pater noster* for the forgiveness of sins, before the presentation of your gift "at the altar" (Mt 5:23–24).

The Peace is thus shared with all the choir, following the hierarchical order. It is the Peace given by the Father to his Son, after the propitiatory sacrifice has been sealed by the Resurrection; the Peace transmitted to the apostles, represented by the deacon; the Peace that is shared among the clergy in the choir to bear witness to this communion comprising the unique flock, with Jesus Christ, the unique Shepherd. Its transmission resembles that of the sanctifying grace that flows from the *gratia capitis*, the "grace of the Head," which fills the human soul of Jesus Christ on account of the hypostatic union, and which flows down into the soul of Christians who have been justified:

> Now we must note that Jesus Christ our Lord gives us his peace only after having drawn it from God his Father. The Father in the person of his Son blesses us, consoles us, and sanctifies us, and every blessing and sanctification comes to us from him in Jesus Christ, not only as man, but also as God and as the Word; for the Son of God, in the embrace of his Father, receives everything from him; and his sanctified humanity is entirely filled with blessing by its union with the Word who allows everything to flow into it. It is the first basin to receive the fullness of the spirit and of grace that this infinite source pours out.[12]

25 THE COMMUNION

Two other prayers of the *apologia* type follow (*Domine Jesu Christe, Fili Dei vivi* . . . and *Perceptio corporis* . . .), addressed like the preceding prayer (*Domine Jesu Christe, qui dixisti Apostolis tuis* . . .) to Jesus Christ and uttered in the first person by the celebrant. There are analogous prayers preparing for the celebrant's communion in all the liturgies.

The prayer *Domine Jesu Christe, Fili Dei vivi* . . . (O Lord Jesus Christ, Son of the living God, who, according to the will of thy Father, through the cooperation of the Holy Ghost, hast by thy death given life to the world, deliver me by this, thy most holy Body and Blood, from all my iniquities and from every evil; and make me always cleave to thy commandments, and never suffer me to be separated from thee) is without doubt a prayer of private devotion focused on participation in the Body and Blood of Christ. The prayer *Perceptio corporis* . . . (Let not the receiving of thy Body, O Lord Jesus Christ, which I, all unworthy, presume to take, turn to my judgment and damnation: but through thy lovingkindness may it avail me for a safeguard and a remedy, both of soul and body) expresses an attitude of reverential fear that can be found in the most ancient liturgies, especially in those attested by the *Apostolic Constitutions*, which themselves are an expansion of the warning of St Paul:

> Therefore whosoever shall eat this bread, or drink the chalice of the Lord unworthily, shall be guilty of the

12 Olier, *L'esprit des cérémonies*, Bk. 8, ch. ii.

> body and of the blood of the Lord. But let a man prove himself: and so let him eat of that bread, and drink of the chalice. For he that eateth and drinketh unworthily, eateth and drinketh judgment to himself, not discerning the body of the Lord.[13]

In all rites the celebrant is the first to communicate, followed by the clergy according to their degree and the faithful (originally, also according to their degree, starting with the magistrates, because *ordo* is of the essence of divine worship). If a traditional papal Mass were celebrated today, the deacon and subdeacon would receive communion in both kinds.

The celebrant's communion is accompanied by five short prayers. The first, *Panem caelestem accipiam* . . . (I will take the bread of heaven, and call upon the name of the Lord), draws attention to the fact that the celebrant is about to communicate in the sacred bread. The second, a triple *Domine non sum dignus* . . . (Lord, I am not worthy that thou shouldst enter under my roof; but only say the word, and my soul shall be healed), repeats the prayer of the centurion who had asked for his servant to be healed (Mt 8:8). The third precedes the communion in the chalice: *Quid retribuam Domino* . . . (What return shall I make to the Lord for all he hath given unto me? I will take the chalice of salvation, and call upon the name of the Lord. Praising I will call upon the Lord, and I shall be saved from my enemies). Finally, while communicating in each kind, the celebrant makes the sign of the cross on himself, first with the consecrated host and then with the chalice, asking each time to be made holy, just as he, the celebrant, has contributed, as the instrument of Christ, to making holy the consecrated elements (May the Body of our Lord Jesus Christ preserve my soul unto life everlasting, Amen . . . May the Blood of our Lord Jesus Christ keep my soul unto life everlasting. Amen).

The communion of the faithful in one kind was introduced in the West progressively for reasons of convenience. In the time of St Thomas Aquinas, it was not yet universal. Communion in two kinds disappeared gradually, along with the communion of young baptized children in the form of a drop of

---

13 1 Cor 11:27–29.

wine placed on their lips (apart from some very rare survivals of the communion of the faithful in the chalice, such as the communion of the emperor or king at the coronation Mass, done with a gold pipe in the manner of the pope).

For the communion, the usual practice was to use the elements consecrated at the Mass itself. The sick and those who were absent used to receive pieces of consecrated bread from that which was reserved (with the result that communion in a single kind was always the practice for the sick and the absent). It was during the time of the Hussite movement and of the Council of Trent that the present discipline of communion in one kind was approved as being equivalent, so far as the fruits of communion are concerned, to communion in both kinds.[14]

For communion in both kinds, alongside the altar chalices, or *calices minores*, there used to exist, before the thirteenth century, larger chalices for communicating the faithful, or *calices ministeriales*, from which the faithful, one after the other, could extract a few drops of consecrated wine by means of pipes of precious metals (the large Merovingian chalices with handles were probably *calices ministeriales*). But it is not certain that they contained consecrated wine: they may just have contained ordinary wine to which some consecrated wine had been added.

It is possible that receiving wine from a *calix ministerialis*, in which a small amount of consecrated wine had been mixed with unconsecrated wine, was not really considered to be communion with the Blood of Christ. It might be a ceremony for the purification of the mouths of communicants who had just received the Body of Christ. This purification following the reception of the Body of Christ had always been provided for – even though not practiced – in the *Caeremoniale Episcoporum* when the bishop was administering communion at a pontifical Mass.[15] Lebrun notes the custom, which survived outside of pontifical Masses in certain French churches until the eighteenth century, of presenting wine, or wine mixed with water,

14 DS 1198, 1725–27.

15 The purification was carried out with wine and water, without the addition of consecrated wine (*Caeremoniale Episcoporum*, Bk. 2, ch. xxix, 3). This usage is as a matter of fact preserved in the ordination Mass for new priests who have taken communion only in the form of consecrated bread, since it is prescribed by the *Pontifical*.

or water, to ecclesiastical and sometimes lay communicants, at least on some occasions.[16]

So, not communion in both kinds but just a purification of the mouth? Unless it is in fact the opposite: might purifications of communicants' mouths with wine at a pontifical Mass be a relic of communion in both kinds from *calices ministeriales*?[17] In any case, at each Mass, as we will see, the celebrant purifies his mouth with wine added to any drops of the consecrated wine that may remain in the chalice.

There is a ceremony that lies in between the Commixture, the addition of consecrated elements to unconsecrated matter, and the purification of the mouth: before the reforms of Holy Week in 1955, in the Mass of the Presanctified on Good Friday, a small portion of the second host that had been consecrated on the evening of Maundy Thursday was dropped into a chalice filled with unconsecrated wine, which the celebrant drank after having received the Body of Christ.

In the East, communion is still practiced in two kinds, but in a controlled fashion (a drop of wine from the chalice is put into the mouth with a small spoon, or communion is given by intinction, that is, by dipping the piece of consecrated, not unleavened, bread into the Precious Blood).

In any case, since the end of antiquity it had become rare for the faithful to take communion,[18] to the point where the rules

---

16 Lebrun, *Explication litérale*, 506–8.

17 A passage of the *Summa theologiae* (IIIa q77, a8) could refer to this ancient practice. The question is raised, what happens if one mixes a liquid (for example, wine) with consecrated wine, whose substance changed at the moment of consecration. St Thomas Aquinas's solution indicates that if a large quantity of wine is added to consecrated wine, the wine finally produced by this mixture is a different wine from the consecrated wine, since it has at least changed its individual character: it is no longer the wine that was consecrated, and it no longer has the same quantitative measurement which would indicate its identity. This allows us to conclude that if the practice of *calices ministeriales* really consisted of mixing a little consecrated wine with a much larger quantity of unconsecrated wine, this would not constitute communion in both kinds.

18 We may recall that, until 1953, the Eucharistic fast was severe and made communion by the faithful at a late hour in the morning very difficult ("Communion Masses" were held in the morning): a total fast from midnight was required and excluded all food or drink, including medicines, apart from certain exceptions which became more common during the war. In 1953, the fast was reduced to three hours for solid foods and

for communicating the faithful are not given in the missal itself. In fact, on days when the people took communion, use was often made of an altar other than the altar of the Mass, as is prescribed by the *Caeremoniale Episcoporum.*[19] If communion is given to the faithful during the Mass, which has become the rule since the time of Pope Pius XII, use is made of ceremonies intended by the *Rituale Romanum* for the communion of the sick: recitation of the *Confiteor* by the communicants[20] followed by the prayers *Misereatur* (May Almighty God have mercy upon you, forgive you your sins, and bring you to life everlasting) and *Indulgentiam* (May the almighty and merciful Lord grant you ✠ pardon, absolution, and remission of your sins), by the presentation of the host by the celebrant saying the *Ecce Agnus Dei* (Behold the Lamb of God, who takes away the sins of the world) and repeating three times the *Domine non sum dignus* of the centurion (Lord, I am not worthy that thou shouldest enter under my roof: but only say the word, and my soul shall be healed).[21] Then the celebrant blesses each communicant with a host that he places on his lips, while pronouncing this deprecatory formula, similar to that of a blessing: *Corpus Domini nostri Iesu Christi custodiat animam tuam in vitam aeternam. Amen* (May the Body of our Lord

alcoholic drinks, and one hour for other liquids, with no prohibition on water and medicines. In 1964 it was reduced to one hour before communion for all foods. We should also recall that in antiquity there was a fast *following* communion as well.

19 On Easter Day, when the number of communicants is very large, the cathedral chaplain, in the absence of the bishop, or the priest sacristan gives the people communion before, during, and after the high Mass, at an altar separate from that used for the high Mass (*Caeremoniale Episcoporum*, Bk. 2, ch. xxx, 5).

20 Unlike the earlier *Ritus servandus in celebratione missae* (X, 7), the *Ritus servandus in celebratione missae* of 1962 (X, 6), does not allow for the *Confiteor* of the communicants, although the custom has tenaciously survived. The *Caeremoniale Episcoporum* in use in 1962 presupposes, however, the singing of the *Confiteor* by the deacon, which is done at every solemn Mass.

21 A bishop celebrating a pontifical Mass does not present the host like this, but gives communion in a very specific way: he takes the host in the chalice carried by the deacon, and then extends his hand to be kissed before he gives the host to the communicant. This practice, stipulated in all the ceremonial manuals and encountered even until the 1970s in some places, has nevertheless disappeared almost without a trace. It is still followed in the pontifical Mass of priestly ordination, in which newly ordained priests kiss the bishop's hand before receiving communion.

Jesus Christ keep thy soul unto life everlasting. Amen). The specific grace of the sacrament is the unity of the mystical Body and of each soul to that mystical Body, without which the soul cannot be saved. From that follows not just the importance of receiving the *viaticum* – communion when death is approaching, in preparation for the final voyage – but also the fact that each communion represents, in a certain way, a *viaticum*, a "safeguard for the soul with a view to eternal life": "Then Jesus said to them: Amen, amen I say unto you: Except you eat the flesh of the Son of man, and drink his blood, you shall not have life in you. He that eateth my flesh, and drinketh my blood, hath everlasting life: and I will raise him up in the last day" (Jn 6:54–55).

Communion in the hand seems to have disappeared no later than the ninth century, probably for two reasons: certainly because the marks of respect for the sacrament had been strengthened, and possibly because communion in the hand recalled the ceremonies of the late antique court for receiving a gift from the monarch, which had fallen out of use.

The *Confiteor* is in some respects the *apologia*, the *excusatio*, appropriate for the faithful (rather as the rosary replaced the recitation of the psalms for monastic lay brothers). There are a certain number of occurrences of this prayer during the Mass. Many manuscripts place a "General Confession" (a *Confiteor*) between the Gospel and the Offertory (the *Confiteor* that has already been mentioned on p. 70, used at the prayers of the homily). Examples of a communion *Confiteor* have also been found after the *Pater noster*.

Communion by the priest is ceremonially necessary to accomplish the rite in its totality. The faithful do not have to communicate, but if the priest does not communicate, there can be no Mass. This is not a matter of the validity of the Mass, but has an essential spiritual reason: the communion by the priest demonstrates his interior participation in the sacrifice that he offers in the name and in the person of Christ. St Thomas Aquinas gives an explanation based on St Augustine: "Because the outward sacrifice he offers is a sign of the inner sacrifice whereby he offers himself to God, by partaking of the sacrifice he shows that the inner sacrifice is his also."[22] Aquinas adds that the priest,

22 St Thomas Aquinas, *Summa theologiae* IIIa, q82, a4.

"dispenser of divine gifts to the people," ought to be the first to partake of these gifts, and so ought to receive the Body and Blood of the sacrifice, with reference to St Paul: "Are not they, that eat of the sacrifices, partakers of the altar?" (1 Cor 10:18). The communion of the faithful is therefore greatly to be encouraged for analogous reasons: it is their deepest participation in the Eucharistic sacrifice, and the best method for them, by uniting their persons with that of Christ, Son of God, to receive its fruits. Olier says that in this way they participate in the "third sacrifice" of Christ, the first being that of Golgotha, the second being that of the passage through fire of the Resurrection. In uniting themselves with the third, that of the altar, they clothe themselves with the state of Jesus Christ in the two other sacrifices. It is a state in which they become a sacrificial victim, dying to sin, as well as a state in which they yearn for a vision of glory,

> in order to become victims sacrificed to God, and to start on making all the Church's faithful into one single sacrificial victim in Jesus Christ, a purpose that will one day be completed and perfected in heaven. That is why although Christ is only one in himself, he is nevertheless multiplied in these hosts, to be one sacrifice in many sacrifices, and by means of himself to make out of many sacrifices one single sacrifice, living, holy, acceptable to God, and performing a reasonable and spiritual service.[23]

26 THE PURIFICATIONS AND THE COMMUNION ANTIPHON

The celebration moves towards its close, at which point the missal has returned to the epistle side, since the Mass as a whole finishes where it started.

Two prayers in the form of an *apologia* accompany the two purifications. In the first purification, the celebrant who has just communicated in the wine purifies his mouth: the prayer *Quod ore sumpsimus*... (Grant, Lord, that what we have taken with our mouth we may receive with a pure mind, and that from a temporal gift it may become for us an eternal remedy) resembles an old Roman prayer. In the second purification, the celebrant uses water and wine to purify the fingers that have touched the consecrated bread: the prayer *Corpus tuum, Domine,*

23 Olier, *L'esprit des cérémonies*, Bk. 8, ch. iii.

quod sumpsi, et Sanguis, quem potavi . . . (May thy Body, O Lord, which I have received, and thy Blood which I have drunk, cleave to my inward parts; that no stain of sin may remain in me, whom thy pure and holy sacraments have refreshed) comes from the *Missale Gothicum*, a Gallican sacramentary dating to the end of the seventh century.

While these ceremonies take place, the celebrant faces the epistle side. The missal is then brought back to that side. The celebrant is therefore now where he started the Mass, on the Jewish side. He returns to that side in the same way as Jesus, after his Resurrection, returned to Jerusalem and Galilee to rejoin his disciples. The return to this side underlines Jesus's reappearance in the areas where he preached prior to his redemptive sacrifice. Jesus completes his task where he began it.

The Communion antiphon that follows is, we should recall, one of the three processional antiphons of the Mass: the Introit antiphon, the Offertory antiphon, and the Communion antiphon. The last of these was often the Vulgate of Ps 33:9: *Gustate et videte quoniam suavis est Dominus* (O taste and see that the Lord is sweet). It has been preserved in the Mozarabic liturgy, where this antiphon, *Gustate et videte quoniam suavis est Dominus*, is entitled *Ad accedentes* (because of verse 6 of this Psalm, *accedite ad eum et illuminamini*, "Approach him, and be enlightened"). The thought of "approaching the Lord" invites us to ask whether we can talk about a "Communion procession" and so about an antiphon to accompany this procession. Yes, we can, but it is not a procession of communicants. The reality is that here the Body of Christ draws near to those who are going to receive him and who present themselves to him, as we will recall, in due order, at least as far as the clergy are concerned, but also, normally, as far as the magistrates and the people are concerned. Consequently, if there is a procession, it is rather the Holy Sacrament that processes, accompanied since the High Middle Ages by the torches of the torchbearers.[24] In any case, just as the Introit in fact follows the entry of

24 At a solemn Mass today, one will usually see the priest, accompanied by the deacon and subdeacon, "processing" from one kneeling communicant to the next. In this way Christ is the one who comes to meet us and give Himself to us.

the ministers that it is thought to illustrate, and the *Agnus Dei* follows the Fraction, so the Communion antiphon generally follows (at least, in a low Mass) the Communion itself.

We have also observed above that these three antiphons of the Mass are composed of borrowings from the liturgical use of the psalms, that is to say, they comprise (or are composed of, or are considered to be composed of) an antiphon (a text taken from a psalm, or from another source, and serving as an introduction), then of a verse of a psalm, then of the doxology (*Gloria Patri et Filio . . .*), and then of a repeat of the antiphon.[25] The practice of two choirs responding to each other alternately, preserved in some churches until a fairly late date, especially for the Communion antiphon, additionally used to underline the similarity of this antiphon to the celebration of the Daily Office. Moreover, the first Mass of Easter Day, that of Holy Saturday, introduces a shortened form of the office of Lauds (or of the office of Vespers before the reforms of Pius XII). Instead of the Communion antiphon and the following prayer, the pattern is: first, a triple Alleluia is sung as an antiphon; second, Psalm 150 is sung (*Laudate Dominum in sanctis eius*, Praise the Lord in his sanctuary); third, the antiphon consisting in the triple Alleluia is repeated; fourth, the *Benedictus* from the morning office is sung, preceded and followed by its own antiphon (or the *Magnificat* with its antiphon, before the reform of Pius XII, when the first Mass of Easter, closing the Vigil, was celebrated on the Saturday morning); finally, the Postcommunion prayer follows, serving as a sort of prayer concluding the current Hour, instead of the Collect. The altar, the clergy, and the people are incensed during the singing of the *Benedictus* (or of the *Magnificat* before the reform of Pius XII), as happens during the singing of this canticle in the Daily Office.

The Communion antiphon signifies the joy of the communicants, which resembles that of the apostles at the Resurrection

25 In many places today, verses are sung along with the Communion antiphon, as prescribed in the Solesmes books. The antiphon is repeated after every verse or pair of verses, and the whole is concluded with the *Gloria Patri*. Similarly, the Solesmes *Offertoriale* makes available long-lost verses for some of the most ancient Offertory antiphons, which may be used to extend the chant over a longer period of time. These have more the form of responsories.

of Christ ("The disciples therefore were glad, when they saw the Lord"—Jn 20:20), a joy so strong that it left them amazed (Lk 24:41), stunned, like people in a trance. The alternating chant of some churches, mentioned just now, recalled the disciples telling each other of their joy at the Resurrection. In just this way, when the disciples of the road to Emmaus had announced to the apostles, assembled with others, that they had seen the Lord, the apostles replied that he had really risen and that he had appeared to Peter. The disciples at Emmaus had, what is more, recognized him from the way he had broken bread, from the *fractio panis*, from the Eucharist (Lk 24:33–35), even if he had not strictly speaking celebrated a Eucharist.

27 THE POSTCOMMUNION, THE DISMISSAL, AND THE LAST GOSPEL

The Postcommunion has become the accepted name for the last priestly prayer of the Mass, the collect following the Communion.

We must not forget that the Postcommunion is one of what can be called, strictly speaking, the three prayers of the Roman Mass: the Collect, the Secret, and the Postcommunion. Each of these brings a complete ritual structure to a close: the Collect brings the entry of the ministers to a close; the Secret brings the Offertory to a close; and the Postcommunion brings the Communion to a close (one could argue that the *Pater noster*, the priestly prayer *par excellence*, plays a similar role for the Canon). The correct original name for the Postcommunion is the *Complenda*, or the *Oratio ad Complendum*, the concluding prayer, the one that completes the Mass.

During weekdays in Lent, the Postcommunion is reinforced by another prayer, called *Super populum*, a prayer over the people (dating to the fifth century?), which was really a blessing of the clergy and people when they were ready to disperse.[26] The prayer has survived only on weekdays in Lent, preceded by an invitation to bow the head before God, *humiliate capita vestra Deo*, an attitude that in itself in fact suits a blessing. Perhaps the transfer of the solemn blessing preceding the communion

26 Like the distribution of bread on Sunday, the prayer was also regarded as a substitute for communion.

to the end of the Mass led to the prayer *super populum* losing the nature of a blessing and becoming more penitential in tone.

In reality the celebrant here gives a double greeting: one *Dominus vobiscum* before the prayer, and another after. The first greeting prepares for the prayer, the second precedes the *missus*, the dismissal of the assembly. But these two transmissions of the Peace, which is what, as we have seen, the celebrant's greetings resemble, also correspond to the two utterances of *Pax vobis* pronounced by Christ when he appeared on the evening of Easter Day (Jn 20:19–21).

In saying these words, the priest, like Christ, extends his hands for a final time, while warning his assistants, as the Lord warned Peter, that they will have to do the same in prayer and in sacrifice: "when thou shalt be old, thou shalt stretch forth thy hands" (Jn 21:18).

When the prayer is over, the missal is closed[27] but without being moved away. The *Oratio ad Complendum* is therefore said on the Jewish side of the altar, on the other side from the Gentile or New Testament side (which covers those who convert to Christ). This is because the preaching of Christ and of his Gospel started with the Jews, then transferred to the Gentiles, and will at the end return to the Jews, who will enter the Church of Jesus Christ. In between the two, the middle of the altar represents the faith in Christ that draws the two peoples together and makes them into one (Eph 2:14), "the people of God" (1 Peter 2:10).

We recall that the dismissal of the faithful, *Ite missa est*, is the counterpart of the old dismissal of the catechumens, before or after the Gospel. It has been suggested that it was probably the *missa catechumenorum*, the dismissal of the catechumens and of the public penitents, rather than the *missa fidelium*, the dismissal of the faithful, which gave its name to the celebration of the holy mysteries, the Mass. The sacred *synaxis* (which occupies all the space between the *Credo* and the *Pater noster* inclusive) succeeds the completion of the solemn act of dismissal of those who do not yet have (catechumens) or for a

27 The missal is left with the spine facing south and the fore-edge facing north, so that it is ready to be opened again to face those without faith in order to spread the warmth of the Word.

certain time no longer have (penitents) the quality of friends of Christ. With the words, *missus*, *missa*, Mass, we are moreover using the purest Roman vocabulary: the Byzantines say, "Let us go in peace"; the Syrians, "Go in peace. Be happy, be joyful, and pray for me."

The word "Mass" therefore designates the intimate friendship of the reunion in the Upper Room, where the Savior celebrated the Last Supper, where he found the apostles on the evening of Easter Day and the following Sunday, where they all, gathered around the Holy Virgin with the disciples and the holy women, finally prayed after the Ascension. The Mass brings together those to whom he said, "I will not now call you servants.... But I have called you friends" (Jn 15:15), a saying that is sung at the ordination of a priest between the Communion antiphon and the Postcommunion.[28]

Sometimes *Benedicamus Domino* replaces *Ite missa est* as the formula of dismissal. This formula was doubtless borrowed from the Daily Office, where it plays this role, but from at least the eleventh century until the missal of 1962, it was reserved for Masses without a *Gloria*.[29]

In a high Mass the priest delegates the singing of the *Ite missa est* or *Benedicamus Domino* to the deacon (in various French churches this delegation was formally granted by the priest giving the deacon a blessing). This triumphal dismissal strongly recalls the dismissal given at the Ascension: "and behold I am with you all days, even to the consummation of the world" (Mt 28:20). The glorious Christ, with his sacrifice completed and death conquered, returns to sit at his Father's right hand.

---

28 Commentators from the 1930s to the 1960s saw *Ite missa est* as the sending out of the assembled Christians as missionaries, connecting the word *missa* with the word missionary. The suggestion is well meant, but it would be wrong to dismiss as pure imagination the allegorical etymologies of St Thomas Aquinas, who supposed that the *missa* takes its name from the fact that the priest sends (*mittit*) his prayers to God, or from the fact that Christ is the victim whom God sends (*mittit*) to us (*Summa theologiae* IIIa, q83, a4, ad 9).

29 These Masses, if they were Masses of the temporal cycle, used to correspond also to Matins without the *Te Deum*: in this way the three ritual "solemnities" were linked: the *Gloria*, the *Ite missa est*, and the *Te Deum*. Since the missal of 1962, the *Benedicamus Domino* has replaced the *Ite missa est* at Masses which are followed by a linked liturgical action, such as the Maundy Thursday and Corpus Christi processions.

The final blessing also has a triumphal tone. It either replaced or reinforced the blessing given after the *Pater noster* (the final blessing is absent in the rite of Lyon and the Carthusian rite and was unknown in a certain number of French churches). It is accompanied by an *apologia*, the *Placeat*, which has its equivalent in all liturgies. Before the time of Pope St Pius V (1566–1572), the *Placeat* used to follow the blessing. Since then, it has preceded it. But this *apologia* preserves the character of a final conclusion: *Placeat tibi, sancta Trinitas, obsequium . . .* (May the homage of my service be pleasing to you, O holy Trinity, and grant that the sacrifice that I, though unworthy, have offered in the sight of thy majesty, may be acceptable to thee: and through thy mercy win forgiveness for me and for all those for whom I have offered it. Through Christ our Lord).

Like all liturgical blessings, this blessing recalls that of the High Priest Aaron, who is a type of the Priest King, Jesus Christ (Lev 9:22), or that of Moses and Aaron, who entered the Tabernacle after completing the offerings of victims and the holocausts, and then, after coming out again, blessed the people (Lev 9:22–23). This moment represents mystically the end of the story of Jesus Christ on earth. And this blessing repeats that which Christ gave finally on the Mount of Olives before ascending to the right hand of his Father: "And he led them out as far as Bethania: and lifting up his hands, he blessed them" (Lk 24:50). But this blessing prepares us also for the blessing that he will give to the "blessed of my Father" (Mt 25:34) when he returns in the same way as he ascended (Acts 1:11).

We must insist for a last time on the influence that the mystical meaning has had on the composition or organization of the rite, an influence at least as strong as any influence in the reverse direction: the allegorical meaning of the end of the Mass (the departure of Christ to heaven) has strongly aided the integration of a final ceremony, the reading of the beginning of the Gospel according to John. "Ye men of Galilee, why stand you looking up to heaven? This Jesus who is taken up from you into heaven, shall so come, as you have seen him going into heaven" (Acts 1:11): that is exactly what the assistants, the clergy and the people do spiritually, after the Christ who has blessed them through the hands of the celebrant has left them. This raised gaze, plunged in the embrace of God, is expressed by the beginning of the Gospel according to John, which becomes here the "Last Gospel": *In principio erat Verbum, et Verbum erat apud Deum, et Deus erat Verbum. Hoc erat in principio apud Deum.* "In the beginning was the Word, and the Word was with God, and the Word was God. He was with God in the beginning" (Jn 1:1–2).

In a pontifical Mass, the bishop thus starts to recite the beginning of John's Gospel from the Gospel side, and he continues to recite it when he has made his way to his seat or to the *secretarium* where he will be divested of his ceremonial vestments; he waits until he is in front of the altar of the *secretarium* before he genuflects and says: *Et Verbum caro factum est* (And the Word was made flesh). This magnificent formula of thanksgiving spread in the thirteenth century, and then in the fifteenth century moved from the thanksgiving after Mass into the Mass itself, a move approved by the missal of St Pius V. But it is also an especial feature of this missal, unknown to many of the non-Roman diocesan Ordinaries of the eighteenth century.

The Mass is now finished, complete: the Word of God, who came down to earth, has ascended to the bosom of the Father with his mission achieved and his victory proclaimed. The disciples gaze on him in the sky, overcome with joy at the reality of the victory that he has won through his death. They have thus obeyed his instruction once again, in commemorating him by accomplishing the Holy Sacrifice of the Mass and the ceremonies in which it is enshrined, thereby bringing his work of salvation to perfection.

Bibliography

Selected works in English and other details added by translator.

ACCESSIBLE *EXPOSITIONES MISSÆ*

Amalarius of Metz. *On the Liturgy, by Amalarius, Archbishop of Lyon*. Edited and translated by Eric Knibbs, 2 vols. Cambridge, MA: Harvard University Press, 2014.

Ambrose of Milan. *"On the Mysteries" and the Treatise "On the Sacraments" by an Unknown Author*. Translated by T. Thompson, edited by J. H. Srawley. London: SPCK; New York: MacMillan, 1919.

Durandus of Mende. *"Rationale Divinorum Officiorum," Book 4: On the Mass and Each Action Pertaining to It*. Translated by Timothy M. Thibodeau. Turnhout: Brepols, 2013.

Germanus of Paris. *Epistolae de ordine sacrae oblationis et de diversis charismatibus ecclesiae Germano Parisiensi episcopo adscriptae*. Edited by Philippe Bernard. Turnhout: Brepols, 2007.

Innocent III. *De sacro altaris mysterio*. In *Patrologia Latina*, ed. J. P. Migne, vol. 217, cols. 773–916.

——. *Mysteriorum evangelicae legis et sacramenti Eucharistiae libri sex*. Amiens: Lenoel-Herouart, 1860.

Olier, Jean-Jacques. *L'esprit des cérémonies de la messe: Explication des cérémonies de la grand'messe de paroisse selon l'usage romain*. Edited by Abbé Claude Barthe, with Michèle Debaecker. Perpignan: Artège, 2009.

Thomas Aquinas. *The "Summa Theologica" of St Thomas Aquinas*. Translated by the Fathers of the English Dominican Province. London: R. & T. Washbourne, 1914.

FURTHER READING

Balzaretti, Claudio. *Missa: storia di una secolare ricerca etimologica ancora aperta*. Roma: CLV-Edizione liturgiche, 2000.

Bernard, Philippe. *Du chant romain au chant grégorien (IVe-XIIIe siècle)*. Paris: Cerf, 1996.

——. "La christianisation de l'espace et du temps: le temps de la liturgie." In J.-M. Mayeur, Ch. et L. Pietri, A. Vauchez, and M. Venard, eds., *Histoire du christianisme des origines à nos jours*, vol. III: *Les Églises d'Orient et d'Occident (432–610)*. Paris: Desclée, 1998.

Berthod, Bernard; Favier, Gaël; and Hardouin-Fugier, Elisabeth, eds. *Dictionnaire des arts liturgiques, du moyen âge à nos jours*. Châteauneuf-sur-Charente: Frémur, 1996.

Borella, Jean. *The Crisis of Religious Symbolism & Symbolism and Reality*. Translated by G. John Champoux. Brooklyn NY: Angelico Press, 2016.

Bori, Pier Cesare. *L'interprétation infinie: l'herméneutique chrétienne ancienne et ses transformations*. Translated by François Vial. Paris: Cerf, 1991.

Bradshaw, Paul. *The Search for the Origins of Christian Worship: Sources and Methods for the Study of Early Liturgy*. Second edition. London/New York: SPCK, Oxford University Press, 2002.

Braga, Carlo. *L'espace liturgique: ses éléments constitutifs et leur sens*. Conférences Saint-Serge, 52nd Semaine d'études liturgiques. Roma: CLV-Edizione liturgiche, 2006.

Braun, Joseph. *Die liturgische Gewandung im Occident und Orient nach Ursprung und Entwicklung, Verwendung und Symbolik*. Freiburg. i. Br.: Herder, 1907.

Caeremoniale Episcoporum . . . Benedicti XIV et Leonis XIII auctoritate recognitum. Third edition. Turin and Rome: Marietti, 1948.

Caesarius of Arles. *Saint Caesarius of Arles: Sermons*. Translated by Sister Mary Magdaleine Mueller OSF. The Fathers of the Church: A New Translation, vols. 31, 47, 66. Washington: Catholic University of America Press, 1953–73.

Claudel, Paul. *Le poète et la Bible*. Edited Michel Malicet, Dominique Millet-Gérard, Xavier Tilliette, 2 vols. Paris: Gallimard, 1998–2004.

Fiedrowicz, Michael. *The Traditional Mass: History, Form, and Theology of the Classical Roman Rite*. Translated by Rose Pfeifer. Brooklyn NY: Angelico Press, 2020.

Guéranger, Dom Prosper. *Les Institutions liturgiques*. Le Mans and Paris: Fleuriot & Débécourt, 1840–41.

——. *The Liturgical Year*. 11 vols. Dublin: James Duffy, 1870–1910.

Gy, Pierre-Marie. "Expositiones Missae." *Bulletin du Comité des études de la Compagnie de Saint-Sulpice*, no. 22 (1958), 223–31.

——, ed. *Guillaume Durand: évêque de Mende (v. 1230–1296), canoniste, liturgiste et homme politique*. Paris: Editions du CNRS, 1992.

Hani, Jean. *The Divine Liturgy: Insights into Its Mystery*. Translated by Robert Proctor. Brooklyn, NY: Angelico Press, 2016.

Hébert, Louis. *Leçons de liturgie à l'usage des séminaires*. Vol. I, *Le bréviaire et le rituel*; Vol. II, *Le missel romain*; Vol. III, *Le Cérémonial*. Edited Abbé Auguste Fayard. Paris: Berche et Pagis, 1947–52.

Heim, François. *La théologie de la victoire: de Constantin à Théodose*. Paris: Beauchesne, 1992.

Kwasniewski, Peter. *Reclaiming Our Roman Catholic Birthright: The Genius and Timeliness of the Traditional Latin Mass*. Brooklyn, NY: Angelico Press, 2020.

Lang, Uwe Michael. *The Roman Mass: From Early Christian Origins to Tridentine Reform*. New York: Cambridge University Press, 2022.

——. *Signs of the Holy One: Liturgy, Ritual and Expression of the Sacred*. San Francisco: Ignatius Press, 2015.

——. *Turning Towards the Lord: Orientation in Liturgical Prayer*. San Francisco: Ignatius Press, 2009.

Lebrun, Pierre. *Explication litérale, historique et dogmatique des prières et des cérémonies de la Messe, suivant les anciens auteurs et les monumens de toutes les églises du monde chrétien, avec les dissertations et des notes sur les endroits difficiles & sur l'origine des rits*. Tours: Forts dans la Foi, 1976.

Le Gall, Dom Robert. *Les symboles catholiques*. Paris: Assoulines, 1999.

Lesage, Robert. *Vestments and Church Furniture*. Translated by Fergus Murphy. London: Burns & Oates, 1960.

Lours, Mathieu. *L'autre temps des cathédrales: du concile de Trente à la Révolution française*. Paris: Picard, 2010.

Mazza, Enrico. *L'action eucharistique: origine, développement, interprétation*. Translated by Jacques Mignon. Edited by Marie-Josée Poiré. Paris: Cerf, 1999.

——. *The Eucharistic Prayers of the Roman Rite*. Translated by Matthew J. O'Connell. New York: Pueblo Publishing Company, 1986.

——. *The Origins of the Eucharistic Prayer*. Translated by Ronald E. Lane. Collegeville, MN: Liturgical Press, 1995.

Menozzi, Daniele. "Le symbolisme Gothique." In Daniele Menozzi, ed., *Les Images: L'Eglise et les arts visuels*, 137–43. Paris: Cerf, 1991.

Metzger, Marcel. "La place des liturges à l'autel." *Revue des sciences religieuses*, vol. 45.2 (1971): 113–45.

Mohrmann, Christine. *Liturgical Latin: Its Origins and Character – Three Lectures*. Washington, DC: Catholic University of America Press, 1957; repr. London: Burns & Oates, 1959.

Monti, James. *A Sense of the Sacred: Roman Catholic Worship in the Middle Ages*. San Francisco: Ignatius Press, 2012.
Mosebach, Martin. *The Heresy of Formlessness: The Roman Liturgy and its Enemy*. Revised and expanded edition. Brooklyn NY: Angelico Press, 2018.
Palazzo, Éric. *Liturgie et société au Moyen âge*. Paris: Aubier, 2000.
——. *Le Moyen Âge: des origines au XIII siècle*. Paris: Beauchesne, 1993.
Pépin, Jean. *Dante et la tradition de l'allégorie, de Philon d'Alexandrie à Dante*. Conférence Albert-le-Grand, 1969. Montréal: Institut d'études médiévales; Paris: Librairie J. Vrin, 1970.
Piccolo Paci, Sara. *Storia delle vesti liturgiche*. Milan: Ancora, 2008.
Quoëx, Franck. "Thomas d'Aquin, mystagogue—*L'expositio missae* de la *Somme de théologie* (IIIa, q. 83, a. 4–5)." *Revue Thomiste*, vol. 105 (2005): 179–226, 435–72.
Robinson, Jonathan. *The Mass and Modernity: Walking to Heaven Backward*. San Francisco: Ignatius Press, 2005.
Schneider, Athanasius. *The Catholic Mass. Steps to Restore the Centrality of God in the Liturgy*. Manchester, NH: Sophia Institute Press, 2021.
——. *Dominus Est—It is the Lord: Reflections of a Bishop of Central Asia on Holy Communion*. San Francisco: Ignatius Press, 2008.
Smyth, Matthieu. *Ante altaria: les rites antiques de la messe dominicale en Gaule, en Espagne et en Italie du Nord*. Paris: Cerf, 2007.
——. *La liturgie oubliée: la prière eucharistique en Gaule antique et dans l'occident non romain*. Paris: Cerf, 2003.
Stercky, Louis. *Manuel de liturgie et cérémonial selon le rit romain*. Seventeenth edition. Edited by Joseph Haegy and Louis le Vavasseur. Paris: J. Gabalda, 1940.
Taft, Robert. *The Liturgy of the Hours in East and West: The Origins of the Divine Office and Its Meaning for Today*. Second edition. Collegeville: Liturgical Press, 1993.
Vogel, Cyrille. *Introduction aux sources de l'histoire du culte chrétien au Moyen Age*. New edition. Preface by Bernard Botte. Spoleto: Centro italiano di studi sull'alto Medioevo, 1981.
Wilmart, Dom André. *Auteurs spirituels et textes dévots du moyen âge latin: études d'histoire littéraire*. Paris: Bloud & Gay, 1932; repr. Paris: Études augustiniennes, 1971.
——. "Expositiones missae." *Dictionnaire d'archéologie chrétienne et de liturgie*, vol. V-1, cols. 1014–27. Paris: Letouzey & Ané, 1922.

The Ordinary of the Sunday Mass[1]

ASPERSIO AQUAE BENEDICTAE	ASPERSION WITH HOLY WATER
In Dominicis per annum Asperges me, Domine, hyssopo, et mundabor: lavabis me, et super nivem dealbabor.	*On Sundays through the Year* Thou shalt sprinkle me with hyssop, O Lord, and I shall be cleansed; thou shalt wash me, and I shall be made whiter than snow.
Miserere mei, Deus, secundum magnam misericordiam tuam. Gloria Patri...	Have mercy on me, O God, according to thy great mercy. Glory be to the Father...
Asperges me...	Thou wilt sprinkle me...
In Dominicis Paschalibus Vidi aquam egredientem de templo a latere dextro, alleluia; et omnes ad quos pervenit aqua ista, salvi facti sunt, et dicent, alleluia, alleluia. Confitemini Domino, quoniam bonus; quoniam in saeculum misericordia eius. Gloria...	*On Sundays in Eastertime* I saw water flowing from the right side of the temple, alleluia; and all to whom that water came were saved, and they shall say: alleluia, alleluia. Praise the Lord, for he is good: for his mercy endureth for ever. Glory be...
P. Ostende nobis, Domine, misericordiam tuam.	P. Show us, O Lord, thy mercy,
℟. Et salutare tuum da nobis.	℟. And grant us thy salvation.
P. Domine, exaudi orationem meam.	P. O Lord, hear my prayer.

1 The English translation is that of Abbot Fernand Cabrol OSB, *The Roman Missal in Latin and English*, 13th edition (Tours: A. Mame and Sons, 1949), with minor changes.

℟. Et clamor meus ad te veniat	℟. And let my cry come unto thee.
P. Dominus vobiscum	P. The Lord be with you.
℟. Et cum spiritu tuo.	℟. And with thy spirit.
Oremus. Exaudi nos, Domine, sancte Pater, omnipotens aeterne Deus: et mittere digneris sanctum Angelum tuum de caelis, qui custodiat, foveat, protegat, visitet, atque defendat omnes habitantes in hoc habitaculo. Per Christum Dominum nostrum. Amen.	Let us pray. Hear us, O Lord, holy Father, almighty eternal God; and vouchsafe to send thy holy angel from heaven, to guard, cherish, protect, visit, and defend all that dwell in this house. Through Christ our Lord. Amen.
PROGRESSIO, INGRESSUS AD ALTARE	PROCESSION, ASCENT TO THE ALTAR
P: In nomine Patris, ✠ et Filii, et Spiritus Sancti. Amen.	P: In the Name of the Father ✠ and of the Son and of the Holy Ghost. Amen.
Introibo ad altare Dei.	I will go in unto the altar of God.
℟. Ad Deum, qui laetificat iuventutem meam.	℟. Unto God, who giveth joy to my youth.
P: Iudica me Deus, et discerne causam meam de gente non sancta: ab homine iniquo et doloso erue me.	P. Judge me, O God, and distinguish my cause from the nation that is not holy: deliver me from the unjust and deceitful man.
℟. Quia tu es Deus, fortitudo mea: quare me repulisti, et quare tristis incedo, dum affligit me inimicus?	℟. For thou, O God, art my strength, why hast thou cast me off? and why go I sorrowful whilst the enemy afflicteth me?
P. Emitte lucem tuam, et veritatem tuam: ipsa me deduxerunt et adduxerunt in montem sanctum tuum, et in tabernacula tua.	P. Send forth thy light and thy truth: they have led me, and brought me unto thy holy hill, and into thy tabernacles.
℟. Et introibo ad altare Dei: ad Deum qui laetificat iuventutem meam.	℟. And I will go in unto the altar of God: unto God, who giveth joy to my youth.

P. Confitebor tibi in cithara, Deus, Deus meus: quare tristis es, anima mea, et quare conturbas me?

P. I will praise thee upon the harp, O God, my God: why art thou sad, O my soul? and why dost thou disquiet me?

℟. Spera in Deo, quoniam adhuc confitebor illi: salutare vultus mei, et Deus meus.

℟. Hope in God, for I will praise him still: the salvation of my countenance and my God.

P. Gloria Patri, et Filio, et Spiritui Sancto.

P. Glory be to the Father, and to the Son, and to the Holy Ghost.

℟. Sicut erat in principio, et nunc, et semper, et in saecula saeculorum Amen.

℟. As it was in the beginning, is now, and ever shall be, world without end. Amen.

P. Introibo ad altare Dei.

P. I will go in unto the altar of God.

℟. Ad Deum qui laetificat iuventutem meam.

℟. Unto God, who giveth joy to my youth.

P. Adiutorium nostrum ✠ in nomine Domini.

P. Our help is ✠ in the name of the Lord.

℟. Qui fecit caelum et terram.

℟. Who made heaven and earth.

P. Confiteor Deo omnipotenti, beatae Mariae semper Virgini, beato Michaeli Archangelo, beato Ioanni Baptistae, sanctis Apostolis Petro et Paulo, omnibus sanctis, et vobis, fratres, quia peccavi nimis cogitatione, verbo et opere, mea culpa, mea culpa, mea maxima culpa. Ideo precor beatam Mariam semper Virginem, beatum Michaelem Archangelum, beatum Ioannem Baptistam, sanctos Apostolos Petrum et Paulum, omnes sanctos, et vos, fratres, orare pro me ad Dominum Deum nostrum.

P. I confess to almighty God, to blessed Mary ever Virgin, to blessed Michael the Archangel, to blessed John the Baptist, to the holy apostles Peter and Paul, to all the saints, and to you, my brethren, that I have sinned exceedingly, in thought, word and deed, through my fault, through my fault, through my most grievous fault. Therefore I beseech the blessed Mary ever Virgin, blessed Michael the Archangel, blessed John the Baptist, the holy apostles Peter and Paul, all the saints, and you, my brethren, to pray to the Lord our God for me.

℟. Misereatur tui omnipotens Deus, et dimissis peccatis tuis, perducat te ad vitam aeternam.	℟. May almighty God have mercy upon you, forgive you your sins, and bring you to life everlasting.
P. Amen.	P. Amen.
℟. Confiteor Deo omnipotenti, beatae Mariae semper Virgini, beato Michaeli Archangelo, beato Ioanni Baptistae, sanctis Apostolis Petro et Paulo, omnibus sanctis, et tibi Pater, quia peccavi nimis cogitatione, verbo et opere, mea culpa, mea culpa, mea maxima culpa. Ideo precor beatam Mariam semper Virginem, beatum Michaelem Archangelum, beatum Ioannem Baptistam, sanctos Apostolos Petrum et Paulum, omnes sanctos, et te Pater, orare pro me ad Dominum Deum nostrum.	℟. I confess to almighty God, to blessed Mary ever Virgin, to blessed Michael the Archangel, to blessed John the Baptist, to the holy apostles Peter and Paul, to all the saints, and to thee, father, that I have sinned exceedingly, in thought, word and deed, through my fault, through my fault, through my most grievous fault. Therefore I beseech the blessed Mary ever Virgin, blessed Michael the Archangel, blessed John the Baptist, the holy apostles Peter and Paul, and all the saints, and thee, father, to pray to the Lord our God for me.
P. Misereatur vestri omnipotens Deus, et dimissis peccatis vestris, perducat vos ad vitam aeternam.	P. May almighty God have mercy upon you, forgive you your sins, and bring you to life everlasting.
℟. Amen.	℟. Amen.
P. Indulgentiam, ✠ absolutionem, et remissionem peccatorum nostrorum tribuat nobis omnipotens et misericors Dominus.	P. May the almighty and merciful Lord grant us ✠ pardon, absolution, and remission of our sins.
℟. Amen.	℟. Amen.
P. Deus tu conversus vivificabis nos.	P. Thou shalt turn again, O God, and quicken us.
℟. Et plebs tua laetabitur in te.	℟. And thy people shall rejoice in thee.
P. Ostende nobis, Domine, misericordiam tuam.	P. Show us, O Lord, thy mercy.
℟. Et salutare tuum da nobis.	℟. And grant us thy salvation.

P. Domine, exaudi orationem meam.	P. O Lord, hear my prayer.
℟. Et clamor meus ad te veniat.	K. And let my cry come unto thee.
P. Dominus vobiscum.	P. The Lord be with you.
℟. Et cum spiritu tuo.	℟. And with thy spirit.
P. Oremus.	P. Let us pray.
Aufer a nobis, quaesumus, Domine, iniquitates nostras: ut ad Sancta Sanctorum puris mereamur mentibus introire. Per Christum Dominum nostrum. Amen.	Take away from us our iniquities, we beseech thee, O Lord: that we may be worthy to enter with pure minds into the Holy of Holies. Through Christ our Lord. Amen.
Oramus te Domine per merita sanctorum tuorum, quorum reliquiae hic sunt, et omnium sanctorum: ut indulgere digneris omnia peccata mea. Amen.	We beseech thee, O Lord, by the merits of thy saints whose relics are here, and of all the saints: that thou wouldst vouchsafe to forgive me all my sins. Amen.
INCENSATIO ALTARIS	CENSING OF THE ALTAR
ANTIPHONA AD INTROITUM	INTROIT ANTIPHON
KYRIE	KYRIE
Kyrie eleison. Kyrie eleison. Kyrie eleison. Christe eleison. Christe eleison. Christe eleison. Kyrie eleison. Kyrie eleison. Kyrie eleison.	Lord, have mercy. Lord, have mercy. Lord, have mercy. Christ, have mercy. Christ, have mercy. Christ, have mercy. Lord, have mercy. Lord, have mercy. Lord, have mercy.
GLORIA	GLORIA
Gloria in excelsis Deo, et in terra pax hominibus bonae voluntatis. Laudamus te; benedicimus te; adoramus te; glorificamus te. Gratias agimus tibi propter magnam gloriam tuam, Domine Deus, Rex caelestis, Deus Pater omnipotens. Domine Fili unigenite, Iesu Christe.	Glory be to God on high; and on earth peace to men of good will. We praise thee; we bless thee; we adore thee; we glorify thee. We give thee thanks for thy great glory, O Lord God, heavenly King, God the Father almighty. O Lord, the only-begotten Son, Jesus Christ: O Lord God,

Domine Deus, Agnus Dei, Filius Patris: qui tollis peccata mundi, miserere nobis. Qui tollis peccata mundi, suscipe deprecationem nostram. Qui sedes ad dexteram Patris, miserere nobis. Quoniam tu solus sanctus. Tu solus Dominus. Tu solus altissimus, Iesu Christe, cum Sancto Spiritu, ✠ in gloria Dei Patris. Amen.

Lamb of God, Son of the Father, who takest away the sins of the world, have mercy on us; who takest away the sins of the world, receive our prayers: who sittest at the right hand of the Father, have mercy on us. For thou only art holy: thou only art Lord: thou only, O Jesus Christ, art most high, ✠ together with the Holy Ghost, in the glory of God the Father. Amen.

COLLECTA

P. Dominus vobiscum.

℟. Et cum spiritu tuo.

P. Oremus. [Oratio.]

COLLECT

P. The Lord be with you.

℟. And with thy spirit.

P. Let us pray. [Prayer.]

EPISTOLA

EPISTLE

GRADUALE ET ALLELUIA [NONNUMQUAM SEQUENTIA], VEL GRADUALE ET TRACTUS, VEL ALLELUIA ET ALLELUIA

GRADUAL AND ALLELUIA [SOMETIMES SEQUENCE], OR GRADUAL AND TRACT, OR ALLELUIA AND ALLELUIA

EVANGELIUM

P. Munda cor meum, ac labia mea, omnipotens Deus, qui labia Isaiae Prophetae calculo mundasti ignito: ita me tua grata miseratione dignare mundare, ut sanctum Evangelium tuum digne valeam nuntiare. Per Christum, Dominum nostrum. Amen.

Iube, Domine, benedicere.

Dominus sit in corde meo et in labiis meis: ut digne et competenter annuntiem Evangelium suum. In nomine Patris, et Filii, et Spiritus Sancti. Amen.

GOSPEL

P. Cleanse my heart and my lips, O God almighty, who didst cleanse the lips of the prophet Isaias with a live coal: vouchsafe, of thy gracious mercy, so to cleanse me, that I may worthily proclaim thy holy Gospel. Through Christ our Lord. Amen.

Pray, Lord, a blessing.

The Lord be in my heart, and on my lips, that I may worthily, and in a becoming manner, announce his holy Gospel. In the name of the Father, and the Son, and the Holy Ghost. Amen.

Dominus vobiscum.

℟. Et cum spiritu tuo.

P. ✠ Sequentia (vel initium) sancti Evangelii secundum *N.*

℟. Gloria tibi, Domine. [Lectio.]

℟. Laus tibi, Christe.

P. Per evangelica dicta deleantur nostra delicta.

The Lord be with you.

℟. And with thy spirit.

P. ✠ The continuation (or the beginning) of the holy Gospel according to *N.*

℟. Glory be to thee, O Lord. [Reading.]

℟. Praise be to thee, O Christ.

P. By the words of the Gospel may our sins be blotted out.

CREDO

Credo in unum Deum Patrem omnipotentem, factorem caeli et terrae, visibilium omnium et invisibilium.

Et in unum Dominum Iesum Christum, Filium Dei unigenitum, et ex Patre natum ante omnia saecula: Deum de Deo, lumen de lumine, Deum verum de Deo vero: genitum non factum, consubstantialem Patri, per quem omnia facta sunt. Qui propter nos homines, et propter nostram salutem descendit de coelis: et incarnatus est de Spiritu Sancto, ex Maria Virgine: ET HOMO FACTUS EST.

Crucifixus etiam pro nobis sub Pontio Pilato, passus et sepultus est. Et resurrexit tertia die secundum Scripturas. Et ascendit in caelum, sedet ad dexteram Patris. Et iterum venturus est cum gloria iudicare vivos et mortuos; cuius regni non erit finis.

CREDO

I believe in one God, the Father almighty, maker of heaven and earth, and of all things visible and invisible.

And in one Lord Jesus Christ, the only-begotten Son of God, born of the Father before all ages: God of God, light of light, true God of true God: begotten, not made, consubstantial with the Father, by whom all things were made. Who for us men and for our salvation came down from heaven; and was incarnate by the Holy Ghost of the Virgin Mary; AND WAS MADE MAN.

He was crucified also for us, suffered under Pontius Pilate, and was buried. And the third day he rose again according to the Scriptures; and ascended into heaven. He sitteth at the right hand of the Father; and he shall come again with glory to judge the living and the dead; and his kingdom shall have no end.

Et in Spiritum Sanctum,
Dominum et vivificantem,
qui ex Patre Filioque procedit:
qui cum Patre et Filio simul
adoratur, et conglorificatur;
qui locutus est per prophetas.

And in the Holy Ghost, the Lord and giver of life, who proceedeth from the Father and the Son, who together with the Father and the Son is adored and glorified; who spoke by the prophets.

Et unam sanctam Catholicam
et Apostolicam Ecclesiam.
Confiteor unum baptisma
in remissionem peccatorum.
Et expecto resurrectionem
mortuorum, et vitam ✠
venturi saeculi. Amen.

And one, holy, catholic, and apostolic Church. I confess one baptism for the remission of sins. And I await the resurrection of the dead, and the life ✠ of the world to come. Amen.

OFFERTORIUM

P. Dominus vobiscum.

℟. Et cum spiritu tuo.

P. Oremus.

THE OFFERTORY

P. The Lord be with you.

℟. And with thy spirit.

P. Let us pray.

ANTIPHONA AD OFFERTORIUM

OFFERTORY ANTIPHON

Suscipe, sancte Pater, omnipotens aeterne Deus, hanc immaculatam Hostiam, quam ego indignus famulus tuus offero tibi Deo meo vivo et vero, pro innumerabilibus peccatis, offensionibus et negligentiis meis, et pro omnibus circumstantibus; sed et pro omnibus fidelibus Christianis, vivis atque defunctis; ut mihi et illis proficiat ad salutem in vitam aeternam. Amen.

Receive, O holy Father, almighty, eternal God, this spotless host, which I, thy unworthy servant, do offer unto thee, my living and true God, for mine own countless sins, offences, and negligences, and for all here present; as also for all faithful Christians, living and dead, that it may avail for my own and for their salvation unto life eternal. Amen.

Deus qui humanae substantiae dignitatem mirabiliter condidisti, et mirabilius reformasti; da nobis per huius aquae et vini mysterium, eius divinitatis esse consortes, qui humanitatis nostrae fieri

O God, who in creating human nature didst marvelously ennoble it, and hast still more marvelously reformed it; grant that, by the mystery of this water and wine, we may be made partakers of

dignatus est particeps, Iesus Christus, Filius tuus, Dominus noster: qui tecum vivit et regnat in unitate Spiritus sancti, Deus; per omnia saecula saeculorum. Amen.

his divinity who vouchsafed to become partaker of our humanity, Jesus Christ, thy Son, our Lord; who liveth and reigneth with thee in the unity of the Holy Ghost, one God, world without end. Amen.

Offerimus tibi, Domine, calicem salutaris, tuam deprecantes clementiam: ut in conspectu divinae Maiestatis tuae pro nostra et totius mundi salute cum odore suavitatis ascendat. Amen.

We offer unto thee, O Lord, the chalice of salvation, beseeching thy clemency, that it may rise up in the sight of thy divine majesty as a savor of sweetness, for our salvation, and for that of the whole world. Amen.

In spiritu humilitatis, et in animo contrito suscipiamur a te, Domine: et sic fiat sacrificium nostrum in conspectu tuo hodie, ut placeat tibi, Domine Deus.

In a humble spirit, and a contrite heart, may we be received by thee, O Lord; and may our sacrifice so be offered up in thy sight this day that it may be pleasing to thee, O Lord God.

Veni, sanctificator, omnipotens aeterne Deus, et ✠ benedic hoc sacrificium tuo sancto nomini praeparatum.

Come, O thou who makest holy, almighty, eternal God, and ✠ bless this sacrifice, prepared for thy holy name.

INCENSATIO ALTARIS

Per intercessionem beati Michaelis archangeli stantis a dexteris altaris incensi, et omnium electorum suorum, incensum istud dignetur Dominus bene ✠ dicere, et in odorem suavitatis accipere. Per Christum Dominum nostrum. Amen.

THE CENSING OF THE ALTAR

Through the intercession of blessed Michael the archangel standing at the right hand of the altar of incense, and of all his elect, may the Lord vouchsafe to bless ✠ this incense, and to receive it for a sweet savor. Through Christ our Lord. Amen.

Incensum istud a te benedictum, ascendat ad te Domine, et descendat super nos misericordia tua.

May this incense which thou hast blessed, O Lord, rise up before thee, and may thy mercy come down upon us.

Diligatur, Domine, oratio mea, sicut incensum in conspectu tuo: elevatio manuum mearum sacrificium

Let my prayer, O Lord, be directed as incense in thy sight: the lifting up of my hands as the evening sacrifice.

vespertinum. Pone, Domine, custodiam ori meo, et ostium circumstantiae labiis meis: ut non declinet cor meum in verba malitiae, ad excusandas excusationes in peccatis.	Set a watch, O Lord, before my mouth, and a door round about my lips; that my heart incline not to evil words, to make excuses in sins.
Accendat in nobis Dominus ignem sui amoris, et flammam aeternam caritatis. Amen.	May the Lord enkindle in us the fire of his love, and the flame of everlasting charity. Amen.
LAVABO	WASHING OF HANDS
Lavabo inter innocentes manus meas: et circumdabo altare tuum, Domine.	I will wash my hands among the innocent: and will compass thine altar, O Lord.
Ut audiam vocem laudis: et enarrem universa mirabilia tua.	That I may hear the voice of thy praise: and tell of all thy wondrous works.
Domine, dilexi decorem domus tuae, et locum habitationis gloriae tuae.	O Lord, I have loved the beauty of thy house, and the place where thy glory dwelleth.
Ne perdas cum impiis, Deus, animam meam; et cum viris sanguinum vitam meam.	Destroy not my soul with the wicked, O God; nor my life with men of blood.
In quorum manibus iniquitates sunt: dextera eorum repleta est muneribus.	In whose hands are iniquities: their right hand is filled with gifts.
Ego autem in innocentia mea ingressus sum: redime me, et miserere mei.	But I have walked in mine innocence: redeem me, and have mercy on me.
Pes meus stetit in directo; in ecclesiis benedicam te, Domine.	My foot hath stood in the straight way: in the churches I will bless thee, O Lord.
Gloria Patri . . .	Glory be to the Father . . .
Suscipe, sancta Trinitas, hanc oblationem, quam tibi offerimus ob memoriam Passionis, Resurrectionis, et Ascensionis Iesu Christi Domini nostri: et in honorem beatae Mariae semper Virginis, et beati Ioannis Baptistae,	Receive, O holy Trinity, this offering, which we make to thee in remembrance of the Passion, Resurrection, and Ascension of our Lord Jesus Christ, and in honor of blessed Mary ever Virgin, of blessed John the Baptist, of the holy

et sanctorum Apostolorum Petri et Pauli, et istorum, et omnium Sanctorum: ut illis proficiat ad honorem, nobis autem ad salutem: et illi pro nobis intercedere dignentur in caelis, quorum memoriam agimus in terris. Per eumdem Christum Dominum nostrum. Amen.

apostles Peter and Paul, of these and of all the saints: that it may avail to their honor and to our salvation: and may they vouchsafe to intercede for us in heaven, whose memory we celebrate on earth. Through the same Christ our Lord. Amen.

ORATE, FRATRES

P. Orate, fratres, ut meum ac vestrum sacrificium acceptabile fiat apud Deum patrem omnipotentem.

℟. Suscipiat Dominus sacrificium de manibus tuis ad laudem et gloriam nominis sui, ad utilitatem quoque nostram, totiusque Ecclesiae suae sanctae.

ORATE, FRATRES

P. Brethren, pray that my sacrifice and yours may be acceptable to God the Father almighty.

℟. May the Lord receive the sacrifice at thy hands, to the praise and glory of his name, to our benefit, and to that of all his holy Church.

SECRETA

[Oratio.]

P. Per omnia saecula saeculorum.

℟. Amen.

THE SECRET

[Prayer in silence.]

P. World without end,

℟. Amen.

PRAEFATIO COMMUNIS

P. Dominus vobiscum.

R Et cum spiritu tuo.

P. Sursum corda.

℟. Habemus ad Dominum.

P. Gratias agamus Domino Deo nostro.

℟. Dignum et iustum est.

Vere dignum et iustum est, aequum et salutare, nos tibi semper et ubique gratias agere: Domine, sancte Pater, omnipotens aeterne Deus; per Christum

THE COMMON PREFACE

P. The Lord be with you.

℟. And with thy spirit.

P. Lift up your hearts.

℟. We have lifted them up unto the Lord.

P. Let us give thanks to the Lord our God.

℟. It is meet and just.

It is truly meet and just, right and availing unto salvation, that at all times and in all places we give thanks to thee, O Lord, holy Father, almighty everlasting

Dominum nostrum. Per quem maiestatem tuam laudant angeli, adorant dominationes, tremunt potestates; caeli caelorumque virtutes, ac beata seraphim, socia exultatione concelebrant. Cum quibus et nostras voces, ut admitti iubeas deprecamur, supplici confessione dicentes:	God: through Christ our Lord. Through whom the angels praise thy majesty, the dominations worship it, the powers are in awe. The heavens, and the heavenly hosts, and the blessed seraphim, join together in celebrating their joy. With these we pray thee join our own voices also, while we say with lowly praise:
SANCTUS	SANCTUS
Sanctus, sanctus, sanctus Dominus Deus Sabaoth. Pleni sunt caeli et terra gloria tua. Hosanna in excelsis. ✠ Benedictus qui venit in nomine Domini. Hosanna in excelsis.	Holy, holy, holy Lord God of hosts. Heaven and earth are full of thy glory. Hosanna in the highest. ✠ Blessed is he that cometh in the name of the Lord. Hosanna in the highest.
CANON MISSAE	THE CANON OF THE MASS
Te igitur, clementissime Pater, per Iesum Christum Filium tuum Dominum nostrum, supplices rogamus ac petimus, uti accepta habeas, et benedicas, haec ✠ dona, haec ✠ munera, haec ✠ sancta sacrificia illibata, in primis quae tibi offerimus pro Ecclesia tua sancta catholica: quam pacificare, custodire, adunare, et regere digneris toto orbe terrarum: una cum famulo tuo Papa nostro *N.* et Antistite nostro *N.* et omnibus orthodoxis, atque catholicae et apostolicae fidei cultoribus.	Wherefore, O most merciful Father, we humbly pray and beseech thee, through Jesus Christ thy Son our Lord, that thou wouldst vouchsafe to receive and bless these ✠ gifts, these ✠ offerings, this ✠ holy and unblemished sacrifice, which in the first place we offer thee for thy holy Catholic Church, that it may please thee to grant her peace: as also to protect, unite, and govern her throughout the world, together with thy servant *N.*, our pope, *N.*, our bishop, as also all orthodox believers who keep the Catholic and Apostolic faith.
Memento, Domine, famulorum famularumque tuarum *N.* et *N.*	Be mindful, O Lord, of thy servants and handmaids, *N.* and *N.*,

Et omnium circumstantium, quorum tibi fides cognita est, et nota devotio, pro quibus tibi offerimus; vel qui tibi offerunt hoc sacrificium laudis, pro se, suisque omnibus: pro redemptione animarum suarum, pro spe salutis et incolumitatis suae: tibique reddunt vota sua aeterno Deo, vivo et vero.

And of all here present, whose faith and devotion are known unto thee; for whom we offer, or who offer up to thee this sacrifice of praise for themselves and theirs, for the redeeming of their souls, for the hope of their safety and salvation, and who pay their vows to thee, the eternal, living, and true God.

Communicantes, et memoriam venerantes, in primis gloriosae semper Virginis Mariae, Genitricis Dei et Domini nostri Iesu Christi: sed et beati Ioseph, eiusdem Virginis Sponsi, et beatorum Apostolorum ac Martyrum tuorum, Petri et Pauli, Andreae, Iacobi, Ioannis, Thomae, Iacobi, Philippi, Bartholomaei, Matthaei, Simonis et Thaddaei: Lini, Cleti, Clementis, Xysti, Cornelii, Cypriani, Laurentii, Chrysogoni, Ioannis et Pauli, Cosmae et Damiani, et omnium sanctorum tuorum: quorum meritis precibusque concedas, ut in omnibus protectionis tuae muniamur auxilio. Per eumdem Christum Dominum nostrum. Amen.

In communion with and reverencing the memory, first, of the glorious Mary, ever a Virgin, Mother of our God and Lord Jesus Christ; also of blessed Joseph, spouse of the same Virgin; likewise of thy blessed apostles and martyrs, Peter and Paul, Andrew, James, John, Thomas, James, Philip, Bartholomew, Matthew, Simon and Thaddeus; of Linus, Cletus, Clement, Xystus, Cornelius, Cyprian, Lawrence, Chrysogonus, John and Paul, Cosmas and Damian, and of all thy saints; by whose merits and prayers grant that in all things we may be guarded by thy protecting help. Through the same Christ our Lord. Amen.

Hanc igitur oblationem servitutis nostrae, sed et cunctae familiae tuae, quaesumus Domine, ut placatus accipias: diesque nostros in tua pace disponas, atque ab aeterna damnatione nos eripi, et in electorum tuorum iubeas grege numerari. Per Christum Dominum nostrum. Amen.

We therefore beseech thee, O Lord, to be appeased, and to receive this offering of our bounden duty, as also of thy whole household; order our days in thy peace; grant that we may be rescued from eternal damnation, and counted within the fold of thine elect. Through Christ our Lord. Amen.

Quam oblationem tu, Deus, in omnibus, quaesumus, benedictam ✠, adscriptam ✠, ratam ✠, rationabilem, acceptabilemque facere digneris: ut nobis Corpus ✠ et Sanguis ✠ fiat dilectissimi Filii tui Domini nostri Iesu Christi.

Which oblation do thou, O God, vouchsafe in all things, to bless ✠, consecrate ✠, approve ✠, make reasonable and acceptable; that it may become for us the Body ✠ and Blood ✠ of thy most beloved Son, Jesus Christ our Lord.

Qui pridie quam pateretur, accepit panem in sanctas ac venerabiles manus suas, et elevatis oculis in caelum, ad te Deum Patrem suum omnipotentem, tibi gratias agens, benedixit ✠, fregit, deditque discipulis suis dicens: Accipite et manducate ex hoc omnes, HOC EST ENIM CORPUS MEUM.

Who the day before he suffered took bread into his holy and venerable hands, and with his eyes lifted up to heaven, unto thee, God, his almighty Father, giving thanks to thee, he blessed ✠, brake, and gave to his disciples, saying: Take and eat ye all of this, FOR THIS IS MY BODY.

Simili modo postquam coenatum est, accipiens et hunc praeclarum calicem in sanctas ac venerabiles manus suas, item tibi gratias agens benedixit ✠, deditque discipulis suis dicens: Accipite, et bibite ex eo omnes: HIC EST ENIM CALIX SANGUINIS MEI, NOVI ET AETERNI TESTAMENTI: MYSTERIUM FIDEI: QUI PRO VOBIS ET PRO MULTIS EFFUNDETUR IN REMISSIONEM PECCATORUM.

In like manner, after he had supped, taking also this excellent Chalice into his holy and venerable hands; again giving thanks to thee, he blessed ✠ and gave it to his disciples saying: Take and drink ye all of this; FOR THIS IS THE CHALICE OF MY BLOOD, OF THE NEW AND ETERNAL TESTAMENT: THE MYSTERY OF FAITH: WHICH SHALL BE SHED FOR YOU AND FOR MANY UNTO THE REMISSION OF SINS.

Haec quotiescumque feceritis, in mei memoriam facietis.

As often as ye shall do these things, ye shall do them in memory of me.

Unde et memores, Domine, nos servi tui, sed et plebs tua sancta, eiusdem Christi Filii tui, Domini nostri, tam beatae passionis, necnon et ab inferis resurrectionis, sed et in caelos gloriosae ascensionis, offerimus praeclarae

Wherefore, O Lord, we thy servants, as also thy holy people, calling to mind the blessed passion of the same Christ thy Son our Lord, and also his rising up from hell, and his glorious ascension into heaven, do offer unto

Maiestati tuae, de tuis donis ac datis, hostiam ✠ puram, hostiam ✠ sanctam, hostiam ✠ immaculatam, panem ✠ sanctum vitae aeternae, et Calicem ✠ salutis perpetuae.

thy most excellent majesty, of thine own gifts bestowed upon us, a pure ✠ victim, a holy ✠ victim, a spotless ✠ victim, the holy Bread ✠ of eternal life, and the Chalice ✠ of everlasting salvation.

Supra quae propitio ac sereno vultu respicere digneris, et accepta habere, sicuti accepta habere dignatus es munera pueri tui iusti Abel, et sacrificium patriarchae nostri Abrahae, et quod tibi obtulit summus sacerdos tuus Melchisedech, sanctum sacrificium, immaculatam hostiam.

Upon which do thou vouchsafe to look, with a propitious and serene countenance, and to accept them, as thou wert graciously pleased to accept the gifts of thy just servant Abel, and the sacrifice of our patriarch Abraham, and that which thy High Priest Melchisedech offered to thee, a holy sacrifice, a spotless victim.

Supplices te rogamus, omnipotens Deus, iube haec perferri per manus sancti Angeli tui in sublime altare tuum, in conspectu divinae maiestatis tuae, ut quotquot ex hac altaris participatione, sacrosanctum Filii tui Corpus ✠ et Sanguinem ✠ sumpserimus, omni benedictione caelesti et gratia repleamur. Per eumdem Christum Dominum nostrum. Amen.

We most humbly beseech thee, almighty God, to command that these things be borne by the hands of thy holy angel to thine altar on high, in the sight of thy divine majesty, that as many of us as, at this altar, shall partake of and receive the most holy Body ✠ and Blood ✠ of thy Son, may be filled with every heavenly blessing and grace. Through the same Christ our Lord. Amen.

Memento etiam, Domine, famulorum famularumque tuarum *N.* et *N.* qui nos praecesserunt cum signo fidei, et dormiunt in somno pacis.

Be mindful, O Lord, of thy servants and handmaids *N.* and *N.* who are gone before us with the sign of Faith, and rest in the sleep of peace.

Ipsis, Domine, et omnibus in Christo quiescentibus, locum refrigerii, lucis et pacis, ut indulgeas deprecamur. Per eumdem Christum Dominum nostrum. Amen.

To these, O Lord, and to all that rest in Christ, we beseech thee, grant a place of refreshment, light, and peace. Through the same Christ our Lord. Amen.

Nobis quoque peccatoribus, famulis tuis, de multitudine miserationum tuarum sperantibus, partem aliquam et societatem donare digneris, cum tuis sanctis apostolis et martyribus; cum Ioanne, Stephano, Matthia, Barnaba, Ignatio, Alexandro, Marcellino, Petro, Felicitate, Perpetua, Agatha, Lucia, Agnete, Caecilia, Anastasia, et omnibus sanctis tuis: intra quorum nos consortium, non aestimator meriti, sed veniae, quaesumus, largitor admitte.

To us sinners, also, thy servants, hoping in the multitude of thy mercies, vouchsafe to grant some part and fellowship with thy holy apostles and martyrs; with John, Stephen, Matthias, Barnabas, Ignatius, Alexander, Marcellinus, Peter, Felicity, Perpetua, Agatha, Lucy, Agnes, Cecilia, Anastasia, and with all thy saints: into whose company we beseech thee to admit us, not considering our merit, but of thine own free pardon.

Per Christum Dominum nostrum, per quem haec omnia, Domine, semper bona creas, sanctificas ✠, vivificas ✠, benedicis ✠, et praestas nobis.

Through Christ our Lord, through whom, O Lord, thou dost create, hallow ✠, quicken ✠ and bless ✠ these thine ever-bountiful gifts and give them to us.

Per ipsum ✠, et cum ipso ✠, et in ipso ✠, est tibi Deo Patri ✠ omnipotenti, in unitate Spiritus ✠ Sancti, omnis honor et gloria. Per omnia saecula saeculorum. Amen.

By him ✠, and with him ✠, and in him ✠, is to thee, God the Father ✠ almighty, in the unity of the Holy ✠ Ghost, all honor and glory. For ever and ever. Amen.

PATER NOSTER

P. Oremus. Praeceptis salutaribus moniti, et divina institutione formati, audemus dicere: Pater noster, qui es in caelis, sanctificetur nomen tuum: adveniat regnum tuum: fiat voluntas tua, sicut in caelo, et in terra: panem nostrum quotidianum da nobis hodie; et dimitte nobis debita nostra, sicut et nos dimittimus debitoribus nostris: et ne nos inducas in tentationem:

℟. Sed libera nos a malo.

THE LORD'S PRAYER

P. Let us pray. Taught by salutary precepts and following the divine commandment, we make bold to say: Our Father, who art in heaven, hallowed be thy name: thy kingdom come: thy will be done on earth as it is in heaven: give us this day our daily bread: and forgive us our trespasses, as we forgive those who trespass against us. And lead us not into temptation:

℟. But deliver us from evil.

P. Amen.

P. Amen.

Libera nos, quaesumus, Domine, ab omnibus malis, praeteritis, praesentibus et futuris; et intercedente beata et gloriosa semper Virgine Dei Genitrice Maria, cum beatis apostolis tuis Petro et Paulo, atque Andrea, et omnibus sanctis, da propitius pacem in diebus nostris: ut ope misericordiae tuae adiuti, et a peccato simus semper liberi, et ab omni perturbatione securi. Per eumdem Dominum nostrum Iesum Christum Filium tuum, qui tecum vivit et regnat, in unitate Spiritus Sancti, Deus. Per omnia saecula saeculorum.

Deliver us, we beseech thee, O Lord, from all evils, past, present, and to come; and by the intercession of the blessed and glorious Mary ever Virgin, Mother of God, together with thy blessed apostles Peter and Paul, and Andrew, and all the saints, mercifully grant peace in our days: that through the help of thy mercy, we may be always free from sin, and safe from all trouble. Through the same Jesus Christ thy Son our Lord, who liveth and reigneth with thee in the unity of the Holy Ghost, one God, for ever and ever.

℟. Amen.

℟. Amen.

P. Pax ✠ Domini sit ✠ semper vobiscum ✠.

P. The peace ✠ of the Lord be ✠ always with you ✠.

℟. Et cum spiritu tuo.

℟. And with thy spirit.

AGNUS DEI

Agnus Dei, qui tollis peccata mundi: miserere nobis. Agnus Dei, qui tollis peccata mundi: miserere nobis. Agnus Dei, qui tollis peccata mundi, dona nobis pacem.

AGNUS DEI

Lamb of God, who takest away the sins of the world, have mercy on us. Lamb of God, who takest away the sins of the world, have mercy on us. Lamb of God, who takest away the sins of the world, grant us peace.

Domine Iesu Christe, qui dixisti Apostolis tuis: Pacem relinquo vobis, pacem meam do vobis: ne respicias peccata mea, sed fidem Ecclesiae tuae: eamque secundum voluntatem tuam pacificare et coadunare digneris. Qui vivis et regnas Deus, per omnia saecula saeculorum. Amen.

O Lord Jesus Christ, who didst say to thy apostles: Peace I leave with you, my peace I give unto you; look not upon my sins, but upon the faith of thy Church; and vouchsafe to her that peace and unity which is agreeable to thy will: who livest and reignest God for ever and ever. Amen.

OSCULUM PACIS	THE KISS OF PEACE
PRAEPARATIO AD COMMUNIONEM	PREPARATION FOR COMMUNION
Domine Iesu Christe, Fili Dei vivi, qui ex voluntate Patris, cooperante Spiritu Sancto, per mortem tuam mundum vivificasti, libera me per hoc sacrosanctum corpus et sanguinem tuum ab omnibus iniquitatibus meis, et universis malis: et fac me tuis semper inhaerere mandatis, et a te numquam separari permittas: qui cum eodem Deo Patre et Spiritu Sancto vivis et regnas Deus in saecula saeculorum. Amen.	O Lord Jesus Christ, Son of the living God, who, according to the will of the Father, through the cooperation of the Holy Ghost, hast by thy death given life to the world, deliver me by this, thy most holy Body and Blood, from all my iniquities and from every evil; and make me always cleave to thy commandments, and never suffer me to be separated from thee: who with the same God the Father livest and reignest God for ever and ever. Amen.
Perceptio corporis tui, Domine Iesu Christe, quod ego indignus sumere praesumo, non mihi proveniat in iudicium et condemnationem; sed pro tua pietate prosit mihi ad tutamentum mentis et corporis, et ad medelam percipiendam: qui vivis et regnas cum Deo Patre, in unitate Spiritus Sancti, Deus, per omnia saecula saeculorum. Amen.	Let not the receiving of thy Body, O Lord Jesus Christ, which I, all unworthy, presume to receive, turn to my judgment and damnation: but through thy lovingkindness, may it avail me for a safeguard and remedy, both of soul and body. Who with God the Father, in the unity of the Holy Ghost, livest and reignest God for ever and ever. Amen.
COMMUNIO SACERDOTIS	THE PRIEST'S COMMUNION
Panem caelestem accipiam, et nomen Domini invocabo.	I will take the Bread of heaven, and call upon the name of the Lord.
Domine, non sum dignus ut intres sub tectum meum; sed tantum dic verbo, et sanabitur anima mea. (3×)	Lord, I am not worthy that thou shouldst enter under my roof; but only say the word, and my soul shall be healed. (3×)
Corpus Domini nostri Iesu Christi custodiat animam meam in vitam aeternam. Amen.	May the Body of our Lord Jesus Christ preserve my soul unto life everlasting. Amen.

Quid retribuam Domino pro omnibus quae retribuit mihi? Calicem salutaris accipiam, et nomen Domini invocabo. Laudans invocabo Dominum, et ab inimicis meis salvus ero.

What return shall I make to the Lord for all he hath given unto me? I will take the Chalice of salvation, and call upon the name of the Lord. Praising I will call upon the Lord, and I shall be saved from my enemies.

Sanguis Domini nostri Iesu Christi custodiat animam meam in vitam aeternam. Amen.

May the Blood of our Lord Jesus Christ keep my soul unto life everlasting. Amen.

COMMUNIO FIDELIUM

℟. Confiteor Deo omnipotenti, beatae Mariae semper Virgini, beato Michaeli Archangelo, beato Ioanni Baptistae, sanctis Apostolis Petro et Paulo, omnibus sanctis, et tibi Pater, quia peccavi nimis cogitatione, verbo et opere, mea culpa, mea culpa, mea maxima culpa. Ideo precor beatam Mariam semper Virginem, beatum Michaelem Archangelum, beatum Ioannem Baptistam, sanctos Apostolos Petrum et Paulum, omnes sanctos, et te Pater, orare pro me ad Dominum Deum nostrum.

THE COMMUNION OF THE FAITHFUL

℟. I confess to almighty God, to blessed Mary, ever Virgin, to blessed Michael the Archangel, to blessed John the Baptist, to the holy apostles Peter and Paul, to all the saints, and to thee, father, that I have sinned exceedingly, in thought, word and deed, through my fault, through my fault, through my most grievous fault. Therefore I beseech the blessed Mary ever Virgin, blessed Michael the Archangel, blessed John the Baptist, the holy apostles Peter and Paul, and all the saints, and thee, father, to pray to the Lord our God for me.

P. Misereatur vestri omnipotens Deus, et dimissis peccatis vestris, perducat vos ad vitam aeternam.

℟. Amen.

P. Indulgentiam, ✠ absolutionem, et remissionem peccatorum nostrorum tribuat nobis omnipotens et misericors Dominus.

℟. Amen.

P. May almighty God have mercy upon you, forgive you your sins, and bring you to life everlasting.

℟. Amen.

P. May the almighty and merciful Lord grant pardon, ✠ absolution, and remission of our sins.

℟. Amen.

Ecce Agnus Dei, ecce qui tollit peccata mundi.

Behold the Lamb of God, behold him who taketh away the sins of the world.

Domine, non sum dignus ut intres sub tectum meum; sed tantum dic verbo, et sanabitur anima mea. (3×)

Lord, I am not worthy that thou shouldst enter under my roof; but only say the word, and my soul shall be healed. (3×)

Corpus Domini nostri Iesu Christi custodiat animam tuam in vitam aeternam. Amen.

May the Body of our Lord Jesus Christ preserve thy soul unto life everlasting. Amen.

GRATIARUM ACTIO

Quod ore sumpsimus, Domine, pura mente capiamus, et de munere temporali, fiat nobis remedium sempiternum.

THANKSGIVING

Grant, Lord, that what we have taken with our mouth we may receive with a pure mind, and that from a temporal gift it may become for us an eternal remedy.

Corpus tuum, Domine, quod sumpsi, et sanguis quem potavi, adhaereat visceribus meis; et praesta ut in me non remaneat scelerum macula, quem pura et sancta refecerunt sacramenta. Qui vivis et regnas in saecula saeculorum. Amen.

May thy Body, O Lord, which I have received, and thy Blood which I have drunk, cleave to my inward parts; and grant that no stain of sin may remain in me, whom the pure and holy sacraments have refreshed; who livest and reignest for ever and ever. Amen.

ANTIPHONA AD COMMUNIONEM

COMMUNION ANTIPHON

POSTCOMMUNIO

P. Dominus vobiscum.

℟. Et cum spiritu tuo.

P. Oremus. [Oratio.]

POSTCOMMUNION

P. The Lord be with you.

℟. And with thy spirit.

P. Let us pray. [Prayer.]

MISSUS FIDELIUM

P. Dominus vobiscum.

℟. Et cum spiritu tuo.

P. Ite missa est.

℟. Deo gratias.

DISMISSAL OF THE FAITHFUL

P. The Lord be with you.

℟. And with thy spirit.

P. Go, you are dismissed.

℟. Thanks be to God.

BENEDICTIO

Placeat tibi sancta Trinitas, obsequium servitutis meae; et praesta, ut sacrificium quod oculis tuae maiestatis indignus obtuli, tibi sit acceptabile, mihique et omnibus pro quibus illud obtuli, sit, te miserante, propitiabile. Per Christum Dominum nostrum. Amen.

P. Benedicat vos omnipotens Deus, Pater, et Filius ✠, et Spiritus Sanctus.

℟. Amen.

BLESSING

May the homage of my service be pleasing to thee, O holy Trinity; and grant that the sacrifice which I, though unworthy, have offered in the sight of thy majesty, may be acceptable to thee: and through thy mercy win forgiveness for me and for all those for whom I have offered it.

P. May God almighty bless you, Father, and Son ✠, and Holy Ghost.

℟. Amen.

EVANGELIUM IOHANNIS

P. Dominus vobiscum.

℟. Et cum spiritu tuo.

P. Initium sancti Evangelii, secundum Ioannem.

℟. Gloria tibi, Domine.

P. In principio erat Verbum, et Verbum erat apud Deum: et Deus erat Verbum: hoc erat in principio apud Deum. Omnia per ipsum facta sunt, et sine ipso factum est nihil quod factum est: in ipso vita erat, et vita erat lux hominum: et lux in tenebris lucet, et tenebrae eam non comprehenderunt. Fuit homo missus a Deo, cui nomen erat Ioannes. Hic venit in testimonium, ut testimonium perhiberet de lumine, ut omnes crederent per illum. Non erat ille lux; sed ut testimonium perhiberet de lumine. Erat lux vera quae illuminat omnem hominem venientem in hunc mundum. In mundo erat, et mundus

THE LAST GOSPEL

P. The Lord be with you.

℟. And with thy spirit.

P. The beginning of the holy Gospel according to St John.

℟. Glory be to thee, O Lord.

P. In the beginning was the Word, and the Word was with God, and the Word was God: the same was in the beginning with God. All things were made by him, and without him was made nothing that was made; in him was life, and the life was the light of men: and the light shineth in darkness, and the darkness did not comprehend it. There was a man sent from God, whose name was John. This man came for a witness, to give testimony of the light, that all men might believe through him. He was not the light, but was to give testimony of the light. That was the true light which enlighteneth every

per ipsum factus est, et mundus eum non cognovit. In propria venit, et sui eum non receperunt. Quotquot autem receperunt eum, dedit eis potestatem filios Dei fieri: his qui credunt in nomine eius, qui non ex sanguinibus, neque ex voluntate carnis, neque ex voluntate viri, sed ex Deo nati sunt: ET VERBUM CARO FACTUM EST, et habitavit in nobis; et vidimus gloriam eius, gloriam quasi unigeniti a Patre, plenum gratiae et veritatis.

man that cometh into this world. He was in the world, and the world was made by him, and the world knew him not. He came unto his own, and his own received him not. But as many as received him, to them he gave power to be made the sons of God: to them that believe in his name, who are born, not of blood, nor of the will of the flesh, nor of the will of man, but of God: AND THE WORD WAS MADE FLESH, and dwelt among us; and we saw his glory, the glory as it were of the only-begotten of the Father, full of grace and truth.

℟. Deo gratias.

℟. Thanks be to God.

Made in the USA
Monee, IL
14 July 2023

39276188R00114